HEY MALAREK!

The True Story of a Street Kid Who Made It

VICTOR MALAREK

Foreword by Michele Landsberg

D1601535

JAMES LORIMER & COMPANY LTD., PUBLISHERS

TORONTO

LORIMER

James Lorimer & Company Ltd., Publishers acknowledges the support of the Ontario Arts Council. We acknowledge the financial support of the Government of Canada through the Canada Book Fund for our publishing activities. We acknowledge the support of the Canada Council for the Arts which last year invested $24.3 million in writing and publishing throughout Canada. We acknowledge the Government of Ontario through the Ontario Media Development Corporation's Ontario Book Initiative.

Library and Archives Canada Cataloguing in Publication

Malarek, Victor, 1948-
    Hey Malarek! : the true story of a street kid who made it / Victor Malarek; foreword by Michele Landsberg. -- 2nd ed.

Issued also in electronic formats.
ISBN 978-1-4594-0047-4

    1. Malarek, Victor, 1948-. 2. Juvenile delinquents--Québec (Province)--Biography. 3. Children--Institutional care--Québec (Province)--Montréal. I. Title.

HV1010.M6M35 2012   364.36092   C2011-908191-1

James Lorimer & Company Ltd., Publishers
317 Adelaide Street West, Suite 1002
Toronto, ON
M5V 1P9
www.lorimer.ca

Printed and bound in Canada.

For my mother, Jennie

ACKNOWLEDGEMENTS

I would especially like to thank Anna Malarek; Oksana Ostapyk, my patient editor; Anne Holloway; and *The Globe and Mail*; and to acknowledge the assistance of the Canada Council Explorations Program.

The names and descriptions of all the individuals in this book have been altered, except for my family, Lorne Furtner, Philip Gillis, Lloyd Roussel, Anna, Rudy Koch, and Maurice Patton. The names of all people mentioned in the Epilogue are real.

CONTENTS

FOREWORD

By Michele Landsberg

*V*ictor Malarek's blunt prose, so fiercely unadorned, is like a hammerblow to the heart. Read this book and be amazed by the author's tough self-discipline: Malarek scorns the softening blur of nostalgia, and not once does he woo the reader by invoking the innocent vulnerability of his child self. It's as though sentimentality would be a disservice to the raw suffering, bewilderment, and helpless rage that dominated the entire childhood and youth of Malarek and his brothers.

Within the first two pages, Malarek, age seven, has heard his mother being beaten to within an inch of her life, found her gone by morning, and her bedroom splattered with blood, and been wrenched away from his home, his brutal father, and his two brothers, and placed into the care of strangers.

Read this book for its exposé of a rotten child welfare system. Read it for its painful human drama. Read it for the redemptive tale of a boy who had the strength to overcome pitiless hardship because of his mother's love, a few humane teachers, and one judge who trusted his intuition. But above all, read it for its bracing timeliness. At the core of Malarek's story is a word he almost never mentions from beginning to end: Poverty. Malarek's mother, by his account a gentle, loving, and devoted person, was unable to keep her three sons with her through no fault of her own. She had to flee her marriage to save her own life; her husband was a violent alcoholic who beat her almost to death. In 1950s Canada, that meant the state saw her as someone who had wilfully turned her back on her husband's livelihood and was not, therefore, entitled to any public support. Her only option was to put her children into "care." She could have them back only if she returned to her husband. (For the boys' sake, she did just that—several times—but every fresh start turned, sooner or later, into more violence and another desperate flight.)

It was poverty that forced the Malarek boys, at ages nine, seven, and five, out of their mother's arms and into the Weredale Home. Their mother eked out her living as a café waitress, seeing her children on rare, snatched visits, while they were consigned to an ugly, loveless childhood in a Dickensian "home for boys." It was an emotional wilderness, where children barely out of their infancy fought grimly for survival. The only victory in Weredale was to learn to be tough, to vanquish one's vulnerability, smother tears, become "hard"—perfect conditioning for society's predestined rejects. For Malarek, who nightly wet his bed in the midst of a recurring nightmare, daily life held endless humiliations, punishments, mockery, and retributions.

Right now, in Canada, income inequality has reached its highest point since the 1920s. The gradual concentration of wealth in the hands of the top 1 per cent is an inexorable result of deliberate government policy. As the lower 99 per cent slip further and further down the income slope, the lives of their children materially worsen. During the past year, international reports have noted Canada's steep decline. The OECD caused shock waves when it reported a new low in Canada's neonatal survival rate, as we slipped from sixth place in the world to twenty-fourth, with 5.1 deaths per 100 live births in the first year of life. Agencies like UNICEF commented sharply on our growing inequality, pointing out that declining parental incomes have a direct impact on the health and well-being of our children.

Read this bleak account of Malarek's childhood and consider that all the loneliness and pain resulted from cold, bureaucratic decisions. No, the state would not support Malarek's mother so she could care for her three children. If she wilfully left her violent husband, it was not the government's responsibility to step into the gap. No one seemed to care that the harshness of life without parental love might foster an entire community of boys who were being groomed for lives as gangsters. By the time they were teenagers, stigmatized in high school by their clumsy institutional clothing and lack of families, they knew that if they wanted to shed their status as threadbare outsiders, they would have to shoplift some stylish clothes.

Out of poverty, want, and lovelessness arises the young tough, the "juvenile delinquent" who will be further punished by a state system that will place him or her in a prison in order to offer further instruction in and incentive for criminality. In his epilogue, Malarek voices his disgust and rage at a child welfare system that so wantonly trampled on children's rights. He reserves his praise and optimism for the Young Offenders Act of 1982, which wiped away decades of punitive paternalism and recognized, at long last, that children were entitled to the same rights in the justice system as adults.

This new edition of *Hey Malarek!* is being published on the very eve of the annihilation of that same Young Offenders Act. What perfect timing! Stephen Harper's government is poised to introduce far more punitive and rigid youth crime laws as part of its Omnibus Crime Bill. Malarek escaped a wasted life and emerged into a stunning career as an investigative reporter, all because a judge felt he had potential and was legally free to send him on his way instead of jailing him. That option will probably not exist after the new crime bill is passed. Most of Malarek's cohort from the boys' home lockstepped numbly into a life of petty crime and a downward spiral of imprisonment. Under the new youth crime laws, there will be fewer and fewer Malareks who will be allowed the chance of a productive life outside the vast new sprawl of privatized prisons. There will be more and more cohorts of youth growing up in pinching poverty, destined to fill those prisons.

Malarek's vivid memoir is preventive medicine. Read it to smell and taste the ugliness and the harm we cause when we vote to let huge numbers of children grow up hungry and underserved. Read it for the ache of knowing we will then punish them further for that crime of being poor and without choices. Read it to make you burn with desire to turn our country around.

1

*M*arch 1956. I remember the violent argument my mother and father were having. I thought I was being jolted out of an ugly nightmare; instead I was slamming head into one. There was shouting back and forth. My mother stood her ground while my father swore repeatedly at her. A beer bottle shattered the dresser mirror. Glass rained onto the floor. Slaps! Punches! My father ripped the clothes from my mother's body. Her muffled screams tore through the cracked plaster walls of the room where my two brothers and I were supposed to be asleep. I didn't know if Freddie and Peter were awake. My head was buried under my pillow. I was sobbing, begging God to make it stop. Another piercing scream. More slaps. There was the thud of a body falling to the floor.

The house became deathly still. The only sound I could hear was my father's uneven, heavy breathing in the hallway. He was drunk. His footsteps approached my room. I was terrified. I curled into a tight ball and clenched my eyes shut, pretending to be asleep as he stumbled through the room to check on us.

The next morning my mother was gone. Her bedroom was a shambles. Bloodstains covered the sheets. Glistening slivers of mirror carpeted the floor. Freddie was pale. I was sure he knew what had happened. He was the oldest and very close to our mother. In his eight short years he had grown to loathe my father. My five-year-old brother, Peter, was cheerful and didn't appear to know what had occurred that night. I kept hoping it had been a bad dream but I knew from Freddie's expression that it hadn't been.

In a subdued voice my father told us my mother had sneaked out during the night to join her lover. He said that she wasn't coming back and that the three of us were to be separated for a short time while he tried to figure things out. I couldn't understand what he was saying. My mother, a lover? Nothing he said made any sense.

My father had arranged for me to be taken in by a couple with four daughters who lived in a wooden-frame house along the river in the town of Lachine, where we lived. I didn't know what my father had said to the man but I had the vague impression he thought I was his to keep. The man said he had always wanted a son but his wife had produced only girls. He slapped his wife on her behind and winked as if I was supposed to know what he was talking about. I didn't want to be someone else's little boy. I was confused and scared. I cried out for my parents. I missed my mother's singing and playing the piano. The gentle way she stroked my head when I was frightened at night. She was a beautiful woman with long, flowing brown hair and deep, soft eyes that always managed a smile for her children even though her life was hell. I missed my father, in spite of his terrifying rages. He would appear often in my sleep. His coal-black, smoldering eyes dominated his Cossack features. A handsome and angry man, he drank too much, and when he was drunk he became ugly. He would fling bottles violently against the walls, dump a full dinner table onto the floor, and kick furniture out of his path. But worst of all were the beatings he gave my mother and the perverse name-calling she had to endure. Even at the age of seven, I knew what every insulting name meant.

Yet in spite of his fearsome temper, my father never beat me or my brothers. Sometimes he got in a solid slap or kick at one of us before my mother jumped into his path, but she bore the brunt of his punishment. He made her suffer.

I missed my brothers a lot. Freddie had been taken in by a Ukrainian family and Peter was staying at his godfather's home. His godfather, a beer-guzzling Ukrainian, was my father's best friend. I hated being away from home. My days were spent listening for the sound of my father's car, my mother's voice. At night I prayed feverishly to God to bring me back. I promised Him I would be good. I felt I must have done something wrong to have been taken away. I wanted Him to make everything better. In the morning I awoke to unanswered prayers.

During my three-month stay, the husband grew to detest me, partly perhaps because I rarely smiled or laughed. My sullenness seemed to provoke him. Mostly though, he hated me because I wouldn't call him "dad". I called him "mister" and that drove him wild. He raved "I'm better than your drunken father. You either learn to call me dad, buster, or get your butt out of my house."

Mister also hated me because I wet the bed.

At first the comforting warmth of wetting the bed felt good, but as the night wore on, it got very cold and clammy. I would lie shivering in the darkness, ashamed and too terrified to move until daylight. I remember darting under a bed one morning when the man slammed his fat hand down on the kitchen table.

"From now on he's sleeping on the cot in the porch, not in my house. Goddamn creep!" he bellowed.

"For Pete sake, George," his wife protested. "He's only a boy. What is wrong with you? Leave the boy alone."

"Shut your mouth. If I want your advice, I'll bark."

"Don't you talk to me – George, George, where are you going?"

I heard his footsteps heading towards my room.

"Where the hell? Get out from under the bed. You little chicken. Only sissies are chicken. Not boys."

I crawled out, crouching towards the far wall. I was afraid he was going to hit me.

"You're sleeping in the porch until you learn to stop pissing the bed. Your room smells like piss. It's disgusting! Babies pee the bed. Not seven-year-old boys. Are you a baby?" he asked in a mocking tone.

"No, mister."

His eyes shot out of their sockets. "Mister! You little son of a bitch. Get out. Get out!" he screamed.

"George, leave him alone. Go for a walk," his wife pleaded as she pushed him out of the room.

The girls in this new family liked having a brother. They enjoyed playing house in the basement and pulling down my pants for a game of doctor. I promised not to tell. We were playing in the basement when my father showed up one afternoon in late summer to take me home. I was so excited. When we arrived, Freddie and Peter were playing with their toy soldiers in the living room. My mother wasn't there.

"Boys, your mother has left me. She's not coming back. I don't know where the hell she is. I can't find her." His voice cracked. Tears welled in his eyes. Freddie ignored him. Peter and I began to cry.

"Tomorrow, some people are coming to take you boys to a new home. The welfare people won't let you stay here without your mother to look after you and I can't be here all the time. I have to work. They spent a lot of time looking for a place to keep you together and they found one."

"Daddy, I don't want to go away again," I begged. "They won't like me because I pee the bed."

My father didn't say a word. He opened the refrigerator and took out a quart of beer. Before the evening was over, he was asleep at the table, dead drunk.

I was sobbing when the welfare woman arrived the next day to take us away.

It was August 27, 1956.

A big, black car pulled up to deliver us to the foster home. It stopped an hour later outside a small cottage with two stately Christmas trees on the front lawn. A black cocker spaniel scampered up to greet us. Then a stout woman charged out of the house, screeching "They're here! They're here! Hello, boys. I'm Mrs. Simson." After a brief chat with the welfare woman, she showed us up to our room on the second floor. It was a large room with a window facing the street. A double bed was in the middle and a single cot was against one wall. Three bureaus lined the wall at the foot of the beds. She helped us put away our clothes and kept telling us how much we would like it there, how happy she was to have us, and that she'd "put some fat on those bones."

"But let's hurry," she insisted. "My husband will be home any minute now and supper still has to be cooked. So let's get washed up!" We did as we were told and then returned to the bedroom, where we sat very quietly, still stunned by the suddenness of what had happened.

"Boys! Come downstairs. I want you to meet someone," Mrs. Simson chirped. Freddie rolled his eyes. Peter and I giggled.

It was her husband, a bald, skinny man with thick bluish veins popping out of his hands and forehead. He was very tall and stooped a little. He was asking our names when the couple's daughter came in from work. She was in her late teens, sandy-haired and quite pretty.

Soon supper was ready and we sat down at the dinner table. I dug right in and received a light rap on the fingers with a wooden spoon. "We must say grace, mustn't we?" Mrs. Simson said. The food – dumplings in stew – was different from what we were used to. There were no seconds and it didn't taste as good as my mother's stuffed cabbage or perogies smothered in cold sour cream. I wondered where my mother was.

Although we had each taken a bath the night before, Mrs. Simson insisted we had to have another. The bathroom was opposite the kitchen. Peter was first. As the tub filled, Mrs. Simson hoisted Peter onto the kitchen table and undressed him. Her husband and daughter sat watching. When Peter was naked, the woman and her daughter took him into the bathroom and scrubbed him from head to toe. They stood him naked on the kitchen table and dried him. I was embarrassed for Peter. I dreaded my turn and retreated upstairs to fetch my pyjamas. Fred was in the tub when I got back. He looked very put off as the matronly woman scrubbed him down. She dried him in the bathroom and refilled the tub. My turn. I slowly began taking off my clothes. She stepped out for a moment, and I tiptoed in my underwear to the bathroom, locked the door, and began taking my bath in private.

She began screeching at me to open the door.

"I can take my own bath. You don't have to wash me."

She was fuming when I came out.

"Never lock the door! It's dangerous," she said, rapping me with a knuckle on the back of the head.

I was assigned the single cot because the welfare people had told her I wet the bed. As a precautionary measure, she had placed a rubber mat under the sheets to protect the mattress. Mrs. Simson assured me that she understood my problem and told me there was nothing to be ashamed of, adding with a smile that she would soon break me of "this silly habit". That night I wet the bed. She wasn't angry. She just smiled and changed the soiled sheets.

We attended Crawford Park School. I was in grade three, Peter in grade one, and Fred in grade four. My teacher, from what I can recall, was nice to me. She let me play the mouse who ate the cheese in a skit called "Who Ate the Cheese?" We performed it for the parents on Open School Day. My father didn't come to see my acting debut. He said he was busy. Every week we had to go to Sunday school at All Saints Church. Fred and I were each presented with a Bible story book for never having missed Sunday school that year. Peter was absent once because he had the flu. As a consequence, he wasn't entitled to an award, and he bolted out of the awards ceremony in tears. He wanted so much to have been called up for a prize like his older brothers.

My father visited us a couple of times a month and always left us five dollars to share for spending money. When he drove off, our foster mother took the money and said she would give us a little each Saturday. We rarely saw more than twenty-five cents among the three of us each week. Sometimes Fred stole milk bottles from in front of nearby homes and cashed them at the local grocery store so he could buy us some candy or ice cream, or a chocolate bar.

The Simsons detested my father. They kept telling each other how rotten and no good he was. Once I yelled at them to stop talking about my father like that and was given the strap by Mr. Simson.

"That will teach you to be rude to your auntie. Now you must apologize to her," he scolded.

After a while, Auntie Simson thought it would be nice if we called her "mother". Fred and Peter didn't seem to mind, but I refused.

Mrs. Simson's feelings about me were fixed forever on that day. Not long after, she began calling me names and no longer smiled when I wet the bed. She forbade me to drink anything after supper, but the remedy failed. She began waking me up at all hours. That too failed. Clutching a long wooden soup spoon, she yanked the sheets off me one morning while I was still asleep. I had wet the bed. The room smelled of urine. Tugging me by the hair onto the floor, she twisted me over the bed and rubbed my face into the soiled sheets, while she beat my backside with the spoon.

I struggled and screamed but she continued to press my face into the clammy sheets. Peter and Fred cried for her to stop. When her daughter tried to help her press my face into the sheets, Fred struck her on the chin with a closed fist. The two women turned their attack on Fred and gave him a severe beating. Mrs. Simson and her daughter submitted me to this treatment every morning for several weeks.

I remember the first time the social worker visited. She was the same woman who had brought us to the Simsons' house. We hadn't seen or heard from her in about four or five months, but I knew she was coming because Mrs. Simson had made us get cleaned up and told us to be on our best behavior. I made up my mind to tell the welfare lady what was going on. Throughout the morning I kept an eye on the walkway from my bedroom window. When her black car finally appeared, I charged down the stairs and out of the house, and blurted out through a blur of tears that Mrs. Simson was torturing me.

"Please . . . please, miss. She rubs my face in the wet bed. Please. I don't want to stay here any more. I'm scared. I hate it here."

The social worker looked down at me in disbelief and then looked toward the house, where Mrs. Simson stood grinning and shrugging her shoulders as if to say, "What can you do with the little fibber? My, how children let their imaginations run wild." She ignored me as we walked up the path.

"Hello . . . hello, Mrs. Simson. How are you today?" the social worker asked awkwardly.

"Fine. The children are a handful. Let me explain about Victor."

"Oh, don't worry. I, of all people, know how children tend to exaggerate. You should be grateful to Mrs. Simson, Victor," the social worker said with a frown, wagging her finger at me. "You shouldn't be naughty and tell such stories. Say you're sorry."

I refused.

"I said, say you're sorry," she repeated more forcefully.

I stood my ground.

"Go to your room and stay there until supper," Mrs. Simson said.

The welfare worker stayed about fifteen minutes, had some tea and doughnuts, and left without speaking to Fred and Peter. It was the only time we ever saw her during our year-long stay.

Mrs. Simson promised us a wonderful surprise at Christmas. She didn't disappoint us. The best Christmas present came with the chimes of the doorbell just after the turkey dinner. Mom! It had been almost nine months since we had seen her. We cried and hugged and cried.

We learned later that she had been recuperating in hospital from the severe beating she'd had from my father. When she was well enough to walk, she had run away from Lachine and disappeared into the bustle of Montreal. She'd found a room and was working as a waitress, saving money frantically to take us away. She'd learned through friends that we had been placed in a foster home, but when she'd contacted the welfare authorities, she was treated with scorn. The head of the agency accused her of desertion and told her she didn't deserve to be a mother. And then he ordered her out of his office. It had taken a lot of tears and begging but she persevered. She had almost given up hope when she remembered a sympathetic-looking captain from the Salvation Army she had served in the restaurant. He listened intently to her story and that very afternoon he marched into the welfare director's office demanding answers.

The Simsons liked my mother right away and boldly asked her how she could possibly have married a bum like my father. My mother didn't want to cause any trouble. She simply shrugged. I wanted to spit at them for talking about my father like that. After the first visit, my mother came every other Sunday with a huge shopping bag of home-cooked goodies.

Late that spring, my parents showed up unexpectedly together. Arm in arm, they were smiling and laughing, and announced that they were going to Niagara Falls for a second honeymoon. When they returned, we would go home, they promised. They kept their word and on June 21, 1957, five days before my ninth birthday, we left for a new beginning.

Life at home was peaceful and pleasant for the first few months. We had moved as far away as possible from Lachine and my father's drinking cronies to an apartment at the eastern tip of Montreal. But the east end also had its share of taverns, and before long my father knew where they all were. He met a new gang of boozers and loafers and within weeks lost his job. My mother went back to work as a waitress. Violent arguments, beatings, and unfounded, filthy accusations awaited her on her return from work. That year, we moved three times from one apartment to another after the landlords turfed us out. My father had used the rent money to entertain his friends.

In the fall of 1958, we moved a fourth time into a dilapidated rooming house near St. Lawrence Boulevard. Living in this slum was degrading for my mother and I could see she was devastated by it. My parents had a room on the first landing and my brothers and I shared a room on the second floor. Three bachelors – a depressed Ukrainian immigrant who spoke no English, a divorced German, and a drunken Pole named Jack – lived in the other three bedrooms. The only fun time I can remember happened when Freddie found a four-foot-long stuffed alligator with gaping jaws and vicious-looking teeth in an abandoned shed. We called the alligator Irving because of his weird grin. He looked as if he had just eaten someone's pet cat before he'd been stuffed. One night as Jack, the Polish boozer, was attempting to manoeuvre the staircase, we stole into his room and hid Irving under his sheets. Minutes later there was a hideous scream, followed by Jack's footsteps clamoring down the stairs. Ten minutes later the police arrived. They searched the room and told Jack to sober up. We played the same trick the next evening, with the same results. On the third night, Jack mutilated Irving with an axe.

Just after New Year's my parents had another of their stormy arguments. My father was angry because my mother forgot to buy his weekend supply of beer. After being slapped a few times, she screamed that she wasn't going to take any more of his abuse. She vowed that she would leave him for good. She was slapped again for talking back but this time she meant what she said.

"So, you're really going through with it, eh?" my father taunted.

"Yes, Mike," my mother answered calmly.

"What about the kids? They'll hate your guts for sending them away again. You'll see, Jennie. You'll see!"

"They'll understand one day. It'll be hard on them now, but one day they'll understand."

There was a pause and then the clatter of dishes being put in the kitchen sink.

"Why?" my father shouted, smashing his fist onto the table.

"Shh, Mike. You'll wake the kids!"

"Don't tell me to shh!" he yelled.

"Look Mike, I can't live with you any longer. I can't take your abuse."

"I'll change. Give me a chance. You'll see!"

"Mike, do you know how many times you've said that? You swore you'd stop drinking the first time I left. And how many times before that did you promise to stop drinking and hanging around with those drunken bums you call your friends? It's no use, Mike. Just leave it as it is. I'm leaving. I can't take it any more. Worrying about you coming home drunk. You scare the children. I can't take your hitting me and calling me names. Insulting and embarrassing me in front of my friends and the neighbors."

"Screw the neighbors!"

"Yes, Mike. That's your answer to everything. Screw them! Well, I'm sorry. It's too late now. I'm tired and I'm fed up. All I do is worry. Why do you always get into fights? Every time you go out you get into a fight. Every time you go to the tavern you come back cut up or the police come here to tell me you're in jail. You can't even hold on to a job! Mike, this isn't the life for me and the kids."

"Then go! Go ahead. Leave! F.O. at the high port. See if I care. But the kids are staying."

"They have to go. The man from the Home is picking them up tomorrow."

"Over my dead body."

"Mike!"

"Don't 'Mike' me or I'll belt you one so hard . . ." A glass shattered against the wall.

"Mike, the kids!" Mom pleaded.

"Shut up, you rotten bitch!"

"I'm going to bed."

"Who with?"

"That's right, Mike. That's right. Keep your filthy mind in the gutter." The bedroom door slammed shut.

"Drop dead! You . . ." A barrage of Ukrainian obscenities followed.

I buried my head in the pillow and sobbed. They couldn't split up. Not again! They loved each other and they loved us. It couldn't happen. Please, God, don't let it happen again. I promise I'll be good, I prayed. But I knew that it was happening, that they were really breaking up. It was over.

"Victor . . . Victor . . . wake up. It's time to get ready," my mother whispered as she ran her fingers gently through my hair the next morning.

I stared up into her red, swollen eyes, forcing myself to hold back the tears.

"Mommy, do we have to go? I don't want to go."

"It's not for long, Victor. The welfare people from the Red Feather thought it would be better if you boys got away from home for a while. They wanted you to stay together and they found this home for boys where you'll be able to live and come home and visit on weekends. I'll come to visit you after work. It won't be for long. You'll be back home this summer. I promise. I promise."

"But I don't want to go. They'll laugh at me."

"Why would they laugh at you?" she asked, stroking my cheek.

"Because I pee the bed."

"You'll get over that, Victor. They won't laugh at you. Now wipe your face and get dressed. Freddie, Peter, wake up," she called softly, tiptoeing over to their bed.

My brothers sat up, rubbing their eyes.

"Are we really going, Mommy?" Peter asked. My mother stared blankly at the wall and didn't answer.

"Mommy?" Freddie called out.

"You'll like it at the boys' home. They have swings, a swimming pool, and you can come home to visit every weekend. It's only for a little while. Now come on, let's get dressed and be quiet. Your father's sleeping."

The doorbell rang.

"Hurry up, Peter, Freddie. That must be the man from the Home."

We dressed quietly and then went downstairs.

"Boys, this is Mr. Johnson," she said as we came down from our room.

The man standing in the passage was tall and heavy-set. He looked like a detective in the movies. His black hair was thinning and silver at the sides. He wore a neatly pressed three-piece grey suit and a friendly smile.

Fred and I had met him three weeks earlier after a brief appearance at juvenile court for an alleged break-in. The charge was so ridiculous that the judge had thrown the case out of court. The three of us had been playing in the burnt-out shell of a store that had been gutted in a fire some months earlier. The owner and a friend nabbed Fred and me in the building and dragged us to the police station, where they laid charges of break and entry. At some point during the court appearance, our home situation had been discussed and arrangements were made for us to be sent to Weredale House, a home for boys in west-end Montreal. It had all happened so fast.

After placing our bags in the trunk of Mr. Johnson's car, we went back into the house to kiss Mom goodbye. She was holding back the tears. We were sobbing.

"Don't go into your father's room. He's sleeping and it's better not to wake him up. I'll see you boys this weekend. Be good."

I wondered what lay ahead for us as the car drove off, and for my mother when my father woke up and found us gone.

CHAPTER

2

The ride to Weredale House was deathly quiet and seemed to take forever. Every time we rounded a corner, I expected to hear the man say, "Well, here it is." He drove through the heart of the city along Dorchester Boulevard and then crossed Atwater Avenue into lower Westmount. A half-block later, the car turned into a tree-lined crescent called Weredale Park. A massive four-storey brown brick institution covered with thick, bare vines dominated the base of the crescent. A gleaming brass plate with WEREDALE HOUSE engraved in large black letters reflected the crisp winter sunlight outside the front entrance. A few low-rise apartment buildings lined one side of the street. On the other was a Protestant church and the Red Feather, the child and family welfare agency my mother had mentioned that morning.

We scooped up our belongings and made our way up a short flight of stairs leading into the home. As Mr. Johnson's hand pulled the door open, a buzzer sounded. A robust woman dressed in a white nurse's uniform scurried into the foyer.

"How do you do? I'm Mrs. Evans," she said.

"Mrs. Evans is one of the nurses on staff here," Mr. Johnson explained. "This is Fred Malarek, Victor, and the little one is Peter. They'll be staying with us for a little while." He then turned to Freddie. "The other boys are at school right now but they'll be back for lunch shortly. So, until then, you boys go and sit in the junior games room while I get you settled into your dormitories and find someone to look after each of you. By the way, while I've got you boys here, you should know that this area is restricted. My office is over there," he said, pointing to a closed wooden door to his right. "The visiting room is down the hall to the left." Mr. Johnson led us down a short, narrow corridor and through a door opening onto a large hallway. "This is the general office," he said, waving his hand at a small room sealed in by a wooden counter. Two desks, a wall of military-green cabinets at the far end, and a row of brown, dented metal filing cabinets under the counter were crammed into the office.

"Oh, while I've got you here . . . I'll be back in a second." Mr. Johnson disappeared behind the door we had just come through. A moment later, he returned with three thin files in one hand and a Kodak camera in the other. "Fred, stand up against the wall there. I want a picture of you. Victor, you'll be next, and then Peter."

Three clicks and it was over. Mr. Johnson opened a file, wrote in Peter's name, the number 156, and the date: February 18, 1959. Beside Freddie's name he wrote 157, and 158 next to mine.

"This is the junior games room," Mr. Johnson said as he put the files under his arm. He led us through a door with a wire-mesh window across from the main office. "Lunch will be in another hour, so you boys sit here until the boys get back from school. I'll see you shortly."

The three of us sat on the bench near the door and didn't say a word.

Looking around the shabby, sparsely furnished room, I wondered why it was called the junior games room. Except for two netless ping-pong tables covered with chips, gouges, and cracks, there was nothing to suggest a games room. The spacious room was painted in pale-green speckled paint. A flight of wooden bleachers was jammed into a small alcove to the left, halfway down from the entrance. They faced a caged-in cubicle in an opening in the wall, which contained two counters at right angles to each other – one facing the games room, the other, a similar room on the other side. There was an old, faded Coke cooler on the floor in the back corner and, hovering over it on a triangular unfinished-wood shelf, was a black-and-white television set. I learned later that the cubicle was called the canteen. I walked over to four large windows lining the wall at the back and peered out. One floor below was a yard covered with asphalt. In the centre was a slush-filled hockey rink. Enclosing the yard was a twenty-foot-high fence. On the other side ran two sets of railway tracks. I wondered where the swings and seesaws were that my mother had told me about.

"You're new here, eh?" a brittle voice inquired.

"Yes," I said, turning to face a boy the same size as me but wirier. He was pale and had thick, black, wavy hair. He stared directly into my face, chewing a wad of gum like the gangsters on television.

"What are you in for?" he asked.

"What . . . I don't know what you're – "

"What are you, dumb? What are you in for? How much time did you get? What did you do?"

"I didn't do anything."

"I'm in for car theft. Got three years," he boasted.

"This isn't a place like that," I said nervously.

Two other boys came in through a side door towards the back of the room and strolled over.

"Hargraves and Westfall here got time for robbing a store," he said.

"Yeah, that's why we're in today instead of at school, because we ran away last week. We got nabbed this morning sleeping under a balcony by the cops," said the one called Hargraves, a thin, pimply-faced boy with short sandy hair.

"You're not telling the truth. This place isn't for those kind of boys. It's for – "

"You calling us liars?" challenged Westfall. He was a well-built redhead with loads of freckles.

"No, but my mother said – "

"What does your mother know, kid? What they tell her and what you get in here are two different things. What a jerk!"

"I'm not a jerk," I said, staring up at Westfall.

"Don't get smart, kid," he said, shoving me against the window.

I pushed him back and he walloped me on the side of the head. Hargraves tripped me onto the floor from behind and kicked me in the leg. I hollered as loud as I could. Fred darted over from the bench with Peter close behind.

"Who hit him?" Fred asked.

"Why? What's it to you?" Westfall asked.

"I'm his brother."

"So, big deal. I hit him, runt," Westfall replied coolly.

Before he could get out another word, Westfall crumbled to the floor holding his nose. Hargraves rushed to his buddy's rescue and met the same fate.

"Nobody touches my brothers," Fred warned.

"What's going on here?" Mr. Johnson's voice boomed from the doorway. "What happened to you?" he asked, approaching me.

"Sir, he hit me for nothing and then he kicked me when I was on the floor. He's a dirty fighter." Tears were streaming down my cheeks.

Mr. Johnson turned on my attackers. "You two are supposed to be sick today. That's why you're home from school. Get in the clinic and wait for me there. I'll give you a reason to feel sick."

Their faces blanched as they scurried out of the room.

"Did you have anything to do with it, Reilly?" he asked, addressing the culprit who had instigated the whole thing.

"No, sir! I was just standing here, sir. I swear! I promise! Ask them!"

"Are you all right?" he asked, looking at me.

"Yes, sir," I said, wiping my running nose on my shirt-sleeve.

"You and your brothers go sit down on the bench near the door. The boys will be home for lunch soon. I'll assign one to look after each of you when they get back."

Reilly threw me a dirty look as Mr. Johnson turned to leave. A few minutes later Westfall limped in, grimacing and holding his ass. A whimpering Hargraves followed. Both had been strapped. Mr. Johnson was on their heels.

"Sit on the bleachers until lunch. After lunch the two of you go to school. Now get!"

At noon a loud bell clanged, bringing Mr. Johnson back into the games room.

"Reilly, take the Malarek boys downstairs and show them where to wash up for lunch."

"Yes, sir," he replied.

We followed Reilly out the side entrance, down a short flight of stairs, and into a big, dimly lit locker room. Rows of narrow, army-green lockers with combination locks built into the metal doors lined every available space along the walls. Thick wooden benches were bolted to the floor in front of the lockers. Directly across from the entrance was a line of stained white porcelain sinks with a bar of pink Lifebuoy soap on each. In one corner, adjacent to the sinks, was a small enclosed area with two urinals and two seatless toilets. No doors or dividers separated the toilets.

We washed our hands and started for the dining room, just as half a dozen boys charged into the locker room from outside. Reilly didn't say a word to any of us the whole time.

At the dining-room doors we lined up single file and waited. A small grey-haired woman, dressed in a white uniform, approached from the other end of the corridor.

"Hello. You must be one of the new boys who joined us today. I'm Miss Stewart, one of the nurses on staff here. What's your name?" she asked with a warm smile.

"Victor Malarek. Those are my brothers, Freddie and Peter."

"Hello, Freddie. My, aren't you adorable," she said, holding Peter's chin in the palm of her hand.

"I see you've met the Malarek boys," Mr. Johnson called out as he marched down the hall.

"Yes. Isn't the little one just adorable?"

"They'll be staying with us for a little while," he continued as he opened the doors to the dining room.

It was a large cafeteria-style room with a very high ceiling. The room consisted of four rows of tables with six chairs around each. On the tables were cutlery, a stack of twelve slices of bread, butter patties, and small bowls filled with caramel pudding. The service area occupied the entire upper left corner.

"Now, the route you take in the dining room is between rows three and four here. Up to the top, turn left, pick a tray near the railing, and get your food," Mr. Johnson explained. "You never use the centre aisle." He then strolled up the centre aisle to the front of the cafeteria. "Send them through, Miss Stewart."

The nurse first inspected our hands to make sure they were clean and ushered us in to get our lunch. As we were about to pass Mr. Johnson, he stopped us. He was holding a small black binder in his hand.

"When you come in from school for lunch, check off with me up here or with whomever I leave on duty. Just call out your name, wait till it's checked off, and go and get your meal," he said. "We may as well start right now."

"Fred Malarek," my brother said.

"Sir!" Mr. Johnson said, his polite smile momentarily leaving his face.

"Fred Malarek, sir!"

Mr. Johnson printed his name in the binder, and put a check mark beside it.

"Okay, next."

"Victor Malarek, sir!"

He did the same for me, and Peter followed.

We each grabbed a tray, were handed a plate of stew in the first section, and a bowl of watery soup and a glass of milk in the second section. We sat down at the first table next to a door leading to the kitchen. Throughout the meal Mr. Johnson sat perched on the window sill at the front of the cafeteria ticking off names in the black binder as a steady stream of boys filed in from school. Within twenty minutes, the cafeteria was packed with more than 120 hungry boys.

"Look at all the guys who live here," Fred said.

"I don't like the soup," Peter said.

"The meat in the stew is tough. It tastes too salty," I complained. "Look at the skin over the pudding."

Mr. Johnson cleared his throat loudly and the room fell silent. Three boys were standing beside him.

"Malarek boys, up here on the double."

All eyes were on us as we left the table.

"This is Fred, Victor, and Peter Malarek," Johnson said, introducing us to the boys. "This is Ricky Parsons, John Gray, and Lorne Cutler. They'll be showing you boys around over the next few days. Parsons, you'll show Fred around. Gray, you'll be in charge of Victor. And Cutler, you'll take care of little Peter here. After school they'll meet you in the games room. Now you boys go and finish your dessert and you boys go get your lunch. Scat!"

The three boys assigned to show us around seemed nice enough. Parsons, who was about an inch taller than Fred, looked very athletic. He was blond and well built. Gray seemed serious and pensive. He was skinny, about my size, and wore wrinkled pants. The boy assigned to Peter looked strong and happy-go-lucky. His fierce green eyes and dark-red curly hair reminded me of a picture I'd seen of a Viking.

When we finished our meal, we piled the dishes onto our trays and got up to bring them back.

"Reilly, show them the way," Mr. Johnson shouted.

Reilly grumbled something under his breath and led us between the tables. As we walked by Mr. Johnson, he stopped us for another lecture.

"When you're finished lunch, put up your hand. I'll give you a nod. Then you can go. This way here we'll avoid a traffic jam with boys just coming in from school. Okay?" His smile did not return to his face.

"Yes, sir," I replied. I noticed a brass school hand-bell resting in a corner of the window sill where Mr. Johnson was perched.

"Fine. Go put your dirty dishes in there," he said, pointing to the cubbyhole at the start of the service area.

Miss Stewart was standing a few paces away. She stopped us to inspect our plates to ensure we had eaten every morsel and weren't attempting to smuggle out any unsavory leftovers. She warned Peter that he'd have to finish his soup next time. We returned to the games room.

At about two in the afternoon, Miss Stewart called us into the clinic, which was next door to the general office. An old dentist's chair dominated the tiny room. Beside it was a deep sink. Wooden medicine cabinets with miniature windows lined the opposite wall. Below was a counter with drawers and cupboards.

"I'm going to measure and weigh you boys, so take off your shoes."

We did as we were told.

Fred and I were the same height — four feet, six inches — but I weighed ten pounds more. Peter measured four feet, two inches. Peter and I looked a lot alike. We both had dark hair and deep-brown eyes. Fred had sandy, blond hair with a cowlick, and greenish eyes. We all had fair complexions and slim builds, although Fred was wirier.

"How old are you boys?" Miss Stewart asked.

"I just turned nine on March 1," Peter said.

"I'll be eleven in June," I said.

"I'll be twelve in July," Freddie replied.

She marked the information in a loose-leaf binder and moments later dismissed us. The boys had started to trickle in from school when we returned to the games room.

"Hi," Gray said, coming over to me by the window. "I have to go and check off. I'll be with you in a second." He went over to the canteen, called his name out to an older boy inside the cage, and came back.

"Want me to show you around?"

"I guess so. I'm tired of sitting in this room."

"We can't go upstairs to the dormitories yet. They're closed until bedtime."

"What time do we go to bed?"

"Lights out at 8:30."

"8:30! At home I go to bed around 11:00."

"This isn't home. You get a slip of paper telling you your locker numbers and what dormitory you're in yet?"

"No."

"Let's go get them."

We went to the general office and waited in front of the counter.

"What is it?" asked the secretary sitting in the office.

"Has he been assigned to a dormitory yet and given his locker numbers? Mr. Johnson told me I have to show him around and —"

"Which one are you?" she interjected.

"What?" I asked.

"Which Malrick are you?"

"Victor. Victor *Malarek*. It's Ukrainian."

"Ah, here it is. Malrick, Victor. Here you go."

She handed Gray a small brown envelope. He tore it open.

"You're in the same dormitory as me, junior north, bed 16," he said. "You're in locker 35 downstairs and 16 upstairs. These are the combinations and this," he said, indicating the digits 158 at the bottom of the paper, "is your laundry number. When you've memorized your combinations, throw the paper away. Don't keep it around. And don't tell anyone your combinations. Do you have any stuff to put away? Did you bring any clothes with you?''

"Yes. They're in a bag on the floor in the office.''

"Miss, can I come in and get his bag?'' Gray asked the secretary.

"Okay.''

In the locker room, under the games room, Gray showed me how to open the locker.

"Your combination is 34-10-34 for this locker. Now here's how it works.''

After watching Gray four more times, and a half-dozen attempts later, I finally managed to open the locker by myself. We put away my clothes and went on a tour of the building.

"These locker rooms across from ours are for the seniors and working guys. The games room next to ours is also for them. You aren't allowed in there until you're promoted to the senior side, so stay out of there.''

Gray then pointed to a wide flight of stairs which led up to the general office dividing the front half of the two games rooms and the locker-room area where we were.

"Those stairs are only used by staff. Never use them or you'll get into trouble. Do you want to see the sub-basement?''

"I guess so. Why can't we use those stairs?''

"I don't know. I never asked. We just don't use them.''

We headed down the same flight of stairs which continued from the games rooms. The sub-basement was dark and eerie. It had a very low ceiling. I could touch it if I jumped just a little. The whole area was painted lower half black and upper half silver. It was ugly. Surrounding four pillars in the centre area and jutting out from the walls on opposite sides was steel piping. Hanging from them, attached to link chains, were shoe brushes.

"You brush your shoes down here. Brown shoe polish on this side, black on the other. You shine them with the brushes around the pillars. This place is also for scraps.''

"Scraps?''

"Fights! Most of the scraps take place down here. That way the staff can't hear all the shouting and screaming from the guys watching.''

"Oh.''

"Over there,'' he said, waving to a blackened corner where the light had burned out, "is the gym. It's closed now but you'll see when we have gym. We mostly play floor hockey.''

A bell sounded.

"Time for supper."

Again we lined up outside the dining-room doors waiting for Johnson to arrive. Everyone stopped talking when he appeared. He opened the doors and counted the boys in six at a time, waiting for each group to be served before letting in another half-dozen. I sat down at the dinner table with Gray and four other boys I had not yet met.

"Hey, kid, what dormitory are you in?" asked one of the boys.

"Junior north," Gray said.

"What's your name, kid?" another asked.

"Victor."

"Victor what?"

"Victor Malarek."

"Mala-what?" he asked with a sneer on his lips. The boy sitting beside him laughed.

"Malarek."

"What kind of name is that?"

"It's Ukrainian."

"Wow, a U-ker-anian!" he mouthed mockingly. There was more giggling.

"Ukrainian," I repeated correctly.

"Going to take your initiation, kid?"

"I don't know what you mean."

"You didn't tell him about initiation yet, Gray? Wow! Every new kid has to get initiated. You'll probably get it tonight. Depends who's on staff in the dormitory."

"Knock it off, you guys," Gray said.

"Oh wow, look at the big man! Johnson gives the suck-hole the new kid to show around and he thinks he's tough. Anytime, Gray. I'll meet you in the sub-basement anytime you like."

"This dining room is getting too noisy," Mr. Johnson shouted angrily from his perch on the window sill. Everyone stopped talking and all that could be heard was the clinking of knives and forks scraping the plates.

After supper, Gray and I went to the games room.

"When does Mr. Johnson eat?" I asked.

"After our supper in the staff dining room. It's on the other side of the building."

"Do they eat the same stuff?"

"Are you nuts? They get steak, pork chops, chicken, pie. It's cooked special for the staff."

"Does Mr. Johnson live here?"

"Yeah. Him and his wife do. So do all the staff and nurses. They have quarters on the third floor and in the new wing on the east side."

Another bell sounded. The boys started to empty out of the games room.

"Studies. You don't have to go tonight. You didn't go to school today."

"Go where? What's going on?"

"We go to study rooms for an hour now to do our homework. Stay here and wait for me. I'll see you later." Gray left.

I went over to join Fred and Peter on the bleachers.

"I don't like this place. I hate it."

"Yeah, it's not like Mom said it would be," Fred said.

"I want to go home," Peter moaned. He started to cry.

"It's no use crying, Peter. You can't go home, so quit crying," Fred said.

"But I don't like it here," Peter cried out.

"Do you think I like it here?" Fred snapped.

"Thank God it's only until the summer," I said. "Did you know some of the guys have been here for four years?"

"That's nothing. One of the staff I met has been here for ten years, since he was twelve," Fred added.

"I wouldn't want to live here for ten years," I said.

One of the older boys from the senior side came into the games room, unlocked the canteen door, and turned on the television. Our attention switched to the hockey game. A bell sounded at 8 p.m. and the boys came pouring back into the games room. As I was getting up from the bleachers, a plump, dark-haired boy about my height approached me as Fred and Peter went off together.

"Are you the new kid in junior north?" he asked.

I nodded.

"What's your name?"

"Victor Malarek."

"Malarek, eh? I'm Dave Janigan. What bed you in?"

"Bed 16," I said looking down at the slip of paper with my locker numbers, combinations, laundry number, dormitory, and bed number on it.

"That's next to me. I hear you're a stoolie. You stooled on Hargraves and Westfall today."

"Stoolie? I don't know what you mean."

"Stool pigeon. Squealer. You squealed on Hargraves and Westfall."

"They beat me up," I offered in my defence. "Anyway I didn't squeal on them. Mr. Johnson saw me crying and asked me what happened."

"So you stooled on them. You'd better not stool when you get initiated."

That word again. It made me shiver.

"What do you mean, initiated?" I asked. A small group had gathered round.

"We initiate new guys into the dorm. Everyone goes through it. If you're too chicken, then you'd better watch out. No one here likes chickens and suck-holes."

"I'm not a chicken. What do I have to do?"

"You got a choice. Run the galley, get black-balled, or have the toothpaste treatment."

"Black-balled?"

"We put shoe polish on your nuts, or toothpaste. Pepsodent. The toothpaste stings for a while but it's better than a week of trying to wash off the shoe polish."

"Yeah, you'll wonder where the yellow went when you rub your balls with Pepsodent," one of the boys chanted. The guys burst out laughing.

"Do I have to take that?" I asked nervously. The thought of having guys rub shoe polish or toothpaste on my genitals disgusted me.

"You could run the galley."

"What do you have to do for that?"

"Run three times from one end of the dorm and back. The guys smash you with pillows, punch you on the arm or the back, or kick your ass as you run by. You pass if you make it. Better decide soon, kid," he said as he turned away.

I was biting my nails when Fred came back to investigate the commotion around me.

"Anything wrong?" he asked.

"Did they tell you about initiation?"

"Yeah. Don't worry about it. Just take it. They won't hurt you."

"Are you going to take it?"

"Yeah. I'm going to run the galley."

"I guess I will too," I mumbled.

Another bell sounded.

"Geez! They got a lot of bells here," I said.

"Come on, Malarek," Gray shouted to me from the doorway.

I ran over. "Victor," I said.

"What?" Gray asked.

"My name is Victor."

"Yeah. Do you want to take a shower or go up to the dorm?" he asked.

"Do I have to take a shower?"

"No, they're not compulsory today but tomorrow they are."

"I don't feel like taking a shower. I took a bath at home last night."

"Okay, let's go up to the dorm."

We climbed up the stairs to the fourth floor.

"That's the intermediate floor," Gray said as we passed the third landing. "It's the same as our floor but most of the guys are in high school. You'll be there in a couple of years."

"I won't be here that long. I'll be back home in a few months."

"Yeah, sure you will," he said flatly.

"It's true. I will. My mother said so."

The corridor on the fourth floor was long, wide, and empty. To the left, adjacent to the staircase, was an open wooden door through which I could see the junior dormitories. A few steps down, we took a right turn into a small, cramped locker room. The lockers were about one foot shorter than those downstairs, and lined both sides of the walls, leaving barely enough room for the boys to change without constantly bumping into each other. The doors in the centre on each side cut the locker room in half. One led into junior north, a long, narrow, well-lit room that looked very much like a military barracks with twenty-one identical beds lining two sides of the walls. A strong scent of urine tainted the air. Red woollen blankets with black stripes at either end covered the brown metal cots. Two of the beds had yellow-stained sheets hanging over the head frames like lean-to tents. A three-foot space separated each bed. There was a window at the far end of the room and four more along the north wall. There were no curtains.

"Why are the sheets hung over the bed like that?" I asked Gray.

"To dry them out. The piss-heads pissed them last night. The sheets are only changed on Monday."

"Oh," I whispered faintly.

"You're not a piss-the-bed, are you? Christ, that's all we need is another piss-head. We've got two already," said a tough-looking boy as he barged into the dormitory.

"Uh, no . . . no," I replied, avoiding his cold stare.

"This is McDougal. He's dorm monitor. What he says goes," Gray said, introducing me to the boy who had just asked me the embarrassing question.

"This is Malarek."

"My name is Victor."

He looked me over like a horse at a farm auction.

"I met your two brothers in the games room. The blond guy, is he older or are you?"

"He's older."

"He's in this dorm too. Is he a piss-head?"

"No."

"Good."

"Come on, you'd better get ready for bed," Gray said.

"Are all the dormitories this big?" I asked.

"No, we're the biggest on this floor. Twenty-one beds. Junior south, across from us, has sixteen, and west, down the hall has eleven. The intermediate floor has exactly the same layout. When you hit the senior side you get three or four guys to a room."

I fidgeted with my combination lock a number of times but couldn't get it open. I was still worrying about wetting the bed.

"Here, let me help you," said a smiling face.

I offered the boy the paper with my combination on it.

"Never mind. I'll open it," Gray interrupted, jerking the paper from the boy's grasp. "Don't show anyone your combination," he warned. "Especially him. It's for your own good. If you need help, call me. You show too many guys your combination, you'll find yourself robbed one day. There are a lot of crooks in here."

After I was in my pyjamas, I went to wash up and go to the toilet. The washroom was through the other door dividing the locker room. It was a brightly lit room, tiled in white marble. Six sinks hung off the wall opposite the door. To the right were two urinal stalls, and in a small, indented space beside them was one toilet with no door. McDougal was squatting over it.

"Don't they have doors on the toilets?" I shyly asked one of the boys standing at the urinal beside me.

"Why? You queer or something?" he asked.

"No. It's just that —"

"Kid, they don't even let you shit in peace here," McDougal snarled as he reached for some toilet paper.

"They want to make sure you're not whacking off," one of the boys added.

Everyone broke out laughing. I didn't get it, but I was too shy to ask what he meant, so I laughed along. After I finished washing, Gray showed me to my bed.

"That's bed number 1," he said as we passed the first bed to the left of the entrance. "One to 10 on that side, 11 to 21 on the right. So 11,

12, 13, 14, 15, 16. That's your bed." Janigan was sitting on bed 15.

"Hi, stoolie," he said.

"Cut it out, Janigan," Gray said. "He's new. Don't be such a jerk on his first day."

"Yeah, yeah."

Fred came into the dormitory with the guy who was showing him around.

"Everything all right?" Fred asked as he passed my bed.

"I guess so. I don't know."

"Peter is down the hall in the dormitory they call junior west," Fred said as he continued to his bed, number 12.

"Is that your brother?" Janigan asked.

"Yes."

"Doesn't look like your brother."

"Everybody get into bed! Now! Move!" a voice from the hallway boomed.

The boys still in the locker rooms scrambled into the dormitory and dove onto their beds.

"Damn! Maitland's on staff," Janigan muttered. "You're fuckin' lucky, kid. No initiation tonight."

"What are you doing out of bed, Reilly?" a man with short-cropped brown hair yelled as he came into the dormitory. He was wearing running shoes, white sweat socks, light-blue flannel pants, and a white shirt with the sleeves rolled up below the elbows.

"Sir . . . I . . ." Reilly started nervously.

"Get into bed. Move!"

So Reilly was also in my dormitory. He burst in and jumped into the bed across the aisle from me.

Maitland glared momentarily up and down the room. He was about five feet six inches tall, very hard, sinewy, and mean-looking. He had been in Weredale since he was twelve, a little more than half his life. He became a working senior when he was seventeen and went on staff for free room and board when he was twenty-one. During the day, he worked as a shipper for a clothing manufacturer.

Once the boys were under their sheets, Maitland opened the small black binder clutched in his right hand and began calling out the boys' names by bed number. Each boy shouted out "Sir" when his name was called.

"Malarek, F."

"Sir," Fred shouted. And so on down the roll the staff continued.

"Parsons."

"Sir."

"Boucher."

"Sir."

"Janigan."

"Sir."

"Malarek, V."

"Sir."

This litany continued until he reached bed 21, when he slammed the binder shut and surveyed the room.

"There are two new boys in the dormitory, but there will be no initiation tonight. Is that understood? No initiation."

"Yes, sir," the boys replied in unison.

Maitland stomped out.

"What a prick!" Janigan said as the lights went out.

I hardly slept that night. I kept tossing and turning, wondering what sort of a place I was in. I hated it so much already, how could I stay here until the summer? I started to cry, burying my face deep into my pillow so no one could hear me. What kind of place is this, I kept asking myself over and over. God, please make everything all right. I'll be a good boy from now on. I promise. I want to go back home. Why am I being punished? What did I do wrong? I was sure I had been put here because I was bad. No one had ever taken the time to tell me just what was really going on. Everyone talked in whispers and half-truths. All I had to rely on was my vivid imagination and my deep fear of God. I figured that somehow I had offended Him and now He was paying me back.

My head was reeling as I fell into an uneasy sleep.

CHAPTER

3

"Wakey, wakey,
Rise and shine!
If you don't get up,
I'll boot your behind!"

I opened my eyes slowly, hoping that the day before hadn't happened and that I was home in my own bed. I felt rotten when I saw Janigan's face. But thank God for one miracle, my sheets were dry! The staff on wake-up duty was in the dormitory across the hall.

"Wakey, wakey,
Rise and shine!"

"What time is it?" I asked, turning to Janigan.

"7:30."

"Boy, am I ever tired. I hardly slept last night."

"Who gives a shit," he muttered.

I stumbled out of bed and into the locker room, where I asked Gray once again to show me how to open my locker. After I had washed and dressed, Gray and I headed to the dining room. The same routine held for breakfast as for the other meals, except no one had to wait in line at the door. We had lumpy porridge doused with a heaping tablespoon of brown sugar, two slices of bread with jam, and a glass of milk.

"I guess you'll be going to school today," Gray said. "What grade are you in?"

"Five."

"Too bad! That means you get Morrison!"

"Who's he?"

"A teacher who hates Weredale guys."

We continued eating. As we were bringing up our dishes, Mr. Johnson stopped us.

"You'll be bringing young Malarek here to school today. I have his report card and a letter for you to give to the principal."

"Yes, sir."

"All right. Get going." He didn't break into his polite smile.

"Yes, sir," we replied in unison.

Gray came over to my locker as I was tugging on my rubber boots.

"We have to line up in the corridor for check-off every morning before school," he said.

"Another check-off! Is this some sort of a jail? They're always checking you off and ringing bells."

"Don't let Johnson hear you talk like that. Better get used to it. Check-off for school is in alphabetical order. First the St. Leo's boys. Catholic school starts fifteen minutes earlier. Then senior high school, junior high, then Queen's School. You won't be put in alphabetical order until next month, so go to the end of the line. I'll wait for you."

Peter, Fred, and I were checked off last.

We walked out of the side entrance of the building, along a catwalk called the Boardwalk leading onto Atwater Avenue. Up Atwater hill, west along Dorchester to Greene Avenue.

"Why don't we just go out the front door? It's faster and you don't have to walk up this hill," I asked.

"The front door is for the staff and visitors. We're not good enough to use it," one boy snarled as he trotted by.

"Don't ever use those doors. You'll get a detention or the biffs," Gray warned.

At Greene Avenue, we turned onto St. Catherine Street for a short block, and then right, onto a quaint, tree-lined avenue called Olivier, where a few steps from the corner stood Queen's School. All the Weredale boys in elementary grades, except for a few Catholic boys who attended St. Leo's Academy, went to Queen's along with the boys and girls from lower Westmount. The boys in grades seven, eight, and nine went to Westmount Junior High and those in grades ten and eleven to Westmount Senior High.

"Remember the route we took," Gray said as we reached the school door. "Never take any other way. If you get caught on St. Catherine Street east of Greene, you'll get a detention or the biffs."

Queen's looked much like any other school. A three-storey brown brick structure with pupils' artwork decorating the windows. The play yard was across the street.

After I had spent a few minutes in the general office, the day monitor took me to a classroom on the first landing. He knocked on the door and we entered. A bald-headed man in his fifties was taking attendance. He was wearing a grey flannel suit.

"Yes?" Morrison said, looking up at the monitor over his wire-rimmed glasses.

"I brought a new boy to your class, sir."

"Fine. Leave him here. You may go."

The boy left.

"Where are you from?" he asked with a look of indifference.

"What, sir?"

"Where do you live, young man?" he snapped.

"In Weredale Boys' Home."

"Oh, God! Not another one. What did I do to deserve this?" he mumbled, his eyes rolling up to the ceiling. "Your name is Victor Malarek," he said, looking at the piece of paper the monitor had given him.

"Yes, sir."

"Sit behind David there. Maybe you'll learn something from him," he said, waving to a boy in the second row who was not from Weredale.

As I sat down at my assigned desk, there was another knock at the door. The same monitor entered. He had a smirk on his face. Fred was behind him.

"Sir, I have another new boy for your class."

Morrison took the note from the monitor and waved him out of the room. His eyes fixed on Fred.

"And where are you from?"

"Weredale, sir."

"Good God! Not two in one day."

A few students laughed.

"You're not his brother?" he asked, pointing to me after reading the name on the note the monitor had given him.

"Yes, sir."

"Which of you is the ten-watt bulb? In other words, who failed?"

"I did last year, in grade five," Fred answered angrily.

"Don't use that tone with me, sonny. Go sit down behind one of your Weredale mates over there," he said, nodding towards the fifth row by the window.

At noon, Gray and I and more than one hundred Weredale boys walked the same route home for lunch. We washed our hands. Miss Stewart checked them for cleanliness and Mr. Johnson checked us off.

After lunch, Morrison decided to give Fred and me a test to see where we stood in relation to his grade five class. He ordered us to stand up and fired off a series of history, geography, and mathematics questions. Although Fred didn't have time to answer most of them, he managed to keep his cool. I got muddled up and started to cry.

"Crying won't help. What kind of a school did you boys go to? I'm afraid, Mr. Victor Malarek, that you'll have to pull your socks up or I'll simply have to fail you," he said, staring indifferently at the attendance sheet on his desk. He turned to Fred. "It won't be any use failing you again, but I just might do so if you don't improve."

Fred shot back a look as if he couldn't care less.

"Both of you, sit down. Class, take out your history books."

After school, I didn't wait for Gray and trudged back to Weredale alone. He found me staring out the window in the games room.

"Why didn't you wait for me? I waited for you for twenty minutes. Christ! Tell me next time if you're going to take off without me. I was almost late for check-off."

I didn't answer him.

"Did you check off?"

"Another check-off?"

"Don't get pissed off at me! I don't make the rules. After school, check off at the canteen. You'd better go do it before 4:30 or — "

"Or I'll get a detention or the biffs. I know." I went to check off.

When supper was over, Fred, Peter, and I were summoned to the office.

"The three of you will be in bench studies," Johnson said. "It's on the junior floor. So when the bell rings for studies, you boys go there. Bring your homework with you, or a book to read if you haven't any homework."

We went back into the games room and waited for the study bell.

Bench studies was less a matter of homework than of giggling, passing gross notes, forcing burps and disgusting farts. It was for grade fives and under. A long wooden desk lined each of the two walls. A third one ran down the centre of the room. Long wooden benches on thick steel pipes bolted to the cement floor served as seats. The desk tops were unpainted, stained with ink, and gouged with initials and holes. About fifty boys crammed onto the benches.

Next door was junior studies, another study room, which resembled a typical classroom. Boys in grade six and some grade fives studied there. The junior- and senior-high-schoolers studied in a classroom above the gym called senior studies.

At the start of the one-hour study session, a staff member came in and took check-off. Two monitors from the senior side, who really couldn't give a damn about what was going on, were appointed to keep order as well as to help anyone who had homework problems.

When the bell sounded, there was a mad scramble for the door. I wandered back to the games room to wait for Gray. I was sitting on the bleachers when a voice taunted: "There's the stoolie."

It was Reilly. Beside him was a short, obnoxious-looking kid from my dormitory whose name was Boucher.

I ignored the remark.

"Malarek didn't get initiated last night," Reilly continued. "But he will tonight. Boy, will he get it tonight."

"Mal-o-rick! That your name, kid?" Boucher asked.

"It's Victor *Malarek*," I said.

"Excuse me, Mr. Malarek, sir," Boucher sneered. There was a pause, short but tense. "Hey . . . you know how you got here?" A vicious grin spread across Boucher's pimply face.

"What?"

"How did you get here? You speak English or French?"

"Yeah. The welfare people — "

"No. That's not what I meant. How were you hatched? Do you know how you were born?" Boucher asked.

"The same way we all were."

"Yeah, but how, stupid? How did your parents have you?" Reilly interjected.

"Don't call me stupid."

By this time, a group had gathered. Wry smirks were plastered on most of their faces.

"My mother and father wanted me — "

"Yeah, and?" a voice in the crowd urged.

"They prayed for me and God sent down an angel with me — "

Before I could finish, they broke up in a fit of laughter. A couple dropped to the floor laughing. I couldn't understand what was so funny. Reilly stopped laughing abruptly and glared at me.

"You know how you really got here?"

"I told you."

"Jerk-face! Your parents had a good, hard fuck!"

"Don't talk like that!" I was shocked that anyone could accuse my mother and father of committing such a filthy act. "You shouldn't talk like that!" I was starting to shake.

"You have to fuck, kid, to have babies. You pray to go to heaven," Boucher blurted out between laughs.

"You shouldn't say things like that. My parents wouldn't do anything like that. God sent me to them because they were good and they wanted me." Tears blurred my vision. "Don't talk dirty about my –"

"They fucked, kid. Face it. You have to fuck to have babies," Reilly tormented.

Fred had come into the games room and heard the tail end of what was happening. He pushed his way through the raucous group and hauled me out.

"Don't forget, Malarek. They had a good, hard fuck!" Reilly yelled as we walked away.

"Freddie, how could they talk like that about Mommy and Daddy?" I cried, wiping my running nose with my shirt-sleeve.

"Don't pay any attention to them. They're nuts."

"It's not true what they said, is it?"

"Well, in a way, yeah. But they don't do it the way they put it."

"But Mommy told me a long time ago that God sent us."

"I know, but that's not all of it. You came through them. Whether you're born or not is up to God."

I was shattered. I couldn't believe what Freddie was telling me. To me, my parents were pure and clean. They could never commit that filthy act. My parents didn't fuck. Not them! Fucking was dirty. It was disgusting. How could those animals talk like that and laugh when I mentioned God? What kind of place was this? I fell in a heap in a corner and stared into space.

Gray eventually came to get me. Freddie had taken off with Parsons, with whom he was getting along great. Gray, by this time, was tolerating me.

"Let's go down to the locker room," my escort said.

I followed him downstairs. We had just reached the locker room when someone bolted past yelling: "Fight! Fight! In the sub-basement!"

"Let's go!" Gray said, running out the door. I was on his heels.

I was shocked when I saw who was fighting. It was Fred and Reilly. Fred had Reilly's arms pinned under his knees and was telling him to give up when a much bigger kid punched Fred on the side of the head and then kicked him in the stomach. Freddie rolled on the floor holding his head. I started to cry and ran out of the sub-basement looking for someone to stop the fight. I felt like a coward for not helping my brother, but the other boy was so big. What could I do against him, I kept screaming to myself. I was a chicken. He had kicked Fred. There was two to one. That wasn't the way to fight. My father had taught Fred how to box. He'd taught him that one on one is fair. Don't kick, scratch, or bite! Fight like a man! But there was nothing fair here. I didn't know whom to run to, where to go. I ran to the general office but no one was there. There were no staff in the games room. I scrambled back down to the locker room. Fred was there washing his face.

"Are . . . are you hurt?" I sobbed.

"Christ! You'd think you got beat up! Why do you always cry? No, I'm not hurt."

"Those guys don't fight fair."

"It's okay. I'll fight like they do from now on. I'll get Dad to teach me."

The bell clanged. It was 8:30. I was starting up the stairs when a staff member collared me.

"Where do you think you're going?" he asked in a cheerful British accent.

"Up to my bed, sir."

"Not yet. Compulsory showers tonight. Downstairs, sonny, and get ready."

Outside the locker room, a dozen or so boys were lined up alongside the wall with just their underwear on and red-and-white-striped towels slung over their shoulders.

"Hi, Mr. Douglas. You on duty tonight?" someone shouted to the Englishman behind me.

"Yep," he chirped, unlocking the green door that led to the showers. The line disappeared inside.

At my locker, I stripped to my underwear, wrapped a towel around my waist, and got into an ever-growing line.

"Next three," Douglas shouted from within.

I walked timidly through the narrow passageway and into a bright, white-tiled room. A couple of boys were standing naked drying themselves. The boys I came in with yanked off their underwear and darted into a steam-filled shower room packed with naked bodies.

I was stunned by the scene unfolding before me.

"Come on, come on," Douglas coaxed, sensing my fear and shyness.

I removed my underwear and, with my hand cupped discreetly in front of my penis, tiptoed in. Jets of hot water poured down onto soapy bodies from six shower heads jutting out from the ceiling. About fourteen boys were showering. Some had erections. I washed gingerly, facing the wall. After a brief drenching I made my way to the exit.

"Whoa! Get into line for inspection and check-off," Douglas said.

I joined the line behind four naked bodies. Two other boys got behind me. Someone rubbed a bar of soap between my buttocks, which really upset me and forced me to retreat to the showers for another rinse. I got back into line, but this time I kept one hand behind me for protection and the other as discreetly as I could over my penis. I didn't want it to rub accidentally against the boy in front of me, who was now facing Douglas for inspection and check-off. The boy was an intermediate and about fourteen years old. I watched in amazement as he went through an embarrassing, degrading routine that I would go through countless times before leaving the home for good. He stretched out his hands over his head, spread his legs, and stood in that position for a brief moment.

"Jennings, intermediate south, bed 4," he called out to Douglas, who held a black binder in his hand.

"Turn," Douglas said. The boy turned a quarter with his left flank exposed for inspection.

"Turn." His back was to Douglas and an erection brushed my hand. I jumped backwards and was shoved forward by someone warning me to "watch it".

The boy was now facing Douglas again.

"Back to the showers and cool off," the staff shouted. The boy dashed into the steamy room.

"Hands over your head and spread your legs," he said as I took one pace forward. I stood in front of him, hands stretched over my head, legs spread as he looked me over for signs of dirt.

"Turn." I turned sideways.

"Turn." My back was to him. I was facing another erection. My stomach began to churn.

"Turn. Fine. Name, dormitory, and bed number?" he asked.

"Victor Malarek, junior north, bed . . . I forgot my bed number, sir." I was in a daze.

"No worry. Ah, here it is. Bed 16," he said, putting a check mark next to my name in the black binder.

"Okay. You have time for a short swim or you can go up to your dormitory."

To my left, through a small opening, was a swimming pool. A score of naked boys were jumping, diving, and swimming about. All I wanted was to get my underwear on and go up to the dormitory.

"Tonight for sure!" Janigan said with a menacing grin as I flopped down onto my bed.

"Tonight what?" I asked through a haze.

"Your initiation. Douglas is on staff."

Janigan's words hardly registered. All I could think about was the pigs in the showers.

"All right, all right. Let's keep it down to a low roar," Douglas shouted as he sauntered into the dormitory. He took check-off and headed to do the other dormitories on the floor.

Initiation. The word suddenly clicked in my mind.

"Does everyone on the floor initiate you?" I asked Janigan.

"No, just the guys in the dormitory."

The room went black. There was dead silence for about ten minutes. No one moved.

"Frenchie?" McDougal whispered into the dark.

"Yeah?" he giggled.

"Go keep nix."

"Ah, come on!"

"Don't worry, you'll get your chance. There's two of them."

Frenchie slithered out of bed 2 onto the floor and disappeared into the locker room. A moment later he crept back to the doorway.

"All clear," he whispered.

McDougal got up and went over to Fred's bed.

"You ready?"

Fred crawled out of bed.

"What do you want, toothpaste rubbed on your nuts? No one brought up any shoe polish. Or run the galley?"

"The galley."

"Everyone in front of your beds," McDougal whispered loudly.

Some of the boys took their pillows. Others punched their fists into their open palms. There was a lot of giggling.

"You too, Malarek. Out of bed."

I stood up in front of my bed.

"You run up and down the dormitory three times. Start from whatever side you want," McDougal instructed. "And remember, you guys, punch on the arm, kick his ass. No shots to the guts or nuts. Or else!"

Fred took off, his arms protecting his head. Pillows and fists let fly. Three times up and down the dormitory and it was all over. I never touched Fred as he flew by. He was beaming when he reached the starting point. He looked over towards me and with a glance assured me that it wouldn't hurt. I felt a little relieved.

"Reilly, go relieve Frenchie on nix."

"Ah, come on. I want to get in on this one."

"Go relieve Frenchie."

"Fuck you, McDougal. I want to —"

"Move or I'll kick your fucking head in!" McDougal threatened.

"Okay. Okay. I'm gone."

Reilly tiptoed out, squatting down on all fours when he got to the locker room. Frenchie came in doing a samba. Everyone laughed.

"Shh, not so loud."

"Ready, Malarek?" McDougal asked as he approached my bed.

"I'll . . . I'll run the galley."

"Any time you're ready."

I braced myself at the doorway and took off, my hands covering my head. A couple of pillows hit me. Then a painful punch stung my shoulder as I passed Janigan's bed. The rest of the way down was easy. On the way back I prepared myself for Janigan's next blow and managed to dodge it. Twice more and I was initiated. I had made it and felt proud.

"Way to go, kid," Frenchie said, slapping my back as I headed towards my bed.

He seems like a pretty nice guy, I thought. I had noticed Frenchie in my class sitting beside Freddie. He was always fooling around and getting kicked out of class for one thing or another. He had a loud, infectious laugh and laughed at anything. This drove Morrison around the bend. Frenchie's eyes always sparkled. His black wavy hair and a little scar above his lip gave him the roguish appearance of a French Foreign Legionnaire. He was thirteen and only in grade five.

"You're lucky I missed you with that last shot," Janigan said as I pulled the sheets over me.

"Too bad."

"Nix . . . Nix!" Reilly signalled, rushing in and diving onto his bed. Everyone scampered into bed. Douglas strolled in seconds later with a flashlight.

"What's going on here?"

Frenchie snored loudly and a few boys giggled.

"Okay, but let's keep it to a low roar."

By this time I was tired, very tired. It had been another long, painful day. My eyes closed. I began to tumble into a deep, tortured sleep.

Dreams! They always began the same way.

A beautiful summer day. Hot. Not a cloud in the sky. Birds chirping. I was sitting in the front yard outside our home on Fifth Avenue in Lachine. I was five years old. Freddie and Peter were in bed with the chicken pox, so I had to play by myself. But I didn't mind. I loved being by myself. I could live and play freely in my own little make-believe world. What a beautiful, peaceful little world it was. I flew with Peter Pan to never-never land. Helped plant apple trees with Johnny Appleseed. I would pretend I was a fierce Cossack like my grandfather was or a soldier like my father was. I played house. I was playing house that day. Making mudpies when I saw him coming down the street. The birds stopped singing. They sensed something was wrong. I made believe he was a soldier. He was carrying a rifle but he had no uniform on, so I made believe he was a hunter. He began to kick savagely at the door of the house across the street. He was cursing, swearing. He was mad. An old married couple lived in that house. They were both very, very fat. A horrible scream! Two shots exploded. The fat man stumbled onto the gallery holding the side of his head. His face was covered with blood. He stared towards the sun, a last glimpse, and crashed to the balcony floor.

"Mommy, Mommy!" She ran out of the house and grabbed me from the lawn. My arms locked around her neck.

"You killed them. You killed them, you murderer!" she screamed at the man with the rifle. He was on the street raising the gun in our direction. A man tackled him from behind and wrenched the rifle from him.

The dream drove deeper. I was four.

"Mommy? Why is Daddy crying? Why are Uncle George and Uncle Eli crying? Why are you crying?"

She gazed down at me, stroking my head. Her eyes glistened.

"Your grandmother has left us. She has gone to live with God."

"No . . . no!" Dad screamed.

"Please, Mikey! Don't! It won't bring her back." A man's voice was pleading.

"Why? Why did she have to die like that? Like an animal under the wheels of a streetcar. God! Why? I'll kill that driver. I'll kill him. I swear."

"It wasn't his fault, Mikey. Please, Mikey! Don't drink no more. It's not good."

I began to shake and moan. No, this couldn't happen. Not to Granny. God wouldn't let it happen. The kindly old woman, whose purse was always filled with candy for her fourteen grandchildren, never came to see us any more.

Dark clouds swept in. There was a violent storm . . . lightning . . . thunder . . .

"Victor . . . Victor," my mother whispered. Tears welled in her eyes. "Victor. Dido is going away. He's going to sleep with God. Dido wants to say goodbye to you before he goes."

His room shimmered in a ghostly yellow aura. I tiptoed to the foot of his bed. Dido lay motionless, an old, weathered man. He smiled at me. His eyes seemed distant. I kissed Dido goodbye. An elderly Ukrainian-Orthodox priest covered in black shuffled past. He was carrying a large gold crucifix and a thick black book in one hand. A brass incense-burner on a chain smoked in the other. I bowed and kissed the cross. It was cold and made me shiver.

The storm raged on. . . . Lightning flashed across the skies. The window in my bedroom became a crucifix. A thunderous blast shook the house. A tremor passed over my body.

"Mommy . . . Mommy . . . Mommy!" She rushed in. I was shaking, sweaty.

"Mommy. Somebody was in the room. I'm scared, Mommy. Why is God angry?"

"Everything is all right, Victor. I'm here. Daddy's in the next room. Nobody will hurt you. I'm here."

"Mommy, I don't want to die. I don't want to leave you and Daddy."
"You're not going to die."
"Dido did. Granny did."
"But they were very old. They were tired. They went to live in heaven."
"Mommy, I don't want to live if you or Daddy die."
She was stroking my head gently. I fell asleep.

I was cold. I was shivering. My teeth were clattering. Then . . . that familiar, oozing, penetrating warmth. I stopped shaking and slept soundly, undisturbed.

4

The next morning I woke up ashamed of myself. The boys in the dormitory called me piss-head and held their noses mockingly as I shuffled with my head held down to the washroom to clean up. I hated myself, but I hated those guys who called me cruel names and mocked me even more.

McDougal kicked open the washroom door.

"Jesus Christ! Another fuckin' piss-head! My fuckin' luck! The dorm doesn't stink enough. I get another one. Go put your sheet up!"

"I'm . . . I'm not finished washing. I—"

"Put your fuckin' sheet up! Now! Piss-head! Move!"

"He's not finished washing," Fred said from the door.

"Mind your fuckin' business, Malarek."

"He'll put up his sheet when he's finished washing." Fred's cold stare seemed to unnerve McDougal. He looked back at me for a second, waved his hand in disgust, and stomped out.

"Christ, Victor, can't you stop wetting the bed?" Fred pleaded. "You're not a baby any more. Grow up!"

"I . . . I can't help it." I started crying.

"And quit always crying," he snapped as he walked out.

I walked back into the dormitory, past the boys dressing in the locker room, and placed my wet, stained sheet over the top railing of the bed so that it could dry during the day. Now everyone knows, I thought. God, I wish I could stop.

I was listless the rest of the day. I couldn't pay attention in class. I sat at my desk staring into space, void of thought. At lunch, and later at supper, I ate little. No one spoke to me and I spoke to no one except to call out my name for check-offs.

But as the evening wore on, it brought with it an unexpected escape, a relief from my depression. It was Friday, and Friday meant movie night in the boys' home. Studies were held right after supper, a half-hour early, and at 7:30 we lined up in the games room and marched single file into the auditorium for a two-hour feature film. The auditorium, which was on the east side of the building on the main floor, was packed with rows of wooden chairs. It was a large room, high, with a stage at the front.

As the lights went out, a Woody Woodpecker cartoon flickered onto the screen. I felt the weight ease from my shoulders.

The main event on Saturday was laundry parade. After breakfast, the bell clanged and everyone lined up in the hallway opposite the locker room on the ground floor. The line formed at a closed wooden door and snaked around the corridor. Laundry number 1 was first and so on down the hallway until it ended somewhere in the 170s.

For the first part of laundry parade, the boys filed down a dimly lit, dusty hallway, into a long, narrow room at the far end. The room was packed with neatly piled bundles of clean laundry resting on every bit of available counter space. Shelves over and under the counters were stuffed with new or nearly new shirts, socks, underwear, towels, pyjamas, pants, and sweaters. At the back was a steel rack jammed from end to end with grey suits. Here we received a clean change of underwear, socks, shirts, pyjamas, and a red-and-white-striped towel.

Another bell sounded at 10:30. This was to signal the second part of the laundry parade, bringing in the dirty laundry. Gray came over to my locker and helped me to prepare for the ritual. Once the dirty clothing was packed into a neat roll, we went off to get the articles marked for identification.

"What's your laundry number?" an older boy asked without looking up at me. He was holding a black marker.

"158."

He meticulously printed 158 on the tags and handed them to me. He seemed proud of his handiwork with the marker. He acted as though the job he was assigned gave him some kind of status.

"Attach them to your socks." He then wrote 158 over the waistband of my underwear and pyjama bottoms, and the collars of my shirts and tee shirts. A larger 158 was lettered onto my towel.

"Do you have to mark it so big on my clothes?"

"Yeah, what of it?"

I didn't answer.

We moved into the corridor and joined a weaving line disappearing into the laundry area. This time it was first ready, first processed. After an hour, we shuffled into the main laundry room. It was a large, dingy area cluttered with carts, washers, dryers, and deep sinks. Johnson dutifully recorded each item in a black binder before we dumped the load into bins lining the exit route.

Not too long after, the lunch bell sounded. The cafeteria was filled with an air of celebration and expectation. Halfway through the meal, Johnson tapped on the window sill for everyone's attention. The boys stopped eating and looked his way. He called out half a dozen names.

"These boys have detention today. Hargraves, Ferguson, Green, Westfall, Reilly. No leave. Is that understood? Check off every hour at the office. The rest of you remember, juniors and intermediates, in by 8:30. No later. Seniors, 10:00 p.m."

Saturday afternoon, right after lunch, we got leave. Now I could go home and tell my mother and father what this place was really like. I knew we wouldn't have to come back once I had told them how unhappy I was.

I met Freddie and Peter in the locker room and we raced out together.

"Mommy is working today. We'll go down to the restaurant first. Then we'll go home with her when she's finished," Fred said as we reached the boardwalk.

My mother was busy when we arrived at the small pizza and fast-food restaurant on St. Catherine Street where she worked as a waitress. It was owned and run by a good-natured Greek. We sat in the last booth at the back. She brought Fred and Peter each a strawberry sundae and for me, my favorite, a creamy, saucy banana split. When she got a break, she joined us.

"Mommy, what time do you finish?" Fred asked.

"I'm finishing late tonight. The girl who works nights phoned in sick."

"We have to be back at 8:30," Peter said. His eyes were watery.

"Mommy, do we have to go back? We don't like it in there," I asked, forcing myself not to look her in the face. Reilly's filthy words kept ringing in my ears. "They had a good, hard fuck! You have to fuck to have babies!"

My mother looked at each of us. Her face grew sad. She took a deep breath and cleared her throat.

"You won't have to stay there long. You'll be home this summer," she said, stroking Peter's head.

"Are you going to be home tomorrow?" Fred asked.

"No, no I won't. I have to work. Your father should be there. I'll be visiting you during the week. Wednesday. Is there anything you'd like me to bring you? Peter?"

"Some candy," Peter said.

"Freddie?"

"Oh Henry bar and Glosette Raisins."

"Victor?"

"Some peanuts."

"Okay. Your father's home. Are you going to the house now?"

"Yes," I said.

She got up to give a customer his bill and take an order from another who had just come in. We waited patiently to talk to Mom again but the restaurant became busier.

"We may as well go home. Mom's too busy," Fred said.

"We're going to see Dad," I said to her as we trudged out.

"All right. Be careful on the street and make sure you get back to Weredale on time. I'll see you Wednesday."

A half-hour later, we were outside our home on Evans Street. It was an old grey-stone row house practically in the heart of downtown Montreal.

My father was sitting at the kitchen table, with a quart of Molson's beer in front of him. He looked sad and angry at the same time.

"Hi, Dad," we said as we came in.

"Hi, boys. How are you?" His face grew cheerful.

"Fine."

"Did you see your mother?"

"At the restaurant," Fred said.

"What did she say?"

"Not much. She was busy," Fred said.

The smile left Dad's face. He gulped down a few mouthfuls of beer. Fred and Peter went into the living room and turned on the television. I sat nervously in the kitchen watching my father. After a long silence, he spoke.

"Do you like it there? Is it all right?"

"No," I said, fighting to hold back the tears.

"Anyone hit you?"

"I got into a fight but Freddie beat the two boys up. Mr. Johnson strapped them."

"Did Fred get strapped?"

"No. But Freddie got into another fight and when he was telling the boy to give up, a big guy punched him in the face and then kicked him."

Dad's expression frightened me. His eyes burned. His breathing was uneven.

"Fred!" he shouted. "Get in here!"

"Yes, Dad?" Fred asked as he raced into the kitchen.

"You get beaten up?"

"This other guy smashed me when I was on top of another —"

"He kicked you when you were down?"

"Yes, Dad."

"What did you do?" he asked, turning to me.

I couldn't find any words. I was scared to tell him I ran.

"The guy was too big, Dad. Victor couldn't do anything even if he wanted to," Fred offered in my defence.

"I've alway taught you to fight fair and stick up for your younger brothers. One on one. Fists and no dirty stuff. No kicking, no biting. But if they don't want to fight fair, I'll show you how to fight even dirtier than they could imagine."

For the rest of the afternoon, Fred went through a gruelling drill of kicks, punches, pokes, and jabs. He learned fast, but his heart didn't seem to be in it.

"And if the guy is too big, stick your fingers into his eyes. Gouge the bastard and then boot the shit out of him. Don't ask him to give up once you've got him down. Don't give him a chance to get you. Make sure he'll never bother you again. And you boys stick up for each other."

"Yes, Dad," we replied.

"I don't ever want to hear of anyone jumping any of you boys without the three of you sticking up for each other. You're brothers. Never forget that, and never let anyone else forget that. Fight for each other."

"Yes, Dad."

"Victor, get me a cold one from the back of the fridge. Are you boys hungry?"

"A little," Fred said.

"There's pork chops in the fridge. I'll cook them up in a minute with some beans. Go and watch TV and I'll call you when it's ready."

My father didn't eat with us. He just guzzled down one quart of beer after another. We didn't say a word at supper because he didn't allow any talking at the table. His cold silence scared us.

"What time do you have to be back to that place?" he asked as we cleaned off our plates. My father also did not allow anything to be left on our plates except well-gnawed bones.

"8:30," said Peter.

"Will we see you tomorrow?" I asked.

"I'll call you tomorrow after your lunch. I may have to work. You boys better get ready to go back. It's 7:30." He gave us a dollar each and we kissed him goodbye.

The boys in the dormitory were in great spirits when we got back. Laughing, joking, play-wrestling, pillow-fighting, running up and down the dorm.

"All right, all right. Calm down. Cool it," a staff member yelled from the door. He was a tall, slim blond who looked about twenty-two years old. His name was Ferguson. He raced through check-off. There was an important hockey game on TV he didn't want to miss. The lights were switched off but the boys didn't want to calm down. The giggling and noise got worse. Suddenly the lights came on in a blinding flash.

"Everyone in front of your beds! Who's got a running shoe?" Ferguson shouted. No one answered.

"That's okay. I'll find one on the senior side." Moments later he returned with a size ten running shoe in one hand.

"Bend over your beds." He gave each boy one solid whack with the sole of the shoe. Some of the boys took their punishment without any show of emotion. They didn't flinch when they were hit. Some were sobbing before Ferguson even got to them. Frenchie began to wail and beg. It was obvious that he was putting on an act. Everyone cracked up and he got an extra whack for playing the clown. When he got to Fred, McDougal called out: "Sir, Mr. Ferguson, sir, he's new."

"Okay, get into bed," he said without looking at Fred. He continued down the line.

"He's new also, sir," Janigan said when Ferguson approached me.

"Get into bed." Dead silence followed his exit but it didn't last long. The giggling and joking started again. And not long after, the lights flashed on again.

"Everyone in front of your bed!" Ferguson was livid.

This time each boy got three whacks on the backside. When he got to Freddie, McDougal attempted another rescue.

"Sir . . . he's new."

"Yes, I know. But this time he's not." He gave Fred three stinging blows. I knew that I'd be getting it this time too. It was agony watching him work his way from bed to bed, getting closer and closer to me. My turn. I bent over. Grasping the back railing of my bed and squeezing my eyes shut, I prepared for the first blow. It was searing. I thought my backside had split and was bleeding. The other two whacks landed swiftly and just as painfully. I crept back into bed and buried my face in the pillow to muffle my sobbing.

This time, the dormitory stayed quiet. I couldn't get to sleep. I kept thinking of my father and how sad he looked, about my mother and wondering if she was going to leave him again. If she did, how could we go back home? The welfare people wouldn't let her keep us. I tried to drive the thought out of my mind.

Tossing over onto my back, I witnessed a peculiar sight. The boy in bed 20 got up and scurried over to bed 4. A few seconds later, another boy near my brother's bed got up and joined the boy in bed 9. They were playing with each other! Lying naked on top of each other and rubbing their bodies heatedly together. Blankets moved up and down, beds squeaked. I stared around the room in amazement. I felt funny inside but I didn't understand what was going on. I didn't know what sex was all about. I had heard some stories in the schoolyard but I was still too young to experience an orgasm. These boys seemed to like the feeling they were getting from someone else's warmth, touch, and closeness. They didn't kiss each other or anything like that but one couple, when they felt sure no one was watching, engaged in oral sex.

My stomach turned. Pigs, I thought. I had never witnessed or experienced the kind of things going on in the dormitory darkness. I shuddered as I thought of some boy approaching my bed one night. I shook the thought out of my mind and began to rock myself to sleep.

I woke up feeling miserable. By this time, I loathed the boys' home and everyone in it. I got up slowly and dragged myself into the locker room.

"You have to wear your suit and tie today. It's Sunday. We have church after breakfast," Gray told me as I was taking off my pyjamas. I didn't answer him.

"No, no, a white shirt. You have to wear a white shirt," he said as I was buttoning up a checkered sport shirt.

"What's the difference?"

"Don't get smart with me. That's the way they want it."

"Sorry. Where do we go for church? To the one on the corner?"

"No. Church is in the auditorium. Chief does the service."

"Chief?"

"Mr. Adams. He's the director."

"I thought Mr. Johnson was in charge of Weredale."

"No. He's the assistant director. But really he runs it. Chief is getting old."

"What happens after church?"

"We have lunch. It's shoe leather today. Then we get leave. You have to be back same time as yesterday, 8:30. Don't be late or you'll lose your leave next week. Let's go! Come on!"

45

"What's shoe leather?" I asked, running after him.

"Roast beef."

After breakfast, everyone filed quietly into the games room to stay clean and out of mischief until the bell sounded for church at ten o'clock. I rested on the window sill, idly gazing down at the bleak, run-down slums of Little Burgundy and St. Henri on the other side of the tracks. It was amazing how many Weredale boys came from this area. On Saturday, a small hooting and cheering battalion of guys on leave charged down Atwater Hill to visit their families. Only a few headed up the hill, but they weren't heading for anything better – just the same thing in other parts of the city. The houses in the slums below were all two- and three-storey attached tenements, owned for the most part by absentee landlords. The wooden balconies protruding onto garbage-littered streets in front and rat-infested laneways in back were rotten, unpainted, and weathered with age. Most of the cars looked third-hand, rusted and about to fall apart. I couldn't help thinking that Weredale must have been a step up for most of the boys, yet almost every one of them hated it here and wanted desperately to go home.

The bitter irony for the Weredale boys was that the Home was tucked safely away in the bottom left corner of lower Westmount, a tiny enclave where some of the most powerful and wealthy families in the entire country lived. From the dormitory windows on the north and west sides of the building, we could see the stately mansions of millionaires dotting the steep slope of Mount Royal. We could see the Cadillacs in the driveways and the hired help grooming the landscaped lawns.

"Hi. What you doing?" a voice asked.

I turned around. A plump, milk-white face with wide brown eyes was beaming at me. It was Nelson, a chubby boy who slept two beds over from me.

"Nothing," I said glumly.

"You feeling bad?" he asked in a consoling tone.

"I don't like it here."

"You'll get used to it. Is it your first time away from home?"

"No. We lived in a foster home once for one year when I was eight."

"I stayed in a foster home for a while before coming here. It wasn't too bad."

"The place I stayed in was rotten. They treated me like a dog."

"What do you mean?"

"Nothing. They just did." A vision of my foster mother appeared before my eyes. She was hitting me with a long wooden stick and rubbing my face into soiled bed sheets.

"They just treated me like a dog, that's all!" I squinted my eyes shut to rid my mind of the memory. Nelson's owl-like eyes were staring at me. A puzzled look was on his face.

"How long have you been here?" I asked.

"A few months."

"Do you like it here?"

"No. I can't stand most of the staff and the food's not all that great."

"Yeah, that's for sure." We laughed.

"Why are you in here?" Nelson asked.

"My parents are sort of having problems but we'll be out by the summer. You? Why are you in here?"

"My mother's dead. I'm a half-orphan. My father couldn't take proper care of me so the welfare put me here."

"Do you have any brothers?"

"I had an older brother. He drowned while we were on a picnic when I was six."

Nelson's brother, who was a year older, had gone out on a boat ride with seven other young boys and his dad. Nelson had stayed ashore with his mother and some other women who were preparing the hamburgers, hot dogs, and tossed salad. He could hear the laughter from the lake and was a little angry at himself for not going along, but he was afraid of the water. Suddenly, there were chilling screams. The boat had overturned in the middle of the lake. Frantic mothers rushed to the shoreline. One barrelled into the water, shrieking her child's name. She drowned. Only two boys and Nelson's father survived. Nelson's parents had never gotten over that unfortunate accident. His mother wasted away mourning the loss of her first-born. His father blamed himself for the tragedy and found solace in a bottle. Nelson was placed in Weredale just before Christmas. He'd been scooped up by the welfare authorities when some neighbors had noticed that his father had not been home in more than a week. He hadn't seen his father since.

"That's too bad. I don't know what I'd do if one of my brothers died. Where do you go when you get leave?"

"I sometimes go see my aunt. Most times I just hang around."

"Well, if you sometimes have nowhere to go, you can come with me."

"You mean that?" he said. A wide smile spread across his face.

"Sure."

"Gee, thanks! You're okay. Put it there." We shook hands. I had found a friend.

The bell rang and two staff members came into the games room.

"All right, everyone line up in single file according to height. On . . .

the . . . double!'' one of the staff said, clapping his hands.

"Move . . . move . . . move! Let's go!''

There was a mad scramble of bodies. The line formed rapidly from the front entrance and wrapped around the games room. Nelson took a position behind me. We were the same height.

On the stage was a podium. Below it, a plain wooden gold cross rested on a box. On the left side of the stage, Mrs. Evans sat in front of an upright piano. On each chair was a Bible and a hymn book. When all the boys were seated, someone shouted, "All rise.'' Chief entered and marched up to the podium. He raised his arms, Mrs. Evans struck a chord on the piano, and everyone sang "God Save the Queen'', followed by "O Canada''. On the last note, he raised his arms, then lowered them, and everyone sat down.

"Everyone take out your Bible and together we will read Psalm 119.''

"Blessed are the undefiled in the way, who walk in the law of the Lord. Blessed are they that keep His testimonies, and that seek Him with the whole heart. They also do no iniquity: they walk in His ways.''

After we finished, Chief asked us to turn to hymn 123. He raised his hand. Mrs. Evans struck a chord and we all stood up to sing. Chief motioned us to sit after the song and spoke about the meaning of the psalm we had read earlier and how we should apply it to our everyday lives. I was spellbound. He looked directly at individual boys as he talked. He was like a father talking to a son. I listened to every word and felt eerie as this grey-haired, weathered old man with silver-framed glasses looked down at me sitting in the very front row. He was a gentle, caring man who seemed out of place here.

We sang another hymn, followed by two minutes of silent prayer. I bowed my head and prayed:

"Dear God, dear Jesus. Please bring Mom and Dad back together. I want to go home. Please? I promise I'll be a good boy from now on. I love Mom and Dad and I believe in You. Please let Freddie, Peter, and me go home. We don't like it here. It's a bad place. I don't want to stay here any more.''

The service ended with just enough time to wash up and head back upstairs for lunch. Once in the cafeteria, we remained standing behind our seats until everyone was positioned at a table. Chief came in, said a short grace, and we all sat down to eat. Sunday lunch consisted of a thin, well-done slice of roast beef, potatoes, peas, rice pudding, and milk. That turned out to be my favorite meal in the home, and I traded Sunday lunches against weekly dishes I didn't like but which the other boys preferred to "shoe leather''.

That Sunday there was nowhere to go. My mother was working. I didn't know where my father was. He didn't answer the phone at home when I called after lunch. Fred and Peter decided to go see three movies for thirty-five cents at the Centre Theatre in Pointe St. Charles. Nelson and I asked to tag along. It was strange how the movies made me forget all my troubles. The triple feature ended at 7:30, so we walked back to Weredale. I felt terrible at not having seen my parents that day and had to force myself not to cry as we approached the building.

After check-off and lights out, the dormitory was still, deadly quiet. It wasn't at all like the night before with lots of laughter and joking around. It was the end of the weekend, the end of leave, and for most that meant not seeing their families for another week. It also meant the start of another week in Weredale. A few boys buried their heads into their pillows and wept. Others stared up at the ceiling. Slowly the room began to sway to the even breathing of deep sleep.

CHAPTER

5

Spring took forever to turn into summer. Every day at Weredale was the same as the day before. Waking up unhappy, check-offs, clanging bells, line-ups, being picked on, yelled at, crying, and going to bed unhappy. The only happiness I had to look forward to were weekend leaves, but even those had become severe and bitter disappointments with my mother spending most of her time at work and my father in one tavern or another.

June 26, 1959, finally arrived. My first birthday in Weredale and, I was sure, my last. I woke up whistling and humming. The morning was beautiful. My bed was dry. It was the last day of school. We were going to see Queen Elizabeth parade through Westmount before she set off to open officially the St. Lawrence Seaway. And my brothers and I were leaving Weredale — today or tomorrow. My mother had told us we would get out before camp started and that was only two days away.

There was no school that morning, so after breakfast the boys lounged around the games room playing ping-pong or chatting excitedly about seeing the Queen. Johnson materialized near the entrance and, as usual whenever he appeared, all activity came to a sudden standstill. Beside him was a skinny, copper-colored boy with a pair of frightened eyes set deep in two dark pits. His brown hair was mussed up on top and kinky on the sides. Johnson was looking for someone. His gaze fixed on me and a cheerful smile spread across his face.

"Malarek," he called.

"Yes, sir." I rushed over.

"This is Gillis, Philip Gillis," he said. I shook the boy's limp, icy hand.

"I'm sure you know the routine well enough by now. I want you to show Gillis around. Introduce him to the boys and fill him in on the routine. He'll be staying with us for a while."

"Yes, sir."

"I know you'll do a good job, birthday boy."

"Yes, sir. Thank you, Mr. Johnson." With that, he left the games room.

"You're just in time for camp," I said casually to Gillis.

"When are we leaving?" Gillis asked in a hoarse, apprehensive whisper.

"Two days from now. But I won't be going. We're getting out soon. Me and my brothers. We're going back home," I boasted. "This afternoon we're going to school to get our report cards and then we're heading over to Sherbrooke Street to see the parade. The Queen is coming by here on her way to open the St. Lawrence Seaway. I'll ask Mr. Johnson if you can come to school with us."

The lunch bell couldn't have clanged soon enough for me. My excitement was building as we herded into the dining room. Any moment I would be called up in front of the boys who would sing "Happy Birthday" to me. Most of us were digging into dessert when Johnson began jingling the old brass school hand-bell and cooing: "Come on up here, birthday boy."

"Get up there, Malarek," a few boys from the junior floor egged.

Feigning shyness, I made my way up the forbidden centre aisle: we boys could walk up it only on special occasions like birthdays. Johnson helped me up onto his window-sill perch and handed me the brass bell. I shook it loud and hard. What a feeling it was having one hundred and sixty boys sing "Happy Birthday"! My heart was pounding in my chest. I was happy; for the first time in many long, long months, I was truly happy. Today was *my* day and nothing could spoil it. The song was over and I jumped down only to be nabbed by Mrs. Evans for her traditional birthday kiss. It was also traditional to try to avoid the kiss and just as customary to get caught. Catcalls, assorted *oohs* and *ahs*, and laughs shot out from the tables of boys as Mrs. Evans planted a heavy, lipstick-stained kiss on my cheek.

After lunch, Gillis and I made our way to school. I ran practically all the way in my excitement at seeing the Queen. In class we anxiously waited for Morrison to arrive, issue our report cards, and take us to the parade site. Everyone rose when he entered the class.

"Sit," Morrison commanded. His eyes roamed over the class, fixing on Gillis. "You! Stand up!"

"Sir," I called out, waving my hand frantically in the air. The teacher ignored me.

"What are you doing in my class?"

"I . . . I came with him," Gillis replied meekly, pointing in my direction.

"Then get out!" he bellowed. "You are not one of my students. Therefore, you have no right being in here. That's all I need for my last day, another Weredale hooligan."

I leapt to my feet. "Mr. Morrison, he's new in the Home and Mr. Johnson said —"

"I don't give a hoot what your Mr. Johnson said. Get him out of here. This is my class. You, boy, I said get out."

"But, sir, Mr. Johnson —"

"Look here, Malarek, I'll have no lip from someone who has failed his year."

A shock wave slammed through my body. By the time I realized what he had said, Gillis had been ushered into the corridor and Morrison was ordering me to sit down. Through glassy eyes, I caught Fred staring at me. He looked really pissed off. Tears began to stream down my face. I bolted out of the class and into the washroom, where in a raging, uncontrollable fit, I punched the walls and tore at my hair. I cursed that bastard teacher. It was my first failure at school. "How could he? I'm no dummy," I shouted at the walls. "Why? Why me? My marks were all above average until I entered this garbage heap. I don't deserve to flunk."

I had done all my homework, which was more than I could say for most of the guys in the class. I only had trouble answering verbal test questions from Morrison, who had intimidated me. But in written tests, I knew I'd done well. I swore I'd get even with Morrison somehow. My only consolation was I knew I wouldn't be in this school next year. "Mom will explain to the principal at my new school why I flunked and I'll be put into grade six. Just wait and see," I muttered desperately to myself.

Then it suddenly dawned on me that someone was in the washroom watching me rant and rave. It was Gillis and he looked terrified. "Morrison's a fuckin' bastard. He hates Weredale guys but he'll get his, one day. Wait and see," I shouted.

The bell sounded and all classes lined up in the schoolyard for the march to Sherbrooke Street. At the head of each class was a flag-bearer with the home room's Union Jack fluttering in the breeze. Fred had somehow weaselled his way into carrying the flagpole for our class. We marched in pairs. Most of the kids were in high spirits because they knew they had passed even though the reports hadn't been given out yet. I no longer felt any excitement. Within ten minutes, the school populace was thronged along a small stretch of Sherbrooke Street awaiting the passing of the Queen and Prince Philip. Just as someone shouted, "She's coming," Fred dashed into the middle of the street and began waving the flag frantically and chanting: "Here comes the Queen, here comes the Queen!" Morrison, a staunch monarchist, turned blood red right up to the top of his bald head. He charged into the street and lunged at the scruff of Fred's neck. My brother managed to duck him and dart back into the crowd. Morrison was hot on his heels.

"Get over here," he shrieked. "I want that flagpole, you little imp. You are not mature enough to carry the flag. Give it to me."

"Drop dead, you bald English prick!" Fred yelled.

"You . . . you insolent little . . . I said give me that flag!"

"You really want it?" Fred asked. A wry smile cracked at the corner of his lips.

"Give me the flagpole!" He lunged at Fred, just as my brother hurled the flagpole at the teacher's chest. Morrison fell flat on his butt trying to avoid the blow. Fred made a snappy exit. Queen Elizabeth and Prince Philip passed sedately by.

When we returned to class, Morrison threw the report cards at each student. He tossed me Fred's with a threat that Johnson would soon be apprised of the despicable incident during the parade. Frenchie cut him off in mid-sentence with a mighty, "Shit!" He too had failed his year. So had six other Weredale boys. Only three Weredale boys, including Fred, had passed, and all of them had failed grade five the previous year, so they couldn't be flunked again.

Frenchie got up and headed for the door.

"I haven't dismissed you yet. Sit down," Morrison commanded.

"Drop dead, baldy," Frenchie shot back.

Morrison's jaw dropped, and without warning, Frenchie grabbed an ink-well, threw the contents in the teacher's face, and bolted for the door. Outside, Morrison's car was sabotaged. His tires were slashed, sugar was poured into his gas tank, and obscene notes were plastered onto his windshield.

"We've got leave until 8:30 tonight," I told Gillis after handing in my unopened report card. "I'm going home, so I'll see you later." I grabbed a jacket out of my locker and raced up to Atwater Bus Terminus, hoping to beat Fred and Peter home.

"Happy birthday, Victor," my mother called out as I dashed into the house. My father wasn't home.

"Mom, when are we getting out? Tomorrow?"

She stared at me for a moment. Her eyes were sad.

"Victor, you boys will have to go to camp this summer. Maybe you'll get out after camp. Christmas for sure. I don't like keeping you in there. You know that. But I can't do anything about it. Your father isn't working and he's drinking again. I can't —"

"We're not getting out?" A choking lump swelled in my throat. "But you told us! I told all the guys we were getting out. I hate it in there. I don't want to go back."

"Victor, I can't help it. Your father and I are going to get a separation for a while. I can't live with him the way he is. I'll work and save some money and we'll make a home for ourselves."

"Ah! He beat us," Peter shouted as he charged into the house with Fred.

I sneaked away during the commotion and locked myself in the bathroom and cried. Through the door I could hear my mother trying to explain to my brothers why she couldn't take us out of Weredale. Her voice was shaky.

"I tried, Freddie. But it's no use. I can't live with that man. Peter, please don't cry. You boys know how your father is. I begged the welfare people to let me keep you but they won't let me. I won't be allowed to work if I want to keep you. They said I have to stay home. But they won't give me any money if I stay home. They keep telling me to stay with your father, but I can't take it any more. Here Peter, blow your nose. They said Weredale would be the best place to keep you boys together for now." She began to cry.

"I love my children. I know you hate it there. I want you home with me but they won't let me keep you. I just don't know what to do. . . . I can't take life with your father any more, but I don't want you children to hate me," she blurted between sobs. "I don't want him scaring or hitting me or you kids. Please understand! I pray one day you'll understand." She ran into her bedroom and closed the door. I could hear her muffled cries haunting the hallway as I crumbled helplessly to the cool bathroom floor.

The rest of the afternoon, as on most visiting days, was spent in front of the television. At supper, Mom brought out a glowing birthday cake and sang "Happy Birthday". I forced myself to smile but inside I was crushed. Some birthday. My father didn't even come home.

The following morning was spent preparing for camp. Line-ups formed in all parts of the building. Line-ups for obtaining camp supplies – kitbags, shorts, jeans, running shoes, thick woollen long johns for those especially chilly Laurentian nights, a new towel, and, of course, a bathing suit. Line-ups to take in the city clothes. Line-ups to visit the local barber on St. Catherine Street for a bean shave. And a small line-up in front of the clinic, where six strokes of a leather strap were dished out by Johnson's assistant, Marshall, to whoever had had anything to do with, or was suspected of having had anything to do with, Morrison's misfortunes.

The culprits, including Fred, also had their visiting privileges cancelled for the remaining two days we had in the city before heading off to camp, and that hurt more than any strapping.

"Malarek! V. Malarek in here?" a voice shouted from the centre of the locker room.

"Yeah! What do you want?" I yelled from my locker where I was piling up my city clothes to bring to the laundry room.

"I'm Plager!"

I snapped around and jumped to my feet. Plager was one of the strongest, most feared scrappers on the senior side. A master of street fighting who hated school and loved sports, especially tough, physical-contact sports like floor hockey. With his black wavy hair freshly sheared off, he looked older than his sixteen years and twice as mean.

"Yes?" I asked nervously.

"I'm hut leader for Dakotas. I got stuck with you in my hut."

"Oh."

"I hear you're a fuckin' baby and a piss-the-bed! Get this straight, I hate babies. As for your pissing the bed, you sleep in the lower bunk! Get it? I don't want you dripping on anyone in the night."

"Yes," I replied in a meek, embarrassed whisper.

Plager turned and called out another name. I bowed my head, closed my eyes, and swore through clenched teeth.

On the morning of June 28, the northward migration of Weredale boys began. Three buses arrived at the front entrance promptly at 8 a.m. Johnson delivered a short farewell speech about the joys of outdoor life and wished everyone a good summer. A brisk hand search for hidden knives and money was carried out before each boy boarded, in alphabetical order, for the three-hour ride to the Lake l'Achigan Laurentian mountain retreat.

We had been on the road for about an hour when George Plumber, one of the seniors, who was appointed CIT (counsellor-in-training), leapt up from his seat at the front of the bus. "All right you guys!" he roared. "We're going to camp, not a funeral. Come on! Let's get in the spirit! You old boys, let's show the new kids what Camp Weredale is all about!" He led the old boys in the camp song:

Camp Weredale is a camp, best of them all.
Camp Weredale is a camp to be loved by one and all.
We will remember thee, through all the years.
Camp Weredale is a camp, so altogether, altogether cheer!
Rah! Rah!

McDonald, another senior, with freckles and red hair, bounced into the aisle shouting, ''The camp yell, the camp yell!'' and began jumping and jerking and twisting. A feeble, sporadic attempt followed as the guys tried to recall the barbaric exhortation.

Hi – zumba zumba zumba
Hi – zumba zumba zee!
Hi – zumba zumba zumba
Hi – zumba zumba zee!
Oo – ee-oo-ah-ah!
We are the boys who make the noise!
Yeaaa – WEREDALE!

''Okay! Now that we all know the yell, let's hear it one more time but this time louder. I want the other two buses to hear us!'' Plumber cried, shooting his fist into the air.

Hi – zumba zumba zumba
Hi – zumba zumba zee!
Hi – zumba zumba zumba
Hi – zumba zumba zee!
Oo – ee-oo-ah-ah!
We are the boys who make the noise!
Yeaaa – WEREDALE!

Camp Weredale was a picturesque village of freshly painted orange-and-black wooden huts nestled on one of the many inlets of Lake l'Achigan. The grounds were immaculate, the panorama was breathtaking. Towering spruce, plush maples, and white birch blanketed the campsite. Hundreds of ancient, moss-draped granite boulders hugged the edge of the shoreline. Across the bay, grey cliffs, crowned with evergreens, dove sharply into the black depths of the lake. Orange flat-bottoms and dories rocked gently behind the shelter of an L-shaped dock next to the beach area, while a dozen dinghies, two larger sailboats, and a motor boat bobbed up and down at their moorings a little way from the dock. The swimming area was crystal clear. A three-foot wall at the shallow end protected the shore from being eaten away any further by hungry waves. A deeper swimming section for proficient swimmers jutted out from the heel of the dock. A raft with a diving board and tower was anchored twenty yards out. Along the waterfront was a small library attached to the recreation hall, a canoe shed atop which was the bunkhouse for the junior counsellors and CITs, and a handicrafts cabin housing senior counsellors on the upper floor.

On a bluff overlooking the waterfront stood a row of wooden huts almost hidden from view by spruce trees. There were twelve cabins in all, eleven ranged in alphabetical order and bearing the names of Indian tribes. The first half-dozen were labelled "Braves" for the younger boys, the remainder "Warriors". The twelfth cabin, isolated halfway down the slope on the Warriors' side, was reserved for orderlies, who for the most part were composed of brown-nosers and suck-holes.

All the buildings were painted in the camp colors, black and orange. The huts were identical: two three-tier bunks on each side of a screen door, and two two-tier bunks in the opposite corners. Five storage cubby-holes occupied the space under the second pair of bunks. The two bottom bunks were reserved for piss-heads, weaklings, or those in disfavor with the powerful hut leader. Fitting all three degrading categories, and following Plager's earlier instructions, I got to sleep on the floor bunk.

In the bush, fifty feet behind the row of huts, was a large outhouse nicknamed The Birches. It was a green-fly- and mosquito-infested shack that reeked horribly of excrement and urine. In one area were five stained porcelain bowls with no seats. A grey panel divided the room into a smaller section where two rust-stained urinal stalls were bolted to a wall. On a hot, muggy day, the overpowering stench from the constantly clogged, backed-up toilets forced most of the boys to seek relief in the forest.

A gravel path on the Braves' side led past the clinic and the nurse's quarters to the camp's main gathering point. Here, on the perimeter of a dusty parade ground gripping the edge of the forest, stood the general office, the camp director's cottage, and a large dining room propped up on tree-trunk stilts.

At breakfast, lunch, and supper, we would be summoned to "come and get it" by the clanging of a thick iron triangle dangling from a roof beam over the dining-room verandah. Forever-hungry hordes would line up in alphabetical cabin sequence for roll-call.

"Algonquins!"

"All present and accounted for, sir!" the hut leader would shout.

"Blackfeet!"

"All present and accounted for, sir!"

"Cayugas!"

And so on down the line.

It was at these times that the morning, afternoon, and evening activities would be spelled out.

After roll-call, before breakfast and dinner, the boys would march in single file onto the Big Rock adjacent to the dining room. The Big Rock was a massive slab of granite imbedded into the shoreline. Rammed into its heart was a flagpole flying a Union Jack and the camp ensign, an orange capital "C" engulfing a small black "w" on a white triangular background. During these rituals, there would be a salute for the raising and lowering of the flag, followed by the singing of "God Save the Queen" and "O Canada". The boys would then about-face and march in orderly fashion to the dining room.

Picnic-style tables lined both sides of the spacious interior. The tables on the left were for the Warriors, those on the right for the Braves. In the centre was a long table for the CITs and the junior counsellors. At the head table sat the director, his wife, two pre-teen sons and a tomboyish daughter, the assistant director, the nurse, and the senior counsellors.

After grace, dinner was served. For the most part, the main courses were delivered to the tables by orderlies on a platter or in a pot. A different menu was served to the head table of CITs and counsellors. When they got sausages and eggs, we got cold cereal. When they got pork chops, we got stew.

It was the hut leader's function with help from his seconder, to dish out equal portions. No one complained as Plager and his seconder piled just a little more on their plates. After all, they needed the energy to run the hut.

Everything at Camp Weredale was arranged. You had to have fun whether you wanted to or not. Activities began right after breakfast and didn't let up until it was time to hit the bunks. First there was hut inspection. Plager was determined to win the award for best hut on the Braves' side that summer. No one dared slip up on his assigned tasks. Inspection was carried out in typical military fashion. The boys would line up at attention outside the huts after clean-up detail. A senior counsellor with a junior counsellor and a CIT in tow would police the cabin and grounds with the hut leader and seconder. All infractions were duly noted: a lump of lint on the hut floor, an improperly made bed, a microscopic scrap of paper on the ground within the boundaries of the hut. Half-points from a possible total of ten were deducted from a score sheet for each flubbed detail.

Then came the legislated fun: water safety, swimming instruction, rifle range, boating, canoeing, sailing, handicrafts, and sports appreciation. Boys were broken down into teams of nine or so and assigned to one-week sessions of compulsory morning activities. Each team was also assigned to a week of general camp clean-up detail, which included a thorough scrubbing down of the Birches.

Depending on the weather and the whims of the senior mandarins, we got to have more mandatory good times after lunch. Swimming, waterfront activities, soccer, baseball, volleyball, or a two-hour hike through the woods would be the order of the afternoon. Occasionally we got free time which was somewhat like a long recess at school. Scavenger hunts, bingo, movies, singsongs around a campfire, and amateur variety shows starring the Weredale hams, made up the events for most evenings, except for every other Friday, when we would hike along the narrow Indian Trail for Indian Council. There we would squat cross-legged around a blazing campfire listening to Indian legends, singing traditional camp songs, and bearing witness to the gruelling and sometimes amazing initiation rites of those Warriors selected to become honored members of the Sequoia, the Camp's inner circle. I'll always remember one particular Indian Council. After the Big Chief had welcomed each of the tribes, and the Warrior and Brave hut leaders in turn acknowledged their presence by tossing a ceremonial log on the bonfire, he turned his attention to an urgent problem.

"We have been receiving bad omens from Manitou," the Big Chief began. Very few of us knew what an omen was but we knew you didn't invoke the name of Manitou unless it meant trouble. A serious expression surfaced through his bright-red, orange, and yellow war-paint. "One of our braves is the cause of much disharmony with nature. This person is being unkind to our little forest creatures. Bring Jimmy Gates before me!" Two Sequoia members charged into the horseshoe ring of boys and hauled Gates to his feet.

Gates was a strange guy who enjoyed crushing bugs under his feet, tearing the legs off the daddy-longleg spiders, blowing up frogs by sticking straws in their rear ends and forcing through lungfuls of air, and torturing trapped squirrels and chipmunks. He was one of the weaklings in the Home, pale, sneaky, and evil-looking. He was grinning foolishly as the Sequoia dragged him before the Big Chief.

"The Inner Council has found you guilty of being cruel to our littlest of creatures. You must be punished. Tie him to the stake! You will remain there until the close of Indian Council," the Big Chief ordered as Gates was being led away to a stake ten feet away from the blazing bonfire.

The Indian Council continued for another two hours, and by the end of the first half-hour Gates was no longer grinning. The punishment was having its prescribed effect. He was hot, tired, and very thirsty. Before the Indian farewell, Gates was untied and dragged before the Big Chief.

"You will leave our little creatures to roam in peace. If not, we will punish you more severely at our next Indian Council. Go in disgrace, Brave!" the chief commanded, pointing to the council entrance.

Gates retreated to a chorus of jeers and catcalls. He was bawling. He would have to return to camp alone along the blackened trail without a flashlight. Nor did he know that hiding behind the trees and boulders was a pack of Warriors waiting in ambush to deliver further humiliations.

Every Sunday morning, there was a church service either at the outdoor chapel a short hike from the camp or, if the weather was rotten, in the recreation hall.

With the exception of Indian Council, a few fights, and the occasional runaway, there was nothing exciting to write home about.

Dear Mom,

I hate it here. I have to sleep on the floor. There's so many blackflies. Please bring me some "Bug Off" and some food. I'm starving. The hut leader eats more than the rest of us. I hate hikes. They make you do everything. How are you? I miss you.

Your son, Victor.

Dear Dad,

Hi. I don't like this place. I'm always hungry. The hut leader is a pig. He eats everything. Bring me some food when you come on visiting day. Could I have a flashlight? I'm scared to go out in the dark. They're always telling you to do everything here. I want to go home. Freddie and Peter say hi. I miss you.

Your son, Victor.

I dropped both letters in a camp mailbox – unsealed, as instructed – and strolled over to the play field to have more fun.

"Malarek, Victor! To the general office! On the double!" the camp P.A. system blared early the next afternoon while I was sitting on the Big Rock talking with Nelson.

I rapped briskly on the screen door and waited for permission to enter. The camp director was crouched at his desk reading a letter. A small pile of orange-and-black envelopes was stacked neatly in front of him.

"So, tell me, little boy, why do you hate it here so much?"

My mouth went dry. My heart began to hammer fiercely in my chest. By the tone of his voice, I knew I was in trouble.

"Sir?" I eked out.

"Apparently, little boy, you're starving. You don't look undernourished to me. You also hate going on hikes and, from what I can make out from your scribbles, you don't like most, if not all, other activities."

It suddenly hit me. The letters to my parents. He had read them!

"Little boy, if you want your mommy and daddy to hear from you while you're at my camp, rewrite this childish drivel. And a warning to the wise, little boy, I suggest you change your attitude. Get out of here!" he said, tossing a blank sheet of writing paper at me. I nervously picked up an envelope and the writing paper and scurried out in the direction of the library.

Dear Mommy and Daddy,

How are you. I am fine. I really like it here. The food is real good. I am having fun. Are you coming on visiting day next Sunday?

Love and kisses, Victor
X X X

P.S. I miss you.

The letter was mailed.

There were three official visiting days during the camp season. The second and last Sundays in July and the second Sunday in August. My parents came together on the first. My mother came on the second, my father on the third.

For me, camp was nothing more than penance in the Laurentians. I wanted so badly to get back to the city. At the last supper, an awards night was held. Plaques were presented to boys who had successfully completed a number of activities and achieved the standing of good campers. Very few first-year boys won a camp plaque. I felt proud when Fred's name was called out to receive one. He was such a good athlete that they had to honor him even though he hated camp as much as I did. Plager was awarded a trophy for Best Hut on the Braves' side and our hut got ice cream as a special treat for dinner.

6

When we got back from camp, my mother announced that she had left my father again. She said she was fed up with his drinking and his not being able to hold on to a job. She also detested his latest gang of boozing buddies. Over the summer months, she had moved her clothes to a small, one-bedroom furnished apartment near her work and began living on her own once again.

My brothers took the news in stride, but I was devastated. Her leaving dashed any hopes I had of getting out of Weredale. I knew I'd be stuck there for a long time.

"Now we'll never get out of Weredale," I said, trying hard to make my mother feel guilty. I was really angry and wanted my words to hurt her.

"What am I supposed to do, Victor? Tell me!" she pleaded. "Must I live with a man who drinks, beats me up, doesn't work, spends my hard-earned money on booze, and then calls me a whore when I come home after ten hours on my feet in that smelly restaurant?"

"I hate Weredale. I can't stand it there," I yelled back.

"I . . . I don't know what to do any more," she cried as she ran into her bedroom.

"Why don't you just fuck right off," Fred threatened me. "You're a fuckin' jerk!" He shoved me against the wall. I pushed him back and took off down the stairs. Fred nailed me in the back with one of his shoes before I got out the door.

I hated him, my brother Peter, and my mother and vowed never to see them again as I stormed out of the apartment building. From then on, I allied myself with my father against the three of them. So often I yearned to visit my mother on the weekends but I told myself I couldn't leave my father alone. I became his boy. My mother had Fred and Peter, I reasoned. And even though I didn't see my mother too often during a six-month stretch, I felt deep down that she understood. She never held anything against me. We gradually drifted so far apart that I came to feel uncomfortable around her and my brothers.

My father continued to shift from job to job, a bouncer in a night club, a truck driver, a millwright, a shipper. He rented a two-room flat on a downtown cul-de-sac. He was terribly unhappy and lonely without my mother. At night, he'd drink himself into a stupor and usually pass out. My weekend visits with him left me depressed and feeling guilty because there was nothing I could do for him. On the occasional Saturday, my father refused to let me return to Weredale. He wanted me to stay with him. He'd tell me not to worry and then bring me back Sunday night. A couple of times there were heated verbal clashes between my father and Johnson until my father decked him one evening for calling him a no-good drunk. For a number of weeks after that, I lost my weekend leaves as punishment. My father was warned never to set foot in Weredale again or he would be arrested.

His friends changed radically that year. He no longer hung around with his Ukrainian drinking cronies. A lot of his new friends were big and mean-looking. All were neatly dressed. Some talked in whispers. Others were loud and bragged about beating up some guy or pulling scores. They drank a lot and carried rolls of money in their pockets. My father also carried a hefty roll, which I found puzzling since I knew he wasn't working. One time when he was asleep, I counted more than $2,700 in assorted bills on his night table. I sensed something was wrong but I was too afraid to confront him.

As our first Christmas in Weredale drew nearer, I felt myself becoming more and more anxious. We were allowed a special leave right after breakfast to go home and see our parents. I knew I would be going in one direction while my brothers went in another. I kept pushing the uncomfortable thought to the back of my mind.

Weredale was charged with excitement on Christmas Eve. When the bell rang shortly after supper, the boys hurried into line. We marched single file into the auditorium and took our seats. The room looked like an illustration straight out of a page in a story book. Gifts were piled at least six feet deep around a towering, glittering Christmas tree. The vision was dazzling. Within moments, the faint sound of reindeer bells, followed by a *ho ho ho,* could be heard in the distance. In came a fat man in a Santa Claus suit. Bets were made on which staff member was behind the costume. No one won because no one could find out for certain who it really was. One by one, just as for laundry parade, the boys were called up to receive a large gift-wrapped package. There were no favorites. We all got virtually the same items – a tie, shirt, a tartan-printed wool sweater, and a game, either Snakes and Ladders, Monopoly, checkers, or chess.

On Christmas Day, I didn't even see Fred and Peter dart out the back entrance. I wanted to give them a present for my mother. At my father's apartment, a pile of gifts waited for me on a coffee table in the middle of the living room.

"If Fred and Pete can't come and see me once in a while, then to hell with them," my father said angrily. He had bought nothing for them. I found it hard to smile and act cheerful as I unwrapped my presents. I kept wondering how my mother felt.

When I returned to Weredale that evening, Fred tossed me two gifts from my mother. The tags read: "To my son, Victor. Love and Kisses, Mummy." I felt so terrible for not even having dropped by to see her. I felt worse about the looks on my brothers' faces when they saw what I had received from my father. They knew they had got nothing from him.

The dormitories went wild that night. Everyone was in a festive spirit. Douglas was on duty, so we all knew we could get away with murder. The dorm was dead silent for about two minutes after lights out. Then Janigan gave the signal by ripping a loud, wet fart.

"Sixers . . . sixers," came the cry from all corners of the room. At least a dozen boys leapt from their beds to pound Janigan six times on his arms and legs for breaking wind without first calling safety.

Then it was bedlam. Frenchie volunteered to keep nix for the first half-hour and crawled on his stomach to the stairwell where he could get an advance warning of any staff member lurking in the area. While he was in the hallway, a few of the guys moved his bed for a joke. There were inter-dormitory raids, pillow fights with shoes in the pillow sacks, and an initiation of a new boy who had come in a week earlier. He got his balls rubbed with Pepsodent.

"Nix . . . nix . . . nix," Frenchie shouted in a loud whisper as he dove over a bed and hit the concrete floor where his own bed should have been. A bunch of guys cracked up but quickly stopped when they realized Frenchie was hurt.

Douglas zipped in, scanning the beds with a blinding beam from his flashlight. He found Frenchie moaning on the floor. His lip was bleeding. He had had the wind knocked out of him.

"I hope you jokers learned something from this," Douglas shouted. "You can fool around but think about what the heck you're doing. You're damn lucky he wasn't killed or injured seriously. Now all of you out of bed and bend over. Janigan, go find me a big running shoe!"

Before long, the dormitory quieted down. A few boys crossed over to other beds or sneaked into nearby dorms to visit a friend. I rolled over and went to sleep.

An hour later, I lay shivering in a sheet-soaked bed. I punched the mattress and cursed myself. "You fuckin' piss-head," I muttered through tightly clenched teeth. Tearing the soiled sheet from my bed, I tiptoed into the washroom, rinsed it in the sink, and draped it over a steaming hot radiator to dry.

"What the heck are you doing here?" Douglas asked, lightly kicking my bottom to wake me up.

I had fallen asleep on the washroom floor.

"Sir, I . . . I washed my sheet. I . . ."

"It's okay. It's okay. Bring it into your dormitory. I'll wait a moment and wake the boys up once you're done. Hurry up."

"Thank you, sir."

"Malarek boys, you have a visitor," the evening office boy called out as he trotted through the junior games room. I was perched on the bleachers half watching a hockey game on television. I jumped to the floor and bolted for the visiting room. Fred and Peter arrived seconds later. It was my mother and she looked upset. It was obvious she had been crying. Fred asked her what was wrong.

"Boys, I have some bad news for you. Come and sit down over here beside me."

"It's about Dad. Isn't it, Mom? He's in trouble," I blurted out.

"Yes, Victor. Your father's been put away. He's been sent to prison for two years."

"No! They can't do that. Not to Daddy," I cried.

"Why?" Freddie asked as my mother drew Peter under her arm.

"For stealing. He got caught stealing by the police and the judge gave him two years."

Johnson tiptoed in and cleared his throat.

"It won't be forever, boys. You'll see your father again soon. It's time for showers. I have to speak to your mother for a moment, so say good night to her and run along," he said in a consoling tone.

The showers came as a bit of a relief. I could cry and not be seen or teased by the boys. I washed slowly, facing a corner of the shower room, and cursed God for what had happened to my father. Two years, I thought. He wouldn't be out of prison until February 1962. My world was crushed: I wouldn't be getting out of Weredale for a long time. My father's sentence was *my* sentence. If there had ever been any hope of a reconciliation between him and my mother, it was quashed.

On Saturday I went with Fred and Peter to see Mom. It was the first weekend in a long time that I had gone to visit her instead of my father.

"Mom?" I began hesitantly as we sat quietly in front of the television, "are you going to visit Dad?"

She sighed, stared at me a moment, and said, "No, Victor."

"Why?" I asked, my voice cracking.

"Victor, your father called me some very nasty names in the court-room and embarrassed me after I went out of my way to get a lawyer to help him."

"But he's there all alone!" I pleaded, staring anxiously into her eyes. "How can I see him if you don't come? Please, Mom."

She drew a deep breath. "All right, all right, Victor. We'll visit him next week."

The following Sunday, she came to pick us up in a taxi. The ride was long, almost an hour. The four of us drove through the city, over the Pie IX bridge and down a narrow, winding road along the river bank before turning into a massive penitentiary complex called St. Vincent de Paul. The name sent a cold shiver through my body.

To the left was a huge cold grey-stone wall reaching into the sky. There were turrets and guards with rifles patrolling the catwalks. In a valley to the right was another prison with smaller walls topped with barbed-wire fencing. The taxi driver drove slowly up the road to the main entrance of the maximum-security penitentiary known as St. François Institution. While my mother made arrangements for the ride back, I jumped out of the cab to look around. Further down the road was a minimum-security farm. Prisoners in grey uniforms were working in the fields. Across the street from the St. François prison, I noticed a small burial plot and went to investigate. Surrounded by a black wrought-iron railing was a marble tombstone. A dozen or so serial numbers of convicts buried there were etched into the black slab. There were no names. I shuddered to think anyone could be so all alone that no one would care enough to claim his body for a decent burial.

My mother rang the bell of the main door and a guard opened it. We walked into a small room with two teller's cages looking into a sparsely furnished office where a few guards were sitting on wooden stools.

"We came here to visit my husband," my mother said in an embarrassed whisper.

"What is his number?" a French-speaking guard snarled, seeming a little annoyed at dealing in English.

"I don't know. His name is Mike Malarek. He's new here."

"Ah, oui. C'est ça," he said, pointing to a name in a green ledger on the counter. "4069 his number. You are who?"

"His wife."

"You have identification?"

"Yes, I have identification."

"Well, let me see it."

Mom handed the guard her wallet.

"Bon! Only two people can go upstairs to visit at one time. Regulations! Visiting two times a month. You have thirty minutes. If you wish to leave money or books, leave them with me. I will see that he gets them."

"Can't each of the boys see their father?"

"One could go up for a few minutes, and when he comes down, the other could go up."

"Thank you."

"Wait in the room there until your name is called."

The waiting room was packed with young women cradling babies in their arms and middle-aged mothers and fathers wearing solemn expressions. A few younger guys in their late teens, who were probably brothers of convicts, strutted about the room like hardrocks. One kept flicking out his comb and dragging it through his greasy hair to make sure his duck's ass was in place. Another chewed a wad of gum with the speed of a jigsaw, and a third, wearing mirror sunglasses, moved a cigarillo from one side of his lips to the other. I pretended to take no notice of anyone and sat down in a corner beside my mother.

"They look like jerks," I whispered in her ear.

"Shh," she said.

Fred was roaming about the room and within minutes was waving frantically at me to join him outside the guard's office.

"What do you want?" I asked.

"Come here. You can see the prisoners being brought in through these bars here."

We stood as inconspicuously as we could under the window, craning our necks to get a glimpse at the dozen or so convicts sitting quietly on two benches lining opposite walls of a large cage. A moment later, a buzzer sounded and a heavy grey steel door opened. My father and two other men in green uniforms marched in. My father signed a register and took his place on one of the benches. He looked mean and angry, his eyes cold and hard. A prisoner sitting next to him saw us and tapped my father on the shoulder. He turned, saw me waving, and smiled. After a fifteen-minute wait, a guard handed my father a ticket and the two disappeared behind a wall.

"We just saw Dad, Mom," I said, rushing back to my seat.

"Malarek," a guard called out, coming halfway down the flight of stairs at the far end of the room.

"Peter will come up with me first. Then when I send him down, Freddie, you come up. You'll come up when Freddie comes down. Okay, Victor?"

"Yes, Mom."

The minutes crawled by, then finally Peter appeared on the stairwell wiping a flood of tears from his eyes. Fred's eyes were glassy after his brief visit but he kept himself under control. I walked up the stairs nervously. I thought my legs would buckle before I got to the top of the landing. I didn't know what to expect.

A guard told me to go to booth 18, indicating the direction with a thick, nicotine-stained finger.

The room was filled with hot, stale air and the overpowering tension of caged men. Dense cigarette smoke burned my eyes. It was difficult to breathe. Convicts in faded green uniforms sat on wooden chairs behind the forbidding glass and metal separation sealing off the centre of the chamber. They spoke to their visitors from behind this barrier through a small rectangular metal sheet that was covered with hundreds of tiny pin holes. These quiet murmurings made an eerie hum in the otherwise silent room.

My father forced a sad smile. I burst out crying.

"Come on, Victor. It's not for long. I'll be out soon. You'll see. Come on, stop crying. Jennie, give him a Kleenex."

"I'm . . . I'm sorry. I didn't mean to cry. It's just that . . ."

"It's okay, Victor. How are you doing in school? Are you passing?"

"Yeah. They don't flunk you twice in the same grade. I'm doing okay."

"That's good. Is everything all right in Weredale?"

"Yes. I guess so."

"I guess that jerk Johnson must be happy I'm here."

"I . . . I don't know, Dad. He didn't seem happy about it when he talked to Mom."

A long, uneasy pause followed. My father stared at my mother. His eyes narrowed. I knew he was going to start something.

"Well, I guess you got what you wanted!" he began caustically.

"Don't, Mike," she replied.

"Why not? You afraid of the truth?"

"I didn't come here to argue."

"Why did you come here? Not because you love me, that's for sure."

"Mike, if you keep this up, I'm not going to visit you any more. I mean it."

"So? Who gives a damn? I didn't ask you to visit me, did I? I don't give a damn if you never come!"

"Fine then, Mike. I won't come any more."

"Good. I wouldn't want to tear you away from any of your boyfriends."

"That's right! Think the way you want, Mike. Your mind is always in the gutter. I'm leaving."

"Good! Go! See if I care!"

"Victor, you can stay up here for a moment," she said before leaving. "I'll see you downstairs."

I sat motionless, staring blankly at the top of the counter.

"I guess your mother won't come to see me any more. Do you still want to visit me?"

"Yes, Dad. You know I do." My voice was trembling.

"Fred and Pete won't come. They stick with their mother. But you're my boy. I'll make arrangements for you to visit with one of your uncles. Okay?"

"Okay."

"Now smile! Come on, let's see a smile for your old man."

"I can't." Tears were streaming down my face.

A guard passed and placed a slip of paper in front of my father. "Time's up," he said.

"I have to go now. Write me and I'll see you in two weeks. Remember, you're my favorite boy and I love you."

"I love you too, Dad!"

7

"*M*alarek," Johnson chirped as I was heading into the games room.

"Yes, sir." I could tell by the cheerful tone of his voice that for once I wasn't in trouble.

"You and your brothers are Ukrainian, aren't you?"

"Yes, sir."

"Do you know any songs?"

"Yes, sir. I know 'Hang Down Your Head, Tom Dooley'."

Johnson laughed. "I mean, do you know any Ukrainian songs?"

"Not all the way through, sir. Why?"

"Well, we're going to hold an open house in about two months and we thought it might be nice to have some of the boys sing songs or do dances from their national heritage."

"I think my mother could teach us on the weekends when we visit her. I'll ask her," I said enthusiastically.

"Good, good. We'll be holding a rehearsal sometime next week. I'll be counting on you and Fred and Peter." Johnson mussed my hair playfully before going into his office.

I felt honored and bolted for the phone booth to call home. "Mom. It's me. Mom, do you know any Ukrainian songs?"

"Yes, Victor. Why?"

"Mom. Guess what? Mr. Johnson asked us to sing in Ukrainian on stage for a big night here. Could you teach us a song in Ukrainian?"

"Sure. I'll teach you a couple of songs that aren't too hard to learn when you come over on the weekend."

The ethnic evening was a smashing success. It was "standing room only" as Westmount dignitaries, Weredale's benefactors and board of governors, teachers, and invited parents packed the auditorium.

Judging from the reaction of the audience, the entertainment side was quite hilarious. Frenchie sang a Quebec folk song, and if there was one thing that he could not do, it was carry a tune. Giovanni, a fat-faced, bug-eyed Italian, forgot his lyrics part way through an aria and hummed the last dozen or so bars. The Waters brothers, two full-blooded Mohawk Indians, collided with each other during a frenzied war dance and tumbled unceremoniously onto the stage floor. At the close of the first half, Fred and a few guys put on a side-splitting skit called "Mother I've Been Shot". When the curtains opened for the last half, the audience was greeted by an Irish quintet who performed a screeching version of "When Irish Eyes Are Smiling". The funniest moment came when a Scottish Highland dancer tripped and sent a sword flying off the stage and into the first row. We were third to last. Fred's voice had gone hoarse from shouting like a madman during the skit. Peter got stage fright and froze and I belted out the lyrics alone, hoping to make up the difference. Belov, a chubby Russian from junior south, tried desperately to kick up his heels in a driving Cossack *hopak*. He careened repeatedly on his butt. The audience couldn't contain itself. Johnson should have asked Fred to dance the *hopak*, I thought, instead of mistakenly assuming that these wild dances were Russian when in fact they were Ukrainian. The closing number was done by a black boy who sang a moving rendition of "Chances Are".

I was beaming when Johnson went over to my mother and congratulated her for a fantastic job in teaching us the Ukrainian songs. Johnson was really happy with us and that made me feel good.

Bringing in the sheaves,
Bringing in the sheaves,
We shall come rejoicing,
Bringing in the sheaves.

Chief raised his hands at the end of the hymn for the congregation to be seated. "Before we break for lunch, I would like to conclude this service by asking each and every one of you to look inside yourself for that tolerance towards your fellow man that I talked about in my sermon. Remember always the Golden Rule: 'Do unto others as you would have them do unto you.' Have a good day and I'll see you all at lunch." Respectfully, everyone rose as he and Johnson marched out of the auditorium.

Maitland took charge of dismissing the boys row by row. "Downstairs and wash up for lunch," he instructed before he waved the first row out.

Line-ups of jostling boys crowded around the sinks in the locker room, so I decided to play with my new black eight-diamond yo-yo while waiting for the lines to thin out. I was practising a baby in the cradle when someone yelled: "Look out!" Damned if I thought the warning was meant for me. I wasn't doing anything wrong. My head suddenly snapped back and smashed against the side of an open locker door. I crumbled to the floor. My head was reeling. Towering over me, his face burning in anger, stood Maitland.

"You're supposed to be washing up, Malarek, not playing with your stupid yo-yo. Move! All of you, move!" he boomed. I felt nervously around my face for the cause of a pulsating pain around my left eye.

"Move, you goddamn little baby, or I'll give you another one. Get up and get washed! Move!" Maitland hauled me up by my hair and shoved me in the direction of the sinks. He was like a madman.

"Leave me alone, you fuckin' bastard," I blurted out, my mouth foaming. "I didn't do anything wrong!"

"I'll teach you to swear at me!" A stinging slap caught my cheek. I dropped to the floor. Maitland grabbed me by the scruff of my neck and dragged me towards the sink.

"Clear the way. Clear out!" he shrieked at the line of boys he was bulldozing out of his way.

"Leave me alone!" I screamed, trying to tear away from his painful grasp. "I didn't do nothing!"

"I'll teach you to swear at me!" he repeated, clutching a bar of soap he'd taken from one of the sinks. I clamped my teeth shut as he struggled to jam the bar into my mouth. He slapped me two more times and yanked upwards at the hair on the back of my neck.

"Open . . . open, you little . . ." he threatened in a pique of rage.

The pain was unbearable. As I opened my mouth to cry out, he rammed in a corner of the soap bar.

"Chew! Chew it! I'll teach you to swear at me. You little creep!"

I was shaking violently and, out of fear for my safety, began to chew. Dozens of boys watched spellbound and horrified. Their heads reared back when I began to vomit.

"Clean it up, Malarek, and wash up when you're finished! The rest of you boys wash up. Move! Those of you who are finished, move it into the games room." Maitland's back was turned as he barked out his orders. I seized the moment to make a break and bolted upstairs screaming at the top of my lungs. Johnson charged out of his office to investigate the commotion.

"What happened to you? Who did this?"

"Mr. Maitland. I was playing with my yo-yo and he punched me."

Johnson drew a deep breath and pursed his lips. "You should have been getting ready for lunch, Malarek. You never do what you're told. You'll get no sympathy from me. Go see the nurse. She'll clean you up. Move it!"

Mrs. Evans was shocked when she saw my eye, but when she learned who had accosted me, she became icy and matter-of-fact.

"You should do what you're told and stay out of trouble," she lectured as she rinsed my face with a cool washcloth.

At lunch-time, Johnson cancelled my leave and put me on detention to report every half-hour for the whole weekend. I couldn't even go home to my mother to show her what had happened. Maitland was lucky in one respect, I thought: he would have died for what he'd done if my father had not been locked up in jail. Fred felt badly that there wasn't anything he could do. What could he do? Maitland was a man and he was only a boy. I spent most of the afternoon brooding in the yard. I fantasized about the day when I would be older, bigger, and stronger, of the day when I would be a man. Then I'd get even with Maitland. I'd never forget what he had done to me. I'd stomp the bastard good, kick his teeth down his rotten throat and break every finger in his bloody hands. And I'd get even with Johnson and all the guys who picked on me. I'd get them all!

"Hey, Malarek! Want to play baseball?" one of the boys shouted from the baseball diamond.

"Jesus Christ!" I snapped. "I got a first name. It's Victor. Victor! There's two other Malareks in the home. My name is Victor! Victor!" I was raving.

"Ah, chuck you, Malarek. I only asked you cause we felt bad at what that prick Maitland did to you," the boy yelled back.

"Damn it!" I muttered to myself. "Nobody ever calls me by my first name. It's always Malarek this, Malarek that. 'Hey, Malarek, get over here' or 'Move it, Malarek!' And I'm supposed to know which one they mean. Ha! What a laugh! It isn't hard anyway. When they call Fred, it's 'Malarek' with a tinge of respect. For Peter, it's a sugary sweet 'Malarek'. For me, it's like I'm diseased or something."

"Hey, Malarek! We need an extra guy. You want to play ball or not? Come on."

"Stupid idiot!" I mumbled under my breath. "Ah, what's the use? Yeah, I'm coming. You got an extra glove?"

June 26, 1960. My twelfth birthday and my second in Weredale. So much for my mother's promise that I'd be home before this birthday. She couldn't take us out of Weredale on her own, and my father was still securely tucked away in prison. She had tried but the welfare people wouldn't allow her custody because they felt the boys' home provided us with a better and safer environment. Too bad they don't live here, I thought. Come to think of it, I had never once been visited by a social worker in the whole time I had been in Weredale. Not one ever came to ask me, "How's it going?" Yet the welfare authorities felt this place was better than being at home with my mother. At least at home we'd be with someone who really loved us. No one in Weredale loved us. No one ever told us they even liked us. The dozen or so staff members had their hands full controlling 160 boys. They could care less about our personal problems.

My mother begged the welfare workers to let us come home. They were concerned about how she would look after us. She said she'd work. Then they asked who would take care of us while she was at work. Someone had to be at home, the social workers said. She said she would stay home if she got welfare, but they refused to give it to her, so she couldn't stay home. Later in my life, I wondered if any of those creeps ever considered the cost of keeping three boys in an institution. I'm sure it was much more that what my mother would have received on welfare.

But it was my birthday and I was excited. I was a bit jumpy at lunch waiting to be called up for the birthday song. It had been the high point of last year. When I saw the boys from tables 1, 2, and 3 being dismissed, I brushed any concerns aside, figuring that I'd be called up at dinner. I noticed Peter talking to Johnson, who looked rather put off. Later, out in the yard, a few of the guys teased me about Mrs. Evans's traditional birthday smacker and I cockily assured them that this year there was no way she would catch me.

"Man, they're really saving it for you," Nelson said.

"What do you mean?"

"The full treatment. All the guys will be in at dinner, even the working seniors, and there'll be two nurses to get kissed by. Man, are you ever going to get it at supper," Nelson gloated.

Late into supper, I noticed Fred approach Johnson. I was sitting two tables away with my back to them.

"First Peter at lunch. Now the older one at supper. Are you his booking agents? I know it's his birthday. Now, sit down," Johnson bellowed.

Fred said something else and a booming "NO" brought the room to a leaden silence. Fred returned to his table looking really cheesed off.

"Don't give me any of your looks, sonny," Johnson shouted, waving his index finger in my brother's direction. Fred sat down and continued his supper.

"Tables 1, 2, and 3, dismissed," Johnson called out.

My heart sank. I wasn't going to be called up for my birthday. I got up from table 5 and kept my head down as I passed Johnson.

"Malarek," he snapped as I was putting my tray into the bin.

"Yes, sir?" I replied, meekly heading over to his perch.

"I'm getting a little fed up with your pouting and sulking. You walk around here as if the world owes you an explanation. Well, it doesn't. We all can't have what we want in this world, sonny. So grow up! And I strongly suggest you do something about your attitude soon or else. Until then, I don't think I'm going to ask the other boys to go out of their way to sing you a happy birthday. Now get!"

Tears were flowing down my face as I left the dining room. I could feel dozens of pitying eyes boring into me.

"He's a prick," muttered Fred, who caught up to me in the stairwell. Fred understood how bad I felt and there was nothing he could do about it. He couldn't slap out Johnson for me and that's all I wished someone would do. We were sitting in the locker room when our family name was shouted in the hallway.

"Malarek boys . . . phone call. Phone call for the Malareks." Fred and I bolted for the phone booth on the first floor.

"Happy birthday, Victor," my mother said as I grabbed the phone.

"Mommy." I cleared my throat. Then I began bawling uncontrollably. Fred took the phone.

"Mr. Johnson didn't call Victor so the boys could sing happy birthday to him," he said. "No, he didn't forget, Mom. Peter and I reminded him. He's a prick, Mom. A rotten prick." Fred's eyes were watering. He handed me the phone.

"Mom, he did it on purpose. If Dad weren't in jail, I'd get him to beat up that bastard. Why is he picking on me? I didn't do anything."

"I'll call Mr. Johnson. Don't cry, Victor. I'll be seeing you tomorrow before you go off to camp. I have a little present for you."

"I wish I was dead."

"Don't talk like that. I'll call Mr. Johnson and talk to him."

"Do you want to talk to Freddie again?" I asked. "Peter just came in."

"All right. But don't cry, Victor. It's your birthday. You shouldn't cry on your birthday. Don't worry. Everything will be fine."

I passed the phone to Peter and ran to a secluded spot in the building where I spent the rest of the evening brooding. The next day at breakfast, which was the last day in the city before leaving for camp, Johnson started clanging the birthday bell.

"Come on up, birthday boy," he teased. "Come up here, Malarek."

A few boys called out my name and a number of catcalls followed.

Nelson, who was sitting next to me, nudged me. He smiled broadly and winked.

"Come on. Get up there. It's your birthday," he egged.

"No. It was yesterday." I continued eating my breakfast without looking up.

"Get up here, Malarek," Johnson shouted, when he saw I wasn't budging. He was getting annoyed.

I put down my spoon and walked up the aisle toward the traditional perch on the window sill. Johnson stood in front wearing a fake smile. There was no way I was going to smile back or look happy. Not for Johnson or for anyone. I knew that my mother had called him. But today wasn't my birthday.

"Sir, it's not my birthday today," I said.

"I have you down for June 27. So get up there," he said, half smiling and trying to remain indifferent about my indifference.

"Sir, my birthday was yesterday. I was born on June 26, 1948. My brothers told you it was my birthday yesterday. And you knew. I don't want to have the boys sing happy birthday to me today, when my birthday was yesterday."

"Get under the clock and stay there!" he boomed.

"You're going to get the biffs!" Hargraves heckled as I walked by his table.

"Go to hell!"

"Whoa, Malarek's getting tough!"

Johnson stood with his hands on his hips glaring down at me. He drew a long, deep breath and rubbed his brow. "You then, Malarek. What am I going to do with you? The next time I get a performance like that, you'll visit the clinic! Understand?"

I should have let it go at that, but my stubborn pride decided otherwise.

"Sir, it isn't my birthday today. My brothers told you that yesterday. It's on June 26 and you —"

"Get in the clinic! I'll teach you to talk back to me!"

The clinic! The word shot through me like an electric shock! I was going to get the biffs. Until then, I had never been strapped formally by Johnson or his assistant, Marshall. By formally I don't mean being whacked with a running shoe while bending over the foot of a bed. Any staff member could dish out that form of punishment. Formally meant getting the biffs in the clinic and having my name and the number of biffs inscribed in a black, hard-covered book that had a thick leather strap for a place marker.

Only Johnson and Marshall had the authority to give the biffs.

My hands were sweaty and my legs wobbled as I approached the clinic door. I was scared, yet I caught myself smiling meekly inwardly. I felt as if I had finally made it to a high plateau in my life. As if I were receiving a kind of benediction. As Johnson disappeared behind the door separating the general office and the inner sanctum where his office was, a few heads peered into the hallway.

"Malarek! Malarek!" one of the heads called out. "Don't cry! Johnson hates babies. He only gives three biffs the first time. If you start bawling, he'll give you more!"

I reassured them with a glance that I could take whatever Johnson had to dish out. Inside, I was forcing myself to rein in the tears. I entered the clinic. Johnson barged in through the side door off the office.

"Take your pants down and kneel on the footrest!" he boomed, pointing to the antiquated dentist's chair. "Move it." He flexed the leather strap and I gripped the arm rest.

"Drop your underwear to your knees!" Trembling hands obeyed. "You're going to learn not to talk back, Malarek. I've had it with your sullen attitude."

I swallowed hard. A second later, a stinging length of leather seared across my bare buttocks. I winced but I didn't cry out. Two, three, four . . . four? Five! Tears were drowning my eyes. I couldn't take any more. I thought my skin would split on the next whack. I began to bawl and Johnson stopped. While I pulled up my underwear and pants, my name was officially entered in the black book and beside it Johnson marked the number of strokes.

"Took more than I thought you would," he commented. "I expected you to be crying after one. I usually give three the first time but I guess you wanted to be stubborn. I hope this has taught you a lesson!" Johnson left.

I had learned my lesson. The guys had sucked me in, telling me not to cry. After rinsing my face under the cold-water tap in the sink, I limped out of the clinic, forcing myself to smile.

"Wow, Malarek got the biffs!" Gillis shouted while goggling at my backside during compulsory showers that evening. Thick, foot-long, black, blue, and reddish welts criss-crossed my behind. Even I was astonished at the sight. It damn well hurt but nowhere near as bad as it looked.

"Johnson! He gave me five. Didn't hurt!" I offered nonchalantly. My backside became the novelty of the shower room. I stayed in extra long so most of the guys could get a good look. I wanted them to see that I had made it. The biffs, after all, was an important ritual and there was no way I was going to let my moment in glory go unnoticed.

My uncle Eli came to pick me up the following day to take me to the penitentiary. He was my father's brother, the third of five children – three boys, two girls – and the only one who didn't drink. My father, who was forty, was the second-youngest.

Uncle Eli was short, stocky, and very easygoing. He owned the house I grew up in when we lived in Lachine. He had married a French-Canadian woman just as the war broke out and now had three sons. The one thing that struck me about him was his big hands. My uncle was a riveter on steel bridges.

During the one-hour bus ride, I peppered him with questions about my father. Uncle Eli seemed a little uncomfortable talking about his brother. Maybe he felt it wasn't his place to tell me anything.

"Uncle Eli, why does Dad drink so much?" I began.

"Victor, your father has gone through a lot. I don't want to make excuses for his stealing or not working, but your father was never the same after he came home from the war."

"What do you mean? How was he before the war?"

"Mikey was a real joker. Full of fun. Never mean to anyone. When the war broke out, he was nineteen. The first thing he did was join up. He didn't wait to get drafted. Your father saw a lot of action. He was wounded twice, once very badly. You know your dad is very proud he served this country. He's very proud of being a vet. But Mikey also killed a lot of men in the war. He also saw two of his best friends die in front of him. That changed him. He was never the same when he came home."

"How did he marry Mom?"

"Your mother was in a convent. She was a novice, going to become a nun. Your mother had a terrible childhood. Her parents came from Ukraine after the Russian Revolution and lived in Pointe St. Charles. They were very poor. When she was ten, her mother died. Within two years her brother and three sisters died. I think another brother went crazy and killed himself. Her father just up and disappeared. She was brought to a convent. After the war, her godfather and your grandfather on the Malarek side arranged a meeting. Your father was twenty-six, your mother was fifteen or sixteen. They were married a couple of months later."

The bus stopped outside a snack bar in the town of St. Vincent de Paul. We took a cab the rest of the way.

My father seemed in good spirits. He wished me a happy birthday. I didn't tell him about the biffs.

"How's your mother?"

"Fine," I said.

"Your brothers?"

"They're okay."

"How did you do in school?"

"I passed easy."

"You got some kid named Plager in the home?"

I nodded at my father curiously. "Yes. Why?"

"Did he ever say where his dad is?"

"I heard he works on the boats. A lot of guys' fathers work on the boats," I added.

"I met Plager's father. We're on the same cell block. I also met a few other guys in here with kids in the Home," he said, reeling off four more surnames of Weredale boys.

I was stunned. I never told Plager I knew his dark secret. That summer, his father slit his throat in his cell. Plager left camp for a week. Everyone was told his uncle had died and he'd gone back to Montreal for the funeral.

8

*A*fter another tedious summer at camp, I returned to the city, terrified of going into grade six. Flunking grade five had torn a thick chunk
out of my confidence. And although I blamed Morrison's hate of Weredale
boys for failing me, not too deep down inside I wondered if it wasn't me.
Maybe I was a dummy.

The grade six teacher, Mr. MacGregor, was new to the school, and
because he was new, he hadn't built up any prejudices against Weredale
boys. He seemed like a really nice man. Young, caring, sincere, and
easygoing. He never had a wisecrack or anything nasty to say to anyone
from Weredale. But that didn't mean he was a push-over. MacGregor
was firm in his dealings with us, letting us get away with a little and
reining us in when we got carried away. MacGregor gave us punishments
when we got too rowdy but he was never physical. I don't remember
him ever strapping any of us.

Overall, grade six was a good year for me, even a great year. MacGregor
had a lot of time for me. He seemed to sense my need to prove that I
wasn't a dummy. He also seemed to recognize the hurt behind my aloof-
ness and how Weredale was hardening me, just as it was hardening many
of the other boys in his class. I knew I was becoming hard. I could feel
it and I couldn't help it. I had had so many bitter disappointments. My
trust in people and relationships was paper thin. I had become a loner,
sullen and quite disliked. I didn't get along with many of the guys in the
Home and I really didn't care. I didn't fit in. Most of the boys, and several staff members, didn't like being around me because I was so moody.
I hardly smiled, although I had stopped sobbing and crying at every trauma.
Still, a lot of things bothered me and it showed. My mind was a torrent
of confusing, bewildering thoughts. Nothing made any sense. At times I
felt something was wrong with me. I believed with firm conviction that
I'd been put in Weredale because I had done something wrong. I thought
I had offended God and he was punishing me. What I couldn't deal with

was a terrifying and growing obsession that somehow I was the cause of my parents' breakup.

I needed someone to talk to. Someone I could trust and someone who would listen. The only people I trusted were my parents and my brothers, and I couldn't talk to any of them. Before, when I had tried talking to my mother, I made her cry, and then Fred got really angry. I guess I expressed myself badly. My father was behind bars with his own problems, and I could never talk to him about anything anyway. I was afraid to. Our closest relatives had all but deserted us. To them, our family had simply ceased to exist.

No one in Weredale seemed to care. No one ever asked how I felt or how I was coping. Most of the staff were "old" boys and the only way they knew to deal with problems was the same way they had been dealt with when they were kids in the Home – with a running shoe applied to a rear end. One thing I found rather ironic was that the very social welfare agency that placed most of the kids in Weredale was just up the street, yet I can't recall one social worker ever coming into the home to talk to any of us.

I opened up a bit to MacGregor but I couldn't spill out my deepest feelings. I'd try to find the words to tell him how upset I felt inside, but my throat would swell up and choke off the words. And I couldn't tell him my father was in prison. I couldn't tell anyone that. I realized that a wall was going up around me and it was getting harder and harder for me to open up.

There was one incident that happened early in the school year that cheered me up and gave me something to look forward to. Our history class was interrupted by a visitor, Mr. Davis, a teacher from Westmount High School. His brief lecture about what the high school had to offer gave me the one important thing I desperately needed at the time, a goal. My goal was to be accepted into the Westmount High School music class. This wasn't just any music class, it was a reward for bright students and an opportunity to learn how to play a musical instrument. In the back of my cluttered thoughts I sometimes fancied myself as a musician of sorts. My mind was made up. I wanted in and I was going to make sure I got in.

Mr. Davis played a significant role in convincing me, not by what he said but by how he looked. Dreamy-eyed and somewhat dishevelled, he seemed out of place and out of character in a classroom. He looked like an eccentric musician or composer, and not your run-of-the-mill music teacher with a penchant for scales and silly children's folksongs. His head was in the clouds composing a sonata or conducting a symphony orchestra. I liked him right off.

"Every year, we select graduating grade six students from the three public schools in Westmount to come into the music class," he read from a prepared text. "Their marks have to be exceptional and they must want to learn to play a musical instrument. A violin, a trumpet, flute, saxophone, clarinet, cello, trombone, or percussion. I'm going to hand out these application forms to any of you who want one. Take them home and discuss them with your parents, and if they agree, and if you have the marks, we'll consider you."

By sixth grade, I was well into my second year in Weredale and I was beginning to gain confidence in myself. I wasn't frightened by a lot of things as I had been, like the dark, thunderstorms, and the water. And I noticed I wasn't wetting the bed as much, although I was still known as a piss-head. I wasn't afraid of a lot of the bullies in the home. After a couple of scraps where I came out the victor, I gained a little status, so I wasn't being picked on as much. But I certainly wasn't up there in the rankings by any stretch of the imagination, unlike Freddie, who had developed into a lethal and feared street fighter. He was also a major dissuading force behind anyone's inclination to bully me or Peter.

My life seemed to be taking on some order. It was far from what I wanted, but at least I was dragging myself out of the mire. I even had my first girlfriend, although it didn't last long. Half faint, the girl's mother clutched her huge left breast and looked to the heavens when I told her my address. Our breakup after just two weeks was painless and a relief. For a twelve-year-old, the life of a midget Romeo in the boys' home proved unbearable. Everyone peppered me with catcalls and hoots, embarrassing questions, and crude advice. But that wasn't the real reason our fledgling romance ended. I thought the girl was a pig. I never told any of the guys in the home about this but one afternoon while we were kissing behind some bushes in Westmount Park, she stuck her tongue in my mouth.

My heart began to race when I was told my mother was in the visiting room. Something was wrong, I could sense it. It was the Monday after Ukrainian Easter and we had just spent the entire Sunday with her, digging into a mouth-watering feast of Ukrainian food she had prepared for us. Usually if my mother visited us during the week, she would come on a Wednesday or Thursday. Johnson was standing in the doorway of the visiting room when I arrived. His grim expression turned my stomach into a cauldron of acid. As he turned to leave, he patted me on the head, confirming my worst fears. Freddie and Peter were sitting quietly beside my mother.

Once again she was the reluctant bearer of bad news. Clearing her throat, she began in a whisper. "Your father has a disease called cancer. The doctors said if he doesn't have an operation soon, he'll die within three months. Your father's a strong man. The doctors said they're hopeful he'll make it through the operation."

Her words came to me in a fog. They didn't seem real. I felt as if I was floating in a strange place, totally removed from reality. This wasn't happening. The word cancer hammered in my eardrums. My father's smoldering Cossack eyes flashed in front of my face.

"How did he get sick?" Fred asked.

"A long time ago during the war a shell exploded near your father. Apparently not all the fragments were cleaned out. He had some small slivers of lead and copper embedded in the left side of his jaw. The doctors think that's how the cancer started. They feel they can clean it out."

There was a long moment where nothing was said. "Victor, Victor, come sit beside me." My mother drew her arm around me and stroked my head.

"When will he be operated on?" Fred continued.

"Tomorrow morning. I want you boys to say a little prayer for him tonight. I'm going to visit him at the Veterans' Hospital tomorrow. I'll light a candle at St. Joseph's Oratory and say a prayer before I go to see him."

For two tense, mind-numbing weeks, my father recuperated in intensive care, wavering close to death. The doctors had removed half his lower jaw and a large section of tissue and tendons from the upper left side of his chest. They found the cancer had spread downwards. We visited as often as we could, fearing that each day might be his last. Johnson even gave us special leave to go to the hospital after school and sometimes in the evening instead of making us wait until the weekend. I was surprised by the concern he showed. I had come to think he was a cold, insensitive man. I knew he didn't care for my father, yet he took a genuine interest in his condition.

I was devastated by my father's illness and the terrifying thought that he could die. In class, I would stare into space for hours, thinking about absolutely nothing. It was as if I were in a giant black pit. MacGregor left me to myself.

The day my father was taken off the critical list and moved out of intensive care, I couldn't stop shaking. In my prayers, I thanked God over and over again. My spirits picked up and MacGregor zeroed in, volunteering for me a special project, a class newspaper which would come out at the end of the school year. I was to write an article about Weredale House.

He didn't let me slack off after that. "I want to see you in that music class, Victor. So let's get to it."

During the final school assembly, I was jolted by three announcements. In the first I was called out to receive an award for scoring the second-highest marks out of both grade six classes. As the principal was handing me my prize – an adventure novel with an inscription in it – Mr. MacGregor made the second announcement.

"Victor has also been accepted into the music class at Westmount High when the new and combined high school opens in September."

The assembly applauded and cheered as I jumped down from the make-shift stage and made my way back to my seat. I was thrilled that a lot of Weredale guys were whistling and clapping proudly. After the awards ceremony was over, the principal rose to address the assembly.

"Before we go off for the summer holidays, I would like to close this final school assembly for this school year by reading a composition written by one of your schoolmates. He is a Weredale boy. I'm sure that most of you children are familiar with the Weredale boys. Those of you who are not from Weredale, I'm sure you realize that these boys are not as lucky as you are. Their lives have been struck by misfortune and sadness. I was particularly moved by one Weredale boy's composition when his teacher showed it to me and I feel that I should share it with you. It's called 'A Home Away from Home'."

My eyes flashed wide open in surprise. It was *my* composition.

"'Often when I look out the window of my dormitory at Weredale House, I get jealous when I think about those other kids who live at home with their parents. I miss my mother and father so much but I can't be with them. They split up. But I know they both love me and my two brothers. It's just that they can't be together.

"'Now I have an even bigger family. The Weredale boys are like my brothers. We have fights and call each other names and all that stuff but deep down inside we care about each other. We have to because it feels sometimes that no one else does. Sometimes it feels like everybody outside of Weredale is against us. I think it's because they don't understand us. They think we were put in the boys' home because we were bad.

" 'Sometimes I feel like nothing is going right. I feel so bad inside when I think about home and my mother and father. But I can't help feeling sad for the boys who have no family at all. There are a lot of orphans in Weredale. Some don't have a mother or a father. Some have parents who never visit and never write. Life is very lonely and sad for a boy who has nobody. Weredale made me realize how important a family is. It made me realize how much my parents mean to me. It made me realize how much I love them.

" 'Every night before I go to bed, I say a little prayer that one day my family will be together again. I hope one day my brothers and I will leave Weredale and go to live at home as one happy family. I'm sure every boy wants to leave Weredale one day and live at home. When I leave, I'll never forget my other brothers. I'm proud of being a Weredale boy.'

"This composition was written by Victor Malarek," the principal said, asking me to stand and take a bow. I could feel my face turning beet red as I pushed myself off the bench. I couldn't have asked for a better day.

"Dad . . . Dad?" I whispered, nudging him softly to wake him up. His eyes opened slowly. "Hi, Dad. Guess what?"

"What?" he asked, wincing in pain as he tried to roll over on his side.

"I passed. I got 93.8 percent. I'm going into the music class in West-mount High. I'm going to learn to play trumpet."

"Good . . . good. Then you can play the Last Post for me when I die."

"Why do you talk like that? You're not going to die," I said calmly.

"Promise me you'll play the Last Post? Promise!"

"I promise." I wanted to change the subject so badly. I hated when he spoke about dying. There was a long pause.

"The doctors are thinking about giving me another operation to make me better but it won't be for a while yet. Maybe three months. They want me to get a little stronger first."

"What kind of operation?"

"They want to take out a piece of my hip and form it into an artificial jaw."

"Is it dangerous?"

My father looked at my face for a moment. "No. Don't worry about it. The devil isn't ready for me yet."

"I just want you to be okay!"

"They're transferring me tomorrow to Ste. Anne de Bellevue Hospital to recuperate. It's quite far from here, so I won't be seeing you before you leave for camp."

"Tomorrow? It's my birthday tomorrow. I was going to visit you."

The nurse came in to announce the visiting hour coming to a close. Without looking up from the floor, I mumbled goodbye and started for the door. I was feeling sorry for myself and I was angry at my father for never being around for my birthday, even though I knew it wasn't his fault.

"Victor!" he called as I was leaving the hospital ward.

"Yes, Dad!" I said without turning.

"You too old to kiss your old man goodbye these days?"

"No! No, I'm not!" I ran back and hugged him.

9

By the time the third camp season rolled around, I had become quite a loner. I had no real friends in Weredale or outside. Nelson and I had split up when I found out he had stolen six dollars from my locker, after I gave him the combination so he could borrow my baseball glove. His biggest mistake was taking out the crisp one-dollar bills in front of Gillis, who later that evening reported my good friend's new-found wealth to me. A sour feeling churned in my stomach as I scurried over to my locker to check my hiding place.

"Rotten son of a bitch. That money was for my father. I was going to buy him two cartons of cigarettes as a present. Goddamn thief. How could anyone steal from a friend? Jesus! I don't believe it."

Gillis stood nearby, staring at me with worried eyes, wondering whether he should ever have opened his mouth.

I tackled Nelson as he bounced into the locker room, but before fists could fly, Douglas pulled us apart.

"What's this all about, lads?" he asked.

"Nothing," I said.

"Nothing," Nelson snorted. He avoided my eyes. He knew I had found him out.

"Then shake hands and let's be friends," Douglas suggested.

"Never!" I snapped.

"Then you go stand under the clock until you cool off. Nelson, you get on your way."

Nelson eventually paid me back the six dollars at fifty cents a week, but our friendship was over.

During most of my free time at camp, I would goof off somewhere by myself. I enjoyed those hours alone. I would go for long walks in the forest and sometimes, just for a silly personal dare, I'd venture beyond the camp boundaries, knowing full well that I risked the biffs if caught.

On one of my sorties into the forest, I found an outstanding hide-out

—a towering fir not too far behind the hut line. Often I would sit perched on a limb high above the camp making believe I was an Indian scout on lookout. From there, I could spy, undiscovered, on my fellow campers. I could see all: a camp thief stashing his booty, a group of Warriors whacking off in a clearing, guys going for a crap in the woods because they couldn't stand the stench of the Birches, a frightened, distraught kid looking for a secluded spot to rant and rave.

Late one afternoon, I spied Cooke, a new camp counsellor, darting through the woods with Chapman in tow.

Chapman was thirteen, a few weeks younger than me, and a pisshead. In the middle of the night, a few months earlier, he and another boy in junior south had been nailed by a staff member in the washroom blowing each other off. They got a terrific beating, and from then on, the two were avoided like the plague. Jerking off was cool with the guys, but these two went beyond the limits and were labelled queers.

Cooke was about twenty-three, a real slob that none of the guys liked, especially me. In the first week of camp during a handicrafts workshop, he sneaked up behind on the pretext of showing me how to prepare a piece of leather for a wallet I was making. His hands shaking a little and his eyes glazed, he began rubbing himself against my buttocks. I bolted for the door. When I recounted the incident to Fred, he suggested I forget it. There wasn't a hell of a lot I could do about it, he said. The cold reality was that it was a staffer's word against mine, and my brother spelled out who the loser would be in that confrontation. Fortunately, Cooke never so much as came near me after that. It was as if the incident had never happened.

In disgust I watched Cooke drop his shorts and Chapman kneel down. "Filthy bastard!" I muttered to myself. Quietly I crawled down the tree trunk and made my way towards the staff's quarters above the canoe wharf. I had locked onto an idea to fix Cooke's goose real good. Stealthily I stole into Cooke's room, heading straight for his locker. There was little chance of being caught because I knew where he was. I riffled nervously through his belongings and found a hand-carved, bone-handled hunting knife. With it I ripped through all his clothing. I jammed every valuable, his wallet, pictures, a chain-link bracelet, a high school ring, letters, and a locket, under my tee-shirt and lowered myself out the back window. Making my way cautiously along the path to the Indian Council, I stopped alongside an isolated cove on the lake. I removed a twenty-dollar bill from the wallet and tossed everything else into the deep waters below.

That evening, a dour-faced camp director summoned all the boys over the P.A. system to line up on the parade ground outside the dining hall. All kinds of rumors were floating about as clusters of boys tried to figure out the reason for the emergency line-up.

"We're probably in for a special treat," one Brave surmised.

"Yeah. Maybe ice cream or watermelon," my brother Peter hoped.

"Probably a new movie," said a third from an optimistic group.

"Look at Armstrong's face. He looks pissed off," said a member of a pessimistic entourage from the Warriors' side.

"I bet you someone ran away," Fred interjected.

"Line up. Line up. Let's go. Move it!" Armstrong ordered as he cast intimidating glances at as many boys as possible in a futile attempt to wrest a confession.

"I want the boy who went into Mr. Cooke's room and stole his valuables to step forward right now," the camp director demanded from the dining-hall verandah above.

"Fat chance," I thought to myself.

"I know who did it. I just want to see if the culprit has the guts to show he's a man and own up to it," Armstrong said, slowly surveying the hushed crowd below.

I stood my ground, looking up innocently at Armstrong and Cooke, hoping it was all a bluff. Ten torturous minutes passed. Then Armstrong read out a list of known or suspected thieves in the Home.

"Dubois, Marino, Carter, Page, Russel, Brunet, Nicols . . . line up outside my office."

The rest of us were dismissed and ordered back to our huts. Little did we know that while we were lined up, the counsellors were ransacking the huts, searching for Cooke's possessions.

After an hour's interrogation, the suspects were freed. Cooke hounded the camp throughout the summer, pulling surprise searches. I got a sweet pleasure watching him go through the boys' belongings, knowing he would come up empty.

In my solitude, I spent a lot of time daydreaming and vowing to myself not to allow anyone to push me around any more, even if it meant getting beaten up. I was growing bigger in size and wiser to the ways of Weredale life. Fred had all too often told me to stand up for myself. His message was sinking in.

"You allow these phony hardrocks to pick on you and they'll always pick on you. Kick the shit out of a few of them real good and you'll see how everyone will stop picking on you," my brother counselled.

"Yeah, but I don't like to fight."

"You think I do?"

"But I can't do what you do. I can't stick my fingers in a guy's eyes or grab his balls and squeeze them."

"All you've got to do is do it once or twice. The guys will stay away from you after that. Believe me. Even guys who can beat you up will leave you alone."

I believed Fred. After all, he was one of the best and most revered street fighters in the Home. He was only an intermediate, yet most of the senior guys were scared of him. Almost everyone left me and Peter alone because they feared that Fred might be just around the corner. But there were still some bullies who relished bugging me constantly, like Reilly and Janigan.

Fred's advice was flat and simple. "Boot them in the nuts. I'm not going to take on those two suck-holes for you, Victor. You could take them easily. Just nail one of them. You'll see."

A violent lightning and thunder storm rocked the camp on the second Saturday in August. The boats had to be taken from their moorings on the dock and hauled onto the shoreline to keep them from sinking. The following day was gorgeous. The sun shone brilliantly. There wasn't a cloud to be seen. On such a beautiful day we would normally have hiked to the outdoor chapel for church service, but the forest was too wet. The service was held instead in the recreation hut near the dock. After the service, the boys clambered out into the sunshine for the few free minutes before lunch. Fred and two of his friends were horsing around near the wharf when they were summoned by a CIT.

"You guys put the boats back into the water and tie them back on the other side of the dock," he instructed in an authoritative voice.

Fred pranced over to the pier and heaved one of the flat-bottoms into the lake, jumping in at the same time to guide it over to the other side of the dock.

"Malarek, get in here!" the camp director boomed as he charged down to the dock area from the recreation hall.

"I'm bringing the boat to the other side of the dock, sir."

"Get back in here with the boat!"

Fred turned the boat around and rowed back to shore. As the bow touched the pier, the director hauled him out by his tee-shirt.

"What's with you?" Fred shouted, jerking himself free of the director's grasp.

"Don't you dare talk to me in that tone," he said, slapping Fred across the face. "Who gave you permission to use the boat?"

"He did!" Fred yelled, pointing at the flustered, frightened CIT.

Armstrong slapped my brother again. "Don't you yell at me, sonny boy!" he warned. "Did you give him permission to use the boat?" the director blasted, turning to the CIT.

"No, Mr. Armstrong," he answered nervously.

"You little liar. I'll show you," Armstrong snarled, scouring the ground along the shoreline. His eyes fixed on a broken yard-long length of fibreglass fishing rod. Grabbing Fred by the scruff of the neck, he marched over and snatched it up.

"I'll teach you to lie."

"I didn't lie! He told — "

"And I'll teach you to shout at me, Malarek. I've had enough of you and your escapades around here."

The red-faced director forced Fred to bend over and swung repeatedly at my brother's backside. Two vicious blows split open the skin along the upper part of his legs and blood began to trickle out. Armstrong suddenly stopped.

"That will teach you to lie!"

Fred's face was blue with rage. Perspiration beaded on his forehead but he didn't cry. He just glared defiantly into Armstrong's face.

"Don't you give me any of your smart looks or I'll give you more of the same!"

"Sir?" a hut mate of Fred's called out.

"What do you want?"

"Sir, the CIT lied. He told Malarek to put the boat back."

"That's right, sir," another hut mate put in. "We all heard him."

Armstrong's face contorted.

"Well, he shouldn't have been in the boat. He should have been washing up for lunch like all of you should be doing right now," he said, flinging the fishing rod into the lake. Without saying another word, he stomped off.

Fred limped towards the sheet-white CIT. "You're going to pay for this," he threatened.

"What are you going to do, Malarek?" the CIT responded sarcastically.

Without warning, Fred smashed him in the throat. One of my brother's hut mates tackled the gagging victim from behind, throwing him to the ground while Fred and another one of his friends put the boots to him. I jumped off a rock and got in a solid kick just as two senior counsellors charged into the fray with fists flying to rescue their wailing colleague. Fred and his two accomplices were escorted to the camp office, where Armstrong strapped them. I didn't get nabbed. I guess the staff assumed I was in the area only because Fred was my brother. I guess they also assumed I wouldn't have the nerve to take on a CIT.

While I was crouched over on the Big Rock with my head on my knees brooding about what had just taken place and swearing revenge on Armstrong, Brunet, a new kid who had come into the Home a few weeks before camp started, wandered over to talk to me.

The only word to describe Brunet was cute. He had blond hair, freckles, and an infectious smile. The fourth of seven children, he had three older sisters, two younger brothers and a baby sister. He was the only kid taken away from his family. Brunet had a problem understanding what wasn't his. Dozens of times he was nailed by floorwalkers and sales clerks for shoplifting. Just as often he was caught stealing at school and from friends' homes. His judge at Juvenile Court felt Brunet, at twelve years old, was too young to be sent to training school. He could easily have sent Brunet there just on his lengthy arrest sheet alone, but the kid looked too much like an altar boy. Instead he ended up in Weredale as punishment until camp was over.

At camp Brunet promptly took to raiding cubbyholes. He was to learn that Weredale's justice was much less lenient than the courts'. He was trying to sell a watch to Plager when a hammering right cross careened into his nose. The watch had been stolen from Plager's cubbyhole a week earlier. In the two weeks that followed, Brunet was beaten up at least half a dozen times by his victims and strapped four times by staff members for stealing. All he wanted now was to escape.

"Too bad about your brother," he began hesitantly.

"Armstrong will get it for what he did. My father will kill him when he gets better."

"Can you do anything about it? Can't you tell the cops or something?"

"No. You can't tell the cops. Jerk! Anyway, who'd believe us? I'd like to shoot that bastard. I feel like taking off. Splitting. That's what I'll do. My mother isn't coming for visiting day today anyway. I can get a good head start before anyone knows I'm even gone."

"You're going to run away?"

"Sure. I'm not scared. I hate it here. Anyway, I want to see my father. Want to take off with me?"

"You're kidding!"

"No, I'm not. You chicken?"

"No, but . . ."

"Come on. Let's go. We'll tell our hut leaders we've got visitors and won't be here for lunch. No one will know we're missing until supper time."

Brunet broke out in a wild, nervous laugh. I went to my hideout and retrieved Cooke's twenty dollars and we were on our way.

We decided to follow the stream alongside the road which provided us with some cover. That would lead us to our first goal, the village. The going was slow and rough. Every time we heard the sound of a car, we scrambled into the forest and waited, panting and trembling, until we were sure the coast was clear.

At one point towards late afternoon, we heard a car approaching slowly. Ducking swiftly behind a tree, we waited for it to pass but it didn't. It stopped. We heard the door open, looked at each other wide-eyed, and took off like scared rabbits deep into the woods. We ran until we were burnt out and plunked ourselves down on a tree stump to catch our breath. We listened intently for the sound of pursuing footsteps. No one was chasing us.

"Boy, that was close," I said, wiping my forehead.

"Yeah, it sure was," Brunet puffed, trying to catch his breath.

"We'd better get going," I said. We had trudged on for about half an hour when it hit me that I didn't have the slightest clue where we were! We were lost. I made up my mind then and there not to tell Brunet. At least not right away. I didn't want to scare him. But as the skies got darker and darker, he too got the flash.

"We're lost, aren't we?" he asked glumly. His eyes were glistening.

"I guess so," I replied, slumping down under a spruce tree. I sat for a while staring idly at the greying sky, too pooped to move and too tired to talk. I was hungry and thirsty.

"Did you hear that?" I asked, pulling myself up on one elbow.

"What?"

"Listen!"

The faint, high-pitched drone of a motorboat whined through the trees.

"It's coming from that direction," I shouted joyfully, pointing up the trail we had been following.

Twenty minutes later we scrambled out of the forest and onto a paved road. On the other side was an expansive lake with scores of sailboats and rowboats.

"That's not Lake l'Achigan," I said. "Let's try and hitchhike or we'll never get home."

"What if the cops see us?"

"Bomb into the woods and keep running."

"We might get lost again," he said.

"Come on, turkey."

We were lucky. A driver picked us up within minutes.

"Where are you boys going?" a balding man in his forties asked.

"To Montreal."

"I'm heading there. Hop in."

Brunet slid over beside the driver and I sat down beside him.

"You boys are out late! It's after nine."

"Yeah, well, you see we came out here with our parents for a picnic and they told us if we weren't back from our hike by 7:30, they'd leave," I offered in our defence.

"That's a rather difficult story to swallow,' the driver replied without looking away from the road.

"You don't know our parents," Brunet ventured.

The driver turned and looked at us suspiciously. He reached over and switched on the car radio. We had been driving in silence for a short while when the 10 p.m. edition of the news came on. The third bulletin caught his attention.

"Motorists driving through the Lake l'Achigan area are asked to keep a lookout for nine boys who are missing from a boys' camp near there. The boys were last seen wearing blue jeans, running shoes, and a white tee-shirt with the initials C in orange and W in black on the front. . . ."

I nervously folded my arms over my tee-shirt. Brunet did the same.

". . . Motorists spotting the missing boys are asked to contact the Quebec Provincial Police."

The driver glanced at us. We stared straight ahead.

"You boys are not the runaways the police are looking for, are you?"

"No!" I snapped. "Anyway, there were nine of them," I noted, wondering who else had run away.

"Yeah, that's right," Brunet added. "We're only two!"

The car came to a stop at the shoulder of the road.

"Why are you stopping?" I asked.

"Nothing to worry about. I'm just taking a short rest. My eyes are tired. I've been driving all day," he replied, resting his hand on Brunet's crotch.

Brunet froze. Inching my hand to the door handle, I jerked it upwards and jumped out, hauling Brunet out with me. We dashed into the woods.

"I'm going to call the police and tell them where you are," the angered driver shouted after us.

"Call them, you queer! I've got your licence number. I'll tell them what you did. Queer!" I yelled back.

The car squealed down the road.

"Slimy queer!" I shouted.

"Next time, you sit beside the driver," Brunet said nervously.

No sooner had we stuck out our thumbs again when another driver picked us up. This one was in his early twenties and dressed quite sportily.

"Where are you boys heading?" he asked.

"Montreal."

"Get in. I'm heading straight into the city."

"Great."

"You boys are out awful late," he said as the car pulled out.

"Yeah. We went on a picnic with my older brother and he got mad at us and left us out here," I explained.

"C. W. What does that stand for?" he asked, pointing at my tee-shirt.

"Oh . . . ah . . . Canadian . . ."

"Camp Weredale," the grinning driver interrupted. "I listen to the news."

"What are you going to do?" I asked hesitantly.

The young driver continued down the road for a while without speaking. "Nothing," he said, clearing his throat. "Take you straight into Montreal like I said."

"Gee, thanks! You're really cool," I said.

An hour later we found ourselves in front of my mother's apartment house on Laval Street near Sherbrooke. I charged up the outside stairs taking two at a time and rang my mother's doorbell. No answer. I rang again.

"That's funny," I said, peeking through the holes in her mailbox under the bell. "The letters we sent her from camp are in her mailbox."

The lobby door buzzed and I yanked it open. A strange hairy-chested Greek in pyjama bottoms and bare feet stood in the doorway, blocking the entrance to my mother's apartment on the second landing.

"Who are you? What are you doing in that apartment?" I demanded.

"What is this?" he asked in broken English.

"Where's my mother?" I asked, dodging by him into the apartment. A nude woman screamed as I stormed into the bedroom. She wasn't my mother. The man was hot on my heels. He grabbed me by the arm and yanked me into the living room.

"Look, I'm really sorry."

"Who you are? What you want?"

"I'm looking for my mother. She lives here!"

"Woman live here before move last week. I call police."

At the mention of police, I pulled away from his painful grip and tore out of the apartment, slamming the door behind me to slow down any possible pursuit. Brunet was at the corner when I zipped by. We ran for a number of blocks.

"Christ, my mother moved and didn't tell us."

"Well, how was she to know you'd be paying her a visit tonight?"

"She didn't say anything about moving. Where is she?"

"Let's go to my house."

"Where do you live?"

"In Ville St. Laurent."

"Man, that's far! How will your parents take your running away?"

"I don't know. But we can't stay here."

"And how do we get there? Hitch?"

"By taxi," Brunet replied.

"I've got no money and neither do you." I was careful not to reveal the twenty-dollar bill in my pocket. If we got caught and it ever came out later that I had twenty bucks, Cooke might link it to the ransacking of his room.

"My mother will pay for it. I hope. If she won't, we run like hell in two different directions."

Twenty-five minutes later, sometime after three o'clock in the morning, the car stopped in front of a run-down low-rise apartment slum. Wisely, the distrustful taxi driver accompanied us into the darkened building. Brunet hammered on the door a few times before we heard the sound of shuffling feet. His mother, a short, stocky woman in curlers and a wrinkled robe, fumbled in near panic for the lock when she heard her son's voice.

"Richard! What are you doing here?"

"I ran away. Can you pay the taxi?"

"You took a taxi from camp? Are you crazy?"

"No. From downtown. It's $2.35."

She paid the taxi driver and ushered us inside. By this time, Brunet's father and two older sisters were out of bed.

"Why did you run away? I told you to stay out of trouble," his mother began.

"His brother was whipped by Armstrong, the man in charge of the camp. He's crazy. So we ran away. A lot of other guys took off too," he explained.

After hearing the story through, Mrs. Brunet reached over the kitchen counter and scooped up a telephone book in her pudgy hands. She scribbled down two numbers and dialled the first.

"Who are you calling?" I asked, preparing to bolt for the door if she said Weredale or the police.

"The *Montreal Star* and the *Gazette*. I want them to hear this story." She talked briefly to someone at both newspapers. "People are going to hear about this. They're sending reporters over. Are you boys hungry?"

"I'm starved! I haven't eaten since early this morning."

No one showed up from the *Gazette*. No one need have shown up from the *Star* for all that reporter was worth. He was young, cocky, and apathetic. He asked a few cursory questions and scribbled a series of slashes into his notebook. To him the vicious whipping of a fourteen-year-old boy wasn't newsworthy. He seemed to think Fred must have done something wrong to have been sent to Weredale in the first place and probably deserved what he got.

"Why was this kid, I mean your brother, put in the Home? What kind of trouble did he get into?" the reporter asked.

It was obvious he wasn't listening. He had overlooked the fact that I had told him only moments earlier that I had run away from the Home. "We didn't get into any trouble," I snapped.

"Well, from where I sit, you don't get put into a boys' home for being good kids," he said, flipping his notebook shut. The interview was over.

The insistent ringing of the telephone at 7 a.m. woke me up. It was the Weredale secretary calling to inform Mrs. Brunet that her son had run away. They wanted to know if she had seen him.

"He's here with his friend. I'll bring them back when they wake up. You tell that Mr. Johnson I want to speak to him when I get there!" I heard her say. She banged down the phone and tiptoed into the bedroom. I pretended to be sound asleep.

"Richard . . . Richard . . . wake up," she whispered. "That was the Home. You'll have to go back."

"Mom. They'll kill me," her son pleaded.

"Quiet! They won't kill you. I'm going to speak with Mr. Johnson. And let's have no more of this running away. You stay away from that Malarek boy from now on. He's trouble. I can feel it."

When she left the room, I slipped into my jeans, told Brunet to keep his mouth shut, and quietly stole out the back door. Outside, I could see Mount Royal and St. Joseph's Oratory in the distance. Across the street from the Oratory was the Veterans' Hospital which, after a four-hour exhausting walk, I reached in time for visiting hour.

"Hi, Dad," I said as I strolled into the ward.

My father rolled over and looked up. A smile spread across his pale, gaunt face. "Victor! What are you doing here?"

"I took off," I replied, returning his smile. I kissed him on the cheek.

"You took off. Why?"

"I wanted to see you!" I had resolved not to upset him by telling him about Fred.

"Are you in any trouble?"

"Naw."

"How's Freddie and Peter?"

"They're fine," I said.

Dad hugged me. I gave him the twenty dollars to buy cigarettes or whatever.

"You wouldn't believe my luck. I found it on the sidewalk. I couldn't believe it."

My mother was filling sugar shakers when I strolled into the restaurant.

"Victor!" she gasped, almost dropping the five-pound bag of sugar she was holding. "What are you doing here? You're supposed to be at camp."

"I took off. Mr. Armstrong whipped Freddie with a broken fishing rod for nothing. So I took off."

"Oh my God! Can't you boys stay out of trouble?"

"Freddie didn't do anything wrong. His legs are all cut up. Why didn't you tell us you moved? I went to your place last night and you weren't there," I said angrily.

"I only moved last week to another apartment. That one was too small and the place was too noisy. I wrote you boys the other day and sent my new address, so don't get upset with me. I didn't expect you to show up all of a sudden."

Her Greek boss came out of the kitchen. "Hello, Victor. You supposed to be at camp? Jennie, you have telephone call."

She returned a moment later. "That was Mr. Johnson. The police caught Freddie and his friends sleeping in a laundromat last night. He's in a detention centre. He was wondering if I had seen you."

"What did you tell him?"

"I told him not yet. What are you going to do?"

"I don't know. I haven't really thought about it. I don't want to go back there. I hate it. I can't take it any more."

"You have to go back. Where are you going to stay?"

"I don't know! But I can't go back. Mr. Johnson will send me to training school!''

"No, he won't. I'll take you back with me after work. I'll talk to Mr. Johnson.''

My heart was racing when the main door buzzer sounded. Johnson appeared in the lobby.

"Victor," he called out. A smile spread across his face. "Well, are we glad to see you're safe. Your friend came back this morning."

Turning to my mother, he said, "I would like to talk to you. Victor, go into the games room and wait there until supper. After breakfast tomorrow, I'll drive you and Brunet back to camp." The warm smile never left his face. I figured it was all an act because my mother was with me.

Brunet was staring out the games room window. He didn't hear me come in.

"Brunet!"

"Malarek! When did you get here?''

"Just now."

"My mother brought me back this morning. Boy, was she angry when she couldn't find you.''

"Tough! Did you get biffed?''

"No. Mr. Johnson seemed happy to see me back.''

"Yeah? He's acting real weird. I bet you we get the biffs when my mother leaves.''

We didn't. After supper, we watched television until ten and went to bed in one of the rooms on the senior side. Early the following morning, Johnson, still cheerful and whistling, drove us back to camp. For the life of me I couldn't figure what he was up to.

"Sir? Where's my brother Freddie?''

"He's in detention at Juvenile Court. I'll be going to court tomorrow morning to see if I can get him and his friends out. They should be back at camp by Thursday if Mr. Armstrong agrees to take them back. You two are lucky you weren't put in detention for a couple of days.''

"Sir, will we be punished by Mr. Armstrong when we get back?'' I asked hesitantly as the familiar gravel road came into view.

"No, no. I think your adventure was punishment enough.''

The car stopped in front of the main office. Hordes of boys came running towards the car under the pretext of greeting Johnson. They really wanted to get a glimpse of the fugitives.

"You boys sit down on the steps while I talk to Mr. Armstrong. The rest of you boys get back to what you were doing. Now, scat!'' The crowd broke up but continued to mill about in small groups a short distance from the office.

Johnson stepped out of the office a half-hour later. He was still smiling as he got into his car and drove off. Two of the longest minutes in my life to that point passed before we were summoned to face the camp director.

"You two boys get in here," Armstrong boomed from his office.

He was sitting behind his desk rocking back and forth in a swivel chair. His eyes were narrow slits and his mouth was drawn tight. He was definitely pissed off and we were in for it.

"So the two runaways have returned from their escapade," he said sarcastically. "And why did *you* run away?" he asked, pointing a threatening finger at Brunet.

"Sir, I don't know. I'm . . . I'm sorry." He began to weep.

"Oh, don't worry about that. You'll be sorry all right. Malarek, what's your excuse?"

"Because of what you did to my brother."

His face went red.

"I didn't strap you!"

"I know. You didn't strap Freddie either. You whipped him and for no reason," I blurted out. I couldn't believe what I had said.

Armstrong pulled himself out of his swivel chair and walked over to me. He stared coldly into my defiant face and slapped me. He then returned to his chair and sat down.

"The two of you will kneel at attention on the Big Rock for three days during all activities. Now, get out there!"

"Sir, Mr. Johnson said we weren't going to be punished," I said.

"I run this camp! Not Mr. Johnson!" he shouted. "Get out there and no more of your lip, Malarek, or I'll strap you!"

Instead of doing what I was told, I decided to discuss the matter of punishment further with Chief. He was sitting outside his cabin on a lawn chair reading a newspaper.

"Sir? Can I talk to you for a minute?" I was nervous.

"Certainly, son," Chief said, folding his paper. It was obvious he didn't know who I was, or, if he did, he didn't know I was one of the runaways.

"Sir, Mr. Johnson brought me back this morning. I ran away with another boy on Sunday. Mr. Johnson said we wouldn't get punished and now Mr. Armstrong is making us kneel on the Big Rock for three days. I don't think I deserve it after what he did to my brother."

"Whoa. Hold your horses! You ran away. Remember that. Mr. Armstrong is responsible for the camp and what goes on here. Mr. Johnson is responsible for the boys in the city. If Mr. Armstrong feels you should be punished for causing trouble at camp, Mr. Johnson has no call to interfere.''

''But still, sir. After what he did to Freddie, I don't —''

''What Mr. Armstrong did to your brother does not in any way excuse your actions.''

''Yes, sir,'' I said dejectedly. There was no use in arguing the point any further. Chief had his mind made up. I started for the Big Rock to serve out my punishment. I was kneeling for about half an hour when Armstrong's voice howled my name over the P.A. system. He'd received a call on his intercom from Chief's cabin.

''Don't you ever go and see Chief about the way I run this camp. Do you understand?'' He whacked me solidly across the back of my head.

''Yes, sir,'' I answered crouching away from him.

''Now bend over that chair and drop your pants.'' I obeyed.

Camp dragged to a close, and as usual I couldn't wait to get back to the city. I wanted to see my father so badly.

''Hey, Malarek,'' Reilly called out. There was a spiteful glare in his eyes.

''Yeah, what?''

''The promotion lists are up and guess who's been promoted to the intermediate floor?''

''Me?'' I asked hopefully and half smiling.

''Naw. They don't let piss-heads on the intermediate floor. Your baby brother got promoted.''

I was stunned. I tried not to believe it as I ran down to the bulletin board to see if he was bullshitting me. About a dozen boys were crowded around the board. Reilly was right. Peter had been promoted to the intermediate floor and Fred to the senior side. I was still a junior.

''Hey, guys! Look at this. Malarek's baby brother got promoted before piss-head here,'' Reilly sneered.

The boys looked over towards me and began to crack up.

''It's a mistake. Johnson will fix it when we get back to Weredale,'' I offered in my defence.

''Yeah, sure,'' a few chided.

''No piss-the-bed babies on the intermediate floor,'' Reilly said coldly.

''Drop dead, you stupid ass!'' I shouted. ''Anyway, I haven't pissed the bed in months. So watch it!''

''Oh, tough-guy Malarek wants a scrap,'' he said, shoving me backwards. Before he could shove me again, I planted a shot flush on his nose. Reilly crumbled to the ground screaming. It was the first time I'd had enough courage to fight the bully. I decided to make sure he didn't bother me again and I wanted all the boys around to see me soundly trounce that rotten creep.

I dropped my knees into his stomach and landed a driving blow on his mouth. After pinning down his arms, I hit him a few more times.

"Do you give up?"

Reilly didn't answer. He continued bawling.

"Give up or else!" I warned, tearing at his hair. I grabbed a handful of dirt and pebbles and threw it in his face.

"I give up! I give up!" he sputtered.

"And you better leave me alone from now on or else. I'm not going to take any more crap from you, prick face! Or anyone else!" As I got up I kicked him in the stomach. He rolled over, gagging for air.

I felt proud and confident after the skirmish. Beating up Reilly in front of those guys gave me new status. It meant that a lot of the guys who picked on me who were weaker than him would now leave me alone. It also meant new-found trouble for Reilly, as boys who thought they could take me would first try to improve their ranking by taking on Reilly.

The foremost thing on my mind when the camp buses pulled up in front of Weredale was to speak to Johnson about the obvious mix-up in promotions to the intermediate floor. I had convinced myself that a mistake had been made and that it would be rectified as soon as I pointed it out. I dashed off the bus and made a beeline for Johnson's office.

"Mr. Johnson . . . sir!" I called out after rapping lightly on his office door.

"Come in. Yes, Malarek. What is it?" he asked.

"Sir? I just wanted to know if maybe Peter was promoted to the intermediate floor instead of me by mistake."

Johnson's eyes narrowed. "There was no mistake. Peter is a little more mature than you, and until you grow up, you'll remain on the junior floor. Is that understood?"

"Yes, sir."

"Now, go! Get ready for laundry parade!"

"Rotten bastard," I cursed as I headed for a secluded place to explode into a raging fit. "I hope he gets his one day, and when he does, I hope he gets it good. He thinks he's so cool now that Dad's sick but just let him try and pick on me. I'll get even. One way or another, I'll get even.

The son of a bitch! I hope he gets run over by a dump truck.'' I had forgotten any kindness Johnson had shown me.

"Who are you talking to?" Fred asked at the bottom of the stairwell.

"Me! That's who!" I screamed.

Fred giggled, shaking his head as he left.

A month later, my name was posted on the office bulletin board to be transferred to intermediate north to make way for a new, younger boy coming into the Home sometime later that week. Big deal, I thought. The promotion meant absolutely nothing now!

10

Davis whirled his conductor's baton in a frenzy as he led the West-mount High School Orchestra in a driving interpretation of Bizet's *Carmen Suite*. He was completely engrossed in conducting, oblivious to the commotion on the auditorium floor below as hordes of grade seven, eight, and nine students scrambled about searching for schoolmates they hadn't seen for the whole summer. It was my first day in my new school and my pulse raced as I entered the spacious auditorium. I was spellbound by the professionalism of these young musicians. Thoughts danced through my head that one day I would be up there playing like a virtuoso. This was the year I had worked so hard for and now I was about to harvest my reward. I felt a little sheepish when I broke into enthusiastic applause after the orchestra finished playing, and found that I was the only one clapping. The kids sitting around me rolled their eyes at my display of "bad" taste in music. A moment later, the principal, followed by a troop of teachers, filed onto the stage. The principal welcomed us and then turned the microphone over to the teachers, who, one by one, read out the names of the students in their home rooms. First the grade nines, then the eights, and finally the sevens. My class was first up – 7 MW (musical winds), followed by 7 MS (musical strings). I jumped up and proudly made my way down to the front of the auditorium to join my new classmates.

I smiled at a few of the guys and got a bitter taste of what was to come. They turned their backs on me as if I was some sort of country bumpkin. Before I knew it, I was walking alone at the tail end of a raucous procession weaving through the corridors of the school. Sitting at my desk, I began to discover that I was different from the rest of the kids. I was the only Weredale boy in the class, the odd kid out. I stuck out like a sore thumb. Compared with my classmates, I looked like a wart. I certainly dressed differently, with scuffed Oxford shoes, wrinkled grey pants with cuffs, a general-issue Weredale sweater, a wide clip-on tie, and a white starched shirt with a black laundry number bleeding through the back collar. The boys in my new class, the sons of stockbrokers, lawyers, doctors, and wealthy businessmen, wore the latest fashions – V-neck sweaters, tab-collared shirts, thin ties, pants with no cuffs which rose above the ankles, white socks, and penny loafers. The girls had to wear regulation blue tunics.

I learned where I stood in the social pecking order from that day on. I was to be the butt of cruel jokes and cold snubs. During the first week, I tried to be included in some of the classroom antics. I wanted so much to be one of the guys. During the final period of that week, some of the students in the back row were horsing around. When I turned around to investigate, a couple of girls crossed their eyes at me and giggled. Like a goof I grinned. The kids were passing around a note but it eluded my grasp. They weren't about to let me take part in the fun. When the bell sounded, someone passed by and discreetly dropped the crumpled note on my desk. Eagerly I scooped it up and unravelled the paper. With smirks plastered on their faces, the snotty clique from the back of the class stood at the doorway waiting for my reaction.

The note was captioned: "Weirdo Malrick. Dumb cluck." Below was an obnoxious caricature with protruding ears, crossed eyes, blackheads, and short cropped hair. Attached to the caricature's neck was a convict's serial plate with the number 158 scrawled across it.

"You think you're funny, eh? You better watch it," I said. My voice began to crack. The jokers bolted down the hallway roaring with laughter.

The teachers got into the act as well, treating me from the very first day as if I didn't belong in 7 MW. Some asked right off if I was in the right class, if I hadn't made a mistake and walked into the wrong room, which drew a round of giggles from the students. They knew I was from Weredale and most treated me accordingly, with contempt. It was like being in Morrison's class all over again, except that here I had to contend with several Morrison types who had the same deep-rooted disdain for Weredale boys. My marks took a nose-dive, dropping to the low 50s and mid 40s, where only the year before, I had passed grade six with a 93.8 percent average. My only respectable showing in 7 MW was in music, where I scored a good passing grade.

Music became my refuge, an escape from the torment. At Christmas, the growing hurt briefly faded when I got my very own trumpet, a gift from my parents. I cherished that gleaming brass instrument and always kept it at school so no one could swipe it from my locker at Weredale.

One afternoon at the start of music class, I noticed that the bell on my trumpet was slightly dented. I saw red and was convinced that someone had deliberately damaged it. I stormed into the music room, scanning the class for the culprit, and caught one of the boys in the trombone section pretending very hard not to be looking my way. Whipping a music stand out of my path, I made a beeline for him.

His name was Irwin, a pudgy-faced rich-kid brat who, since my first day in class, always seemed to be quick to laugh loudly at any crack directed at me by the students or the teachers. He was also the twerp behind many of the vicious notes circulated in the classroom at my expense.

"Did you have anything to do with this?" I shouted, pointing to the dent in my trumpet. The class was hushed.

"Get lost!" he replied caustically. A cocky grin spread across his smug face.

"Wipe that smirk off your face, you stupid arsehole!" My fist shot out, grazing the side of his chin.

"What's going on here?" Davis yelled from the doorway.

"Someone dented my trumpet on purpose. This creep had something to do with it. I know it. I swear he's going to pay for this."

"Cool down! You! Did you have anything to do with this?" Davis asked, approaching Irwin, who was massaging his cheek.

"No, sir!" he answered defiantly. "He hit me, sir. These Weredale guys –"

"Shut up! Let me see your trumpet." Davis examined the damage. "It's not that bad. It's only a tiny nick. It won't interfere with the sound. Go and sit down."

"You're going to get yours," Irwin threatened as I made my way to the trumpet section.

"Wow. You really scare me, fink. Can't you see how much I'm shaking?"

"Cool it, you two, or you'll be out for the rest of the week," Davis warned.

I did make one classroom friend, Rudy Koch, a plump kid with blond wavy hair. He was the only boy outside Weredale to befriend me. We didn't hang around all the time, just at recess and for a bit after school. I had to be back at Weredale by four o'clock for check-off, so I couldn't dilly-dally about on the streets. I'll always remember the day Rudy got me invited to a party at the home of his friend Maurice Patton, in the swank upper-crust area of Westmount. My Weredale status didn't faze Rudy or Maurice. To them, I was an okay guy.

There was only one hurdle to overcome before I could give Rudy a firm reply, getting permission. Johnson's answer was a curt no. I unhappily reported to Koch and Patton that I wouldn't be able to go the party that evening.

"Why not?" Koch inquired.

"That creep Johnson told me I couldn't go. He hates my guts. He said no one gets special leave on Fridays."

"We'll see about that," Patton said. "I'm going to speak to my mother."

At 7:30 p.m., as studies were ending and the boys were heading to the games room to line up for the Friday night movie, Johnson summoned me to his office. Mrs. Patton had phoned to personally request my attendance at her son's party. A car would pick me up at 8:15 p.m. sharp. Johnson was in good spirits and didn't seem one bit offended by the call. In fact, he seemed rather impressed that one of his boys was invited to the home of a respectable Westmount family. He hadn't paid any attention when I'd asked permission to go.

"I want you on your best behavior. Is that understood? Mrs. Patton is a very nice lady. If I hear word that you misbehaved, I'll tan your behind. Now go and get ready. Someone will be here to pick you up in forty minutes," Johnson said. "Put on your Sunday suit, your white shirt, and a tie. Don't forget to polish your shoes." His final instructions zapped my euphoria. "How embarrassing. Now I'll really stick out," I moaned inside. I had wanted to dress casual.

Overall, the party was a success. Everyone had a great time, except me. Koch and Patton talked and joked with me, but all the other kids ignored me altogether. Most of them were from the music class. After a bit of friendly coaxing from Koch, I mustered up enough courage to ask one of the girls to dance. It was the first time I had ever asked a girl for a dance and she turned me down. I pretended her rejection didn't bother me but inside I was crushed. What hurt me even more was that she consented to dance with another boy a second later. Koch brushed it off as nothing and tried to talk me into cutting in on a couple. I should never have listened.

"It's all right. Go ahead. They can't refuse," he said.

"I don't feel like dancing. Really."

"It's all right, Victor. Watch. I'll show you." Koch tapped a guy on the shoulder and waltzed in with no trouble.

Taking a deep breath, I tapped a shoulder. The boy was about to break away when his partner yanked him back and whispered a few harsh words into his ear.

"He's Weredale. I don't want my head kicked in," he replied nervously. "It's only one dance . . ."

I left and walked the streets for several hours. I wanted all the guys at Weredale to think I was out having a fantastic time. In a deserted park, I sat on a secluded bench and cried. When I got back to the Home I boasted about my escapades with a bevy of cool chicks at the party. The guys seethed with envy.

One afternoon Koch asked if I would stay behind after school to practise some scales. He squeaked along on clarinet while I angrily re-examined the small dent in my trumpet. As we were leaving, a huge grade eleven boy barrelled between us, blocking my path. On his heels was Irwin, grinning.

"I told you I'd get even," Irwin boasted.

"How much did you have to pay him?" I asked, nodding at Irwin's bodyguard.

"Don't get smart, shithead," Irwin's friend threatened, grabbing me by my sweater and yanking me towards a clenched right fist.

"Go pick on someone your own size, jerk! Or else I'll get one of the senior guys in Weredale to ram the crap out of you."

An open hand stung my cheek. I tore myself out of my assailant's grasp, dropped my books, and pulled the dividers out of my geometry set.

"Look at the tough guy. Come on, chicken. I dare you," he taunted.

A moment later, his shaky hands were fumbling around his stomach. He started to back up very slowly. I had really stabbed him. The small crowd that had gathered froze. They were dumbfounded. Koch was sheet white. Irwin looked green. The bully turned and hobbled out the door, doubled over in pain. Irwin tore off down the hall.

"I think you're in trouble," Koch said in a quivering voice.

I couldn't sleep the whole night. I kept thinking that at any moment the cops would charge into the dormitory and arrest me, that the guy I stabbed had died, that I would be sent to training school. Or worse, the penitentiary. Maybe I would be hanged for murder.

At school the next day I was instructed to report to the vice-principal's office first thing. Lawrence, the vice-principal, looked like Boris Karloff. He was in his fifties, greying, and he talked very slowly in a low gravel voice.

"Young man," be began, clearing his throat. "You're in serious trouble."

"Sir?" I said, pouring on as much innocence and bewilderment as I could possibly muster.

"Don't stand there and pretend you don't know what I'm talking about!"

I swallowed heavily. My heart pounded. My palms were sweaty and my throat was parched.

"Did you stab someone with a knife yesterday?"

"No, sir."

"Don't you lie to me, young man."

"No sir. I . . . I didn't knife anyone. Honest!"

"The boy is in very serious condition in hospital and his mother is going to press charges against you. Did you knife the boy?"

"No, sir."

"Don't lie to me!"

I remained silent. Thoughts of prisons and jail cells flashed through my mind. I resolved that I would never confess.

"Did you stab that boy with a knife?"

"No, sir."

"You stand here on your word of honor and tell me you did not knife that boy."

"I did not stab anyone with a knife, sir. I swear." I wasn't lying, I told myself: I used a pair of dividers.

"Get out! Stand in front of the office in the corridor. And mark my words, you'll stay out there until you're man enough to tell the truth. Liars disgust me. They're cowards."

Every morning and after every lunch hour for two weeks, Lawrence summoned me into his office to confess, and stubbornly I stuck to my defence, admitting nothing. After school, I'd collect my books and home-work assignments and return to the boys' home. A torrent of worries tortured my mind.

Was there a warrant waiting for me? Did Lawrence call Johnson and tell him? Johnson disliked me so much, he wouldn't hesitate shipping me off to training school. My God, I had stabbed someone! He could have died. The reality was sinking in. *He could have died.* I was scared.

At the start of the third week, I resumed my post outside the office. Minutes into the first period, the boy I had stabbed appeared at the far end of the deserted corridor. He seemed tense and nervous as he approached the office area. I pretended to take no notice of him and he too refused to look in my direction. He knocked on Lawrence's door and entered. He was in the office for about half an hour before he reappeared looking even more upset. Again we avoided each other's eyes. Lawrence summoned me. He sat down and began drumming his fingers on the desk. After a while, he began in a disarming tone:

"He's a big boy!"

"Who, sir?" I asked.

"The boy you stabbed."

I didn't answer. I knew a bit about reverse psychology.

"I pieced the story together. Now, why don't you admit to your part in this unfortunate affair and you could go back to your class. I think you've had enough punishment."

"And get sent to training school," I blurted.

"Nobody is going to send you to training school," he reassured me. "I could have phoned Mr. Johnson about this but I didn't."

"Soon as I admit anything, I'm in for it. I'll go to court and Mr. Johnson will make sure I get sent to training school. He hates me!"

"Hogwash. No one is going to court. The matter has been settled. We could clear up this whole mess right now and you could go back you your classes. You've had your punishment. All you have to do is tell the truth. I don't like liars and cowards. Now, tell me. Did you knife him?"

I thought for a moment and calmly looking into his eyes answered, "No, sir."

To my astonishment he chuckled and sent me on my way. The matter was officially closed.

For the longest time I couldn't rid my mind of the incident. It haunted me in my sleep and tormented me throughout the day. Desperately I tried to recreate the split seconds leading up to the stabbing but the entire event had become a blur, lost in a thick fog. It happened so fast, so unexpectedly. I never intended to use the dividers. I was pretty sure of that. I simply hoped the kid would back off and not call my bluff. I almost convinced myself that he had been stabbed by lunging at me. But in my dreams I felt my arm thrusting forward and the dividers puncturing his abdomen. No matter how much or how hard I tried to understand my actions, only one chilling fact remained clear: I could have killed that boy.

A lot of Weredale guys started shoplifting when they reached Westmount High. Their desire to have some of the nicer clothes their well-to-do schoolmates wore far outweighed any fears they harbored about what would happen if they were caught stealing. Until grade seven, I had been too chicken to get involved in shoplifting. Also I was too religious. Deep down, I believed God would punish me. Not so deep down, I dreaded what would happen if the cops nailed me and brought me back to Weredale. I knew I was only one false step away from training school.

In grade six, I had often tagged along with some of the older guys heading out on a shoplifting spree. When they arrived at a department store that carried the merchandise they were in the market for, I would backtrack to safer ground and wait anxiously for their return, hoping to get some leftover booty they had overlifted like a wallet or gloves. By the time grade seven rolled around, those piddly bits and pieces no longer satisfied my wants. I hungered for the big game — the clothes! But that meant taking the risk myself because no one would be crazy enough to do that much for me. All I needed was the guts.

One Saturday in early spring, after I'd wished Fred and Plager a safe and bountiful return outside a large downtown department store on St. Catherine Street, I bumped into Robillard, a French-Canadian kid who had come into the Home shortly after the New Year. Although he was in my dormitory, he had established his own circle of friends, which didn't include me, so we rarely spoke. I was surprised when he accosted me.

"Eh, man. What you doing here?" He asked in a heavy French accent.

"Nothing much. Going for a walk."

"Where did they go?" he asked, pointing at the store's revolving door.

"To get some stuff."

"They got money?"

"They're not going to *buy* the stuff, stupid!"

"Why didn't you go with them?"

"I wanted to, but they work in pairs. It's risky in threes," I said, trying to be cool.

"So let's me and you go. You need some stuff?"

"Yeah, it's just —"

"Chicken!"

"No, I'm not. It's just that . . . ah, what the hell! I'm fed up of wearing Weredale crap."

Robillard grimaced suddenly.

"What's wrong? You chickening out now?" I asked.

"No. No, it's just —"

"Just what?"

"It's a sin to steal. I'm Catholic, you know, and —"

"Big deal. I'm Ukrainian Orthodox. We're in the same boat."

"I don't want to go to hell when I die."

"Man, you're nuts! Forget it!"

"No. No, I need the stuff," he said, pausing to think something out. "You ever hear of Robin Hood?"

"Sure."

"He used to steal from the rich and give to the poor. He never stole for himself."

"I watched the same TV show."

"I'm sure God didn't punish him!"

"So what?" I no longer really wanted to team up with a nut.

"So? So, you're poor and I'm poor. These big stores are really rich. What do you want? I steal it for you. And what I want, you swipe for me."

"You are crazy, man. You know that? I'm not going in there with a friggin' nut. You're playing with forty-eight cards."

"Come on. Come on," he urged tugging at my arm. Hesitantly, I shuffled through the revolving door.

Robillard wanted a pair of pointed leather shoes, a red shirt, a pair of black slacks, and a wallet. He pointed them out while we panned the place for floorwalkers. I wanted two pairs of white socks, a pair of brown pants, no cuffs, a pair of brown penny loafers, and a white tab-collar shirt. I bagged Robillard's order as gingerly and as inconspicuously as possible. He took his sweet time examining the merchandise like some big-time spender and even enlisted the assistance of a sales clerk to answer questions on the quality and durability of some of the fabrics. He was making me bloody nervous, but after a number of pokes, jabs, and dirty looks, he finally bagged the goods and we strolled nonchalantly out of the store.

Not two blocks away, we ran into Fred and Plager. Both were giggling and wearing new blue windbreakers.

"Need a wallet?" Fred said, tossing one to me.

"You want one?" Plager asked Robillard.

"No. Malarek got me one."

"You got him one?" Fred asked, staring at me angrily.

"Yeah. We swiped some stuff for each other. It was easy."

"Do you know what could happen to you if you get nabbed? Are you nuts? You're lucky you didn't get caught," Fred warned.

"You're lucky you didn't get caught," I snapped back.

"I know what I'm doing. Do that again and I'll kick your ass."

We walked quietly up St. Catherine for a few blocks when Fred began chuckling to himself.

"Plager, you want to see something real funny?" Fred asked.

"Yeah, man!"

Fred poured four pieces of Clorets gum into his mouth and began to chew rapidly, spitting out the excess juices. We walked a little further until Fred halted in front of a steak-house window. He removed the wad of green gum from his mouth and placed it between the thumb and index finger of his right hand. He motioned us to stand a little way back and began acting like a starved puppy outside the restaurant window where two middle-class couples in their early thirties were about to dig into a juicy steak dinner.

At first, the people ignored Fred and his mutt-like begging antics. Then, just as they were about to mouth a healthy morsel, Fred stuck his finger deep into his nose. He dug around with an exaggerated movement, trying to capture the foursome's undivided attention. Finally, they glanced up from their plates and Fred plucked out his finger, at the same instant latching onto the lump of gum in his right hand. A long, dangly, green gob stretched from his nose. The two women coughed up their mouthfuls. Then one of the men threw down his knife and fork and charged for the door. We took off, almost tripping from laughing so much.

11

The clanging and hissing of the radiators pumping hot water through the pipes echoed through the dormitories. In the distance, the night watchman shuffled through the corridors on his rounds punching the security clocks. Outside, a forbidding early March blizzard pelted the city with snow and ice. I punched my pillow, cursing it for failing to lull me to sleep. Dawn was creeping into the frosted window over my bed as I lay there knowing that, in a couple of hours, a team of doctors would be slicing into my father once again. This time they would be looking to see if there was any cancerous tissue still there after his first operation. If everything looked fine, they would cut out a piece from his hip bone and use it to replace the part of his jaw they had removed earlier.

From the moment my father had told me about the operation, I was afraid for him. I didn't want him to die, and yet I couldn't help fearing that this time he might not make it. I remembered how I had felt when Mom told me about the first operation. When she'd said Dad had cancer, I hadn't even known what cancer was. It just sounded so bad . . . so deadly. All I knew was that he could die. Until that day I had never imagined him dying. He was so strong that I was sure nothing could kill him. He'd been wounded twice overseas in the war and he didn't die.

But after that first operation, seeing my father in the intensive-care ward, I had realized he wasn't invulnerable. He was pale and weak. His face was bandaged in layers of white gauze. Translucent tubes ran into his nose. A red plastic bag of blood and a bottle of intravenous fed both arms, a drop at a time. A hole, covered by a stainless steel plate, was drilled into his neck so he could breathe. For weeks he lay motionless. He never spoke. He seemed to be in another world. Then, just as the doctors had about given up hope, his strength started to come back. I told myself I knew it all along. Nothing could kill Dad. Nothing. Except this second operation and the pills and drugs to which he was now addicted.

Somewhere through a haze I could hear the sound of muffled giggles and the voice of an angry man yelling. The shouting got louder and louder until I suddenly realized that my math teacher was ordering me to leave his class. Instead of standing in the hallway, I threw on my winter coat and sneaked out of the school. A few minutes later, I was in a snack bar up the street dialling the hospital.

"He's in recovery. He's on the critical list. It's still too early to know," the nurse said.

"Can . . . can I visit him?"

"He can't have visitors for at least a few days. You can come by on Thursday."

My head was spinning as I hung up the receiver. He was on the critical list. *He has got to pull through.* Over and over again I repeated those words. *He's got to make it.*

On Thursday I juked the last period to visit my father. I knew I'd be late for check-off but I couldn't wait until the weekend to see him. He still hadn't regained consciousness but the nurse let me into a small private room where he lay motionless on a bed. "Only for a minute," she said. It was like a replay of the way he had looked after the first operation, his face so puffed up and heavily bandaged I could hardly recognize him. I started to cry, holding his cold, limp hand in mine.

I got back to Weredale just as the bell was clanging for supper. I knew I'd get nailed for not checking off before 4 p.m. but I couldn't give a damn. Before dessert, Marshall made a gesture and silence blanketed the dining room.

"Malarek, V."

"Yes, sir," I called out, rising from my seat. I felt myself go weak in the knees.

"You didn't check off."

"Sir? I checked off as soon as I came in at three o'clock. I know I did. I'm pretty sure I did."

Marshall scrutinized my face with a glare of distrust and ordered me to sit down. That was close. The next time wouldn't be so easy.

Slowly my father began to get better, but he never returned to his old self. When I came to visit, he'd force a smile, talk a little about what I was doing, ask about Peter, Fred, and Mom, and then, for no apparent reason, his eyes would turn sad and moist and he'd drift into a trance. Sometimes he'd just sit in a chair by his bed trembling and crying like a scared child.

I remember forcing myself to hold back the tears, trying to be strong for both of us. I would ask why he was so sad — after all, he was getting better – but he would just stare quietly at me and not answer. One Wednesday afternoon, as I was about to leave, he finally broke his silence.

"Where are all my friends? Where are they? I gave the shirt off my back to my friends. I took a rap in jail for my friends. I would cut off my right arm for my friends. I fought for them when they were in jams. Where the hell are they? Rotten, goddamn bastards!" He swung his arm over his night table. The glass tumbler and the ashtray smashed onto the floor.

My hands began to shake.

"And where is your mother? Can't she even visit me? I nearly died and she didn't even care to visit. Where are your brothers? Are they too good for me too? I'm supposed to be their father. I wish to hell I would have dropped dead on that operating table. Maybe I'll die yet. It's not over. The doctors don't give me much hope. Hope! Ha! For what? Balls all."

"Dad, please don't talk like that. I don't want you to die."

"I have nothing more to live for, Victor. Nobody gives a shit whether I'm dead or alive."

"I do. I don't want you to die." I couldn't hold back the tears any longer. I buried my face in his chest.

"I'm sorry," my father said, rubbing my head. "I didn't mean it. Come on, let's see a smile," he coaxed, turning my face to his.

"I . . . I can't. You don't want to live. What am I supposed to do? All I've got is you. Fred and Peter have Mom. I don't want to live if you die. I'll kill myself. I don't want to live without you."

"I'm not going to die. Okay? I'm going to get better. I promise. I will and maybe soon we'll take off to Vancouver like I promised and to hell with everyone else. Now go and wash your face. Visiting is almost over."

Halfway through dinner, Marshall raised his arm and the dining room plummeted into dead silence. I knew this time I was in for it.

"Malarek, V., when you're finished supper, meet me in the clinic!"

I bowed my head over my dessert. I didn't feel like eating any more. Scores of eyes turned toward me, searching for a clue as to why I was going to get the biffs.

"What did you do wrong, Malarek?" asked Nelson, who was sitting across from me.

"I guess Marshall figured out why I haven't been checking off after school."

"We finish school at three. You have enough time to check off before four!" Robillard, who was also at my table, offered.

"No shit! Fantastic deduction. I'm not hungry any more. Nelson, you want my dessert?"

"You sure?"

"Yeah."

"Thanks, man!" Nelson said, scooping the canned peaches into his bowl.

Our table was dismissed. I trudged past Marshall, who paid no attention to me, and placed my tray in the receiving bin. My mind flashed back vividly to the time Johnson had initiated me in the clinic. In the hallway, Plager had cautioned me not to cry.

"Marshall will only give you three on your first time with him. He hates babies, so don't start bawling or else you'll get more."

There was no way I was going to fall for that scam again. No way! I sat in the old dentist's chair waiting for Marshall and hopped to my feet when I heard his voice outside the door ordering some boys into the games room.

"Malarek, are you aware that leave is granted only on the weekends?" he asked as he came into the clinic.

"Yes, sir."

"I detest liars, Malarek. You lied to me. Drop your pants and kneel down!"

The first whack seared across my backside. It was more painful than all three of Johnson's. The second popped tears from the corners of my squinted eyes and forced a muffled whimper. It hurt. Lord, how it hurt. I was bawling as the third length of leather scorched my buttocks. I groped to my feet to pull my trousers up.

"Get back down," he commanded. "I'm not finished. You're getting one extra for being such a goddamn baby, and if you continue crying, you'll get more!" There was a scuffle outside the clinic door. "If I come out there, you'll all get it!" Marshall yelled to the eavesdroppers. A mad scramble for the games room ensued. The distraction gave me a moment to pull myself together. I grasped the arm rests and held my breath.

Thwack!

"Get up. No leave for you this weekend!"

"But, sir!" I began.

"I said, no leave! Get out!"

Marshall knew where I went after school and he was well aware that Johnson had flatly refused to give me special permission to visit my father during the school week because of the profusion of red circles denoting failed subjects on my report card at the end of the first and second terms.

As far as Marshall was concerned, the issue was clear-cut: I had dis-
obeyed Johnson's order and I had lied.

A first: Fred had been demoted from the senior side to the intermediate
floor for conduct unbecoming a senior. In the three years since I had been
in the boys' home, no one else had ever been demoted. Fred had been
on the senior side about two months and in that time he had gotten into
all kinds of mischief. He'd been nailed a few times for being way out of
bounds, long after the 10 p.m. lights out for seniors. After bed check and
lights out, Fred would stuff his bed to make it appear he was in it and
then he would sneak down a fire escape at the back of the building with a
couple of guys for late-evening petting and necking sessions with some
girls from Summerhill, a smaller, female version of Weredale. Summerhill
was a number of blocks from the boys' home, not too far from downtown Montreal. A few of the Weredale guys had sisters there.

What sealed Fred's demotion was a late-night raid he and two other
seniors pulled on intermediate north in an attempt to initiate McLeod, a
mouthy new kid who had come into the home two weeks earlier.

McLeod had taken to bragging that no one on the intermediate side
had the guts to initiate him because he'd punch out anyone who tried.
Fred, Plager, and Parsons felt no one should come into the Home without
being initiated. After all, it was a tradition. McLeod went into a swinging
fit when he was woken up and told what was going to happen to him.
Plager subdued him with three hammering rights to the head. Fred opened
the tube of Pepsodent and the sobbing newcomer got his nuts rubbed.

The next day Marshall did a double-take when McLeod, his face badly
bruised, passed him in the cafeteria.

"You . . . come here! Who did that to you?"

"I don't know, sir."

"What do you mean you don't know?"

"It was dark. I was asleep and I got initiated. I don't know who it
was."

"What dormitory are you in?"

"Intermediate north."

"Everyone from intermediate north, under the clock after breakfast!"

We stood under the clock for almost an hour before Marshall came
over to interrogate us.

"Who did that to the new boy? Who initiated him?"

No one said a word.

"Gray, you're dormitory monitor. Who did it?"

"Sir, I was asleep. There were no initiations last night."

"I don't believe you. I'll give you an hour to think about it. Then I'll take each one of you in the clinic. Your Saturday leave for today is cancelled!"

Fred and Plager wandered over a few minutes later.

"What's happening?" Plager asked. Gray explained.

Fred and Plager stared at each other for a moment. My brother nodded towards Marshall's office and the two disappeared behind the door. There was a long silence and then Marshall blew up. The only words we could make out clearly were: "Get in the clinic!"

Plager lost four weekends of leaves and had to be in his room by 8:30 p.m. for an entire month. Fred was demoted and was assigned the bed next to mine in intermediate north. Fred immediately pronounced himself dorm monitor, and the once fairly peaceful dormitory, which had been regularly winning the bonus dessert treat of ice cream on Monday evenings for being so orderly, soon gained the reputation of being the rowdiest, most uncontrollable room out of all the dorms on the intermediate and junior floors. Initiations were held for those who had managed to escape them until now. Inter-dormitory raids swung back into full gear. Pillow fights raged into the middle of the night, and teams of pyjama-clad commandos joined forces in the late hours to sneak into intermediate south and west to tip over beds occupied by suck-holes, stoolies, and brown-nosers. For those who really wanted to prove they had guts, small lightning raids were carried out on the junior floor above.

"Nix . . . Nix . . . Nix . . .," Nelson called out in a loud whisper as he raced into the dormitory. Everyone dove into their beds and pretended to be fast asleep.

Jones, a tall, skinny, balding Australian whose veins popped out all over his forehead, loped into the dormitory. He had come on staff three months earlier.

"All right, all right, cut out the racket," he said in a thick accent. He was met with a chorus of snores in a variety of octaves.

"Cut that out!"

The dormitory fell silent. As he was heading out the doorway, Fred let out a ripping snort. I began to giggle. Jones paced slowly down the dormitory corridor and stood over my bed.

"Cut that out, young Malarek."

"I didn't do anything, sir."

"I said, cut it out!"

"Yes, sir."

Fred lay motionless in his bed, pretending to be sound asleep. Jones had just made it to the doorway when Fred sang out "And along came Jones" in a slow descending tenor falsetto. Jones froze dead in his tracks.

"Who said that? Who said that?"

I buried my head in my pillow and cracked up. A heavy finger jabbed into my shoulder blade.

"Out of bed, you!"

"Sir, I didn't do anything," I said, half laughing, half pleading.

"Out of bed!"

One whack over my backside with a running shoe and I was back in the sack. Jones was midway down the dormitory when Fred started to mimic the rhythm of the Australian's kangaroo-like gait.

"Boing . . . boing . . . boing . . . boing."

Jones raced over to my bed and hauled me out.

"Honest, sir, it wasn't me," I shouted, covering my head in case he tried to slap me. I got three more whacks with the running shoe. My bottom stung.

"Boing . . . boing . . . boing . . . boing, boing, boing, boing."

Dead silence.

Jones was hovering over my bed.

"See, I told you it wasn't me."

"Who was it?"

"I don't know."

"All of you boys, out of bed."

Everyone crawled out of their beds vehemently protesting their innocence. Fred remained in his bed pretending to be out cold.

"You too, Fred Malarek," Jones said, leaning over his bed.

Fred didn't budge.

"I said you too!" Jones shouted while shaking Fred to wake him up. Fred lay limp on his mattress.

"Oh, never mind. Everyone bend over your bed."

Each boy received one solid whack with a running shoe.

"Cut it out, Fred! My ass hurts," I whispered as I pulled the sheets over me. Fred grinned from ear to ear. The last boy was biffed and Jones stomped out into the locker room.

"Boing . . . boing," Fred yelled out loudly.

The lights flashed on. A few boys cursed. Jones stormed in fuming.

"Out of bed! All of you!"

The protesting mob threw their sheets from their bodies and stood in front of their beds. Jones stomped over to my brother's bed.

"Out of bed!"

Again Fred didn't move. Jones shook him violently. Fred didn't react. He pulled Fred up by his arms. My brother half opened his eyes and fell back on to the bed. Jones started to pull Fred's feet out on to the floor, then grabbed his arms and jerked him into an upright position.

"What . . . what's going on?" Fred asked, acting half dazed.

"Oh, go back to sleep."

Fred flopped back on to the pillow and almost immediately began to snore.

We had to stand in front of our beds for over an hour and afterwards we got two more whacks of the running shoe.

"You boys should take a lesson from your monitor, Fred Malarek, here," Jones instructed as he left the room.

The lights went out. There was dead silence.

"Boing!"

Thank God, Jones gave up!

When Borman was appointed to the senior staff, all the guys thought he'd be okay: after all, he had been one of the boys for more than eight years. But Borman turned out to be a sadist. He was worse than Maitland, although he didn't have Maitland's vicious temper. Borman was mild-mannered and quiet. He would sneak upstairs slyly in his stocking feet, or make it sound as if he had left the floor after lights out, only to hide in the locker room and nab whoever happened to be on nix. He'd then motion to his startled captive in threatening sign language to give the all-clear signal. Once the fun in the dorm had started, the lanky 22-year-old would saunter in and stand at the doorway until each and every one of us realized he was there.

Borman wasn't a running-shoe man like the other staff. He was a head-bopper. He got his kicks slamming boys' foreheads together.

"Bed 1 meet bed 2. Bed 3 meet bed 4," he said with a peculiar grin as he made his way down the dormitory smashing skulls together. "Bed 21 meet the wall."

One evening, shortly after lights out, Fred got out of bed to go to the washroom. We had decided to keep it cool because Borman was on staff and no one wanted a headache. A hand shot out from the blackened locker room, grabbed Fred by the arm, and hauled him into the hallway. Borman motioned at Fred to keep his mouth shut.

"I'm just going to the washroom, sir," my brother said loudly.

Borman slapped him across the face for blowing his cover.

"Watch who you're slapping. I said I was going to the can."

"Bend over and face the wall. Move it. Now!"

Fred did as he was ordered but pulled back slightly to soften the blow. Borman pulled my brother by the hair. "You'll get three more for that. Bend over, Malarek."

Fred dropped to his knees, holding his throbbing forehead after the second blow.

Borman yanked him up by tugging on a chunk of hair on the back of my brother's neck. "Bend, you little punk. I said bend."

"Up yours, you fuckin' Nazi! Go torture someone else. Too fuckin' bad my father missed you in the war."

"What did you call me?"

"Nazi!"

The boys in the dormitories held their breath. Borman lunged at Fred and began to swing wildly with closed fists. My brother tore into Borman, going for his eyes. Borman won the fight but not before Fred had put home some severe blows to his face. My brother was taken to the clinic and the following morning he was in juvenile court.

It seemed as if the entire staff had it out for Fred after that. Any infraction, no matter how minor, and he got the biffs or a weekend detention. Borman didn't let up either. A week later, he ordered the dormitory to stand in front of their beds and went down the aisle introducing heads. He told Fred and me to bend over.

"I think you two brothers should get to know each other better," he said with a sadistic grin. He rang our chimes good and hard. "Oh, a graze! No good! Got to meet again. Bend over."

My head was reeling. Fred looked into Borman's sneering face. "You fuckin' Nazi! Why don't you beat up on somebody else?"

Borman grabbed Fred by the hair and caught him with a stinging open hand across the face. Fred heaved his knee into Borman's crotch. He went wild. I jumped on his back and dug my fingers into his throat. Borman managed to throw us both off him and raced out of the dormitory. Ten minutes later, Marshall appeared in the doorway and dragged Fred and me to the clinic. He never asked us for our side of the story.

"Drop your pyjamas. The underwear too, and kneel," he said, waving me to the footrest on the dentist's chair. I got six of the best. I was bawling.

"Stay here," Marshall said as I made my way to the door. "I want you to see what you have to look forward to the next time you get out of line. Drop them and kneel." Fred received twelve searing blows from the barber's belt. He winced in pain and dug his hands into the armrests. He didn't cry.

The next day, I had gym at Westmount. During showers, the guys in the class freaked out when they saw my backside.

"Holy mackerel! Victor, what the hell happened to you? Jesus, I can't believe it," Koch said. His eyes almost bulged out of their sockets.

"I got the biffs last night."

"Man, that's not biffs. That's torture. Guys, hey, guys, look at Malarek's rear. I can't believe it," Koch yelled.

The gym teacher came over to examine the damage and shook his head in disgust. "Takes a madman to do that to a kid," he said.

"Are you going to do anything about it?" Koch asked.

"Weredale is not my business. This gym class is. Now finish washing up and get ready for your next class."

"Well, I'm going to tell my parents about this."

"No! Don't, Koch. You'll just make it worse for me," I pleaded. "I have to live in that dump, and if I cause any more trouble, Johnson will get me sent to training school. Forget it. It didn't hurt anyway."

All hell broke loose the following day. I was getting ready for laundry parade when Gillis ran into the downstairs locker room with a terrified look on his face.

"Your brother Fred. He's been hurt real bad. He's upstairs in the intermediate north locker room!"

I charged up the stairs and was horrified by what I saw. My brother's eye had nearly popped out of its socket. Thick blood oozed out of his nose and mouth. He was in a daze.

"Open . . . open your locker," he mumbled, stumbling towards me.

"Who did this to you? I'll kill him, I swear. Who did this, Fred? Who did it?"

"Maloney," Gillis shot back. "Fred was doing his laundry. He was bent over like this near the radiator when Maloney ran in and booted your brother in the head. Fred's face smashed the radiator."

Maloney was a senior. He had apparently taken it upon himself to get even with my brother for a minor scrap Fred had had earlier in the day with one of Maloney's friends.

"Open your locker, Victor."

"Never mind my locker. You've got to get to a hospital, Freddie."

"Open your locker! Now!"

"Why?"

"I want your hunting knife."

Fred pulled the knife out of its leather sheath and took off after his assailant. I grabbed a steel bar from my locker and went to help out. Maloney was in the downstairs locker room bragging about having taken care of Fred Malarek.

"I fixed his ass good," Maloney said.

"Now I'll fix yours, you sneak-attack prick!" Fred yelled as he staggered into the room.

Maloney grabbed a steel bar from an open locker and swung at Fred's head. My brother caught the full force of the blow with his right arm and jabbed his attacker in the stomach with the knife. As Maloney keeled over, I slammed the bar over his head. Peter came out of nowhere, smashing a broken hockey stick across the senior's back.

Two staff members tackled Fred and dragged him upstairs to Johnson's office. A few minutes later, both fighters were rushed to the hospital. I was ordered into the clinic and got strapped by Johnson several hours later. I also got a month of weekend detentions for having a knife in my possession.

Fred never returned to Weredale. He was sent from the hospital to the juvenile court detention centre. Johnson told my mother he was going to see to it that my brother was sent to training school.

12

St. Joseph's Oratory is a gigantic basilica in Montreal where countless miracles are supposed to have happened. Crutches, wheelchairs,
and leg braces, and hundreds of notes of thanks hang from the church
walls as testament to the belief that St. Joseph has interceded to ease
suffering and cure illness.

The Oratory is across the street from the Vets' Hospital, so one Saturday afternoon, before the 3 p.m. visiting hour began, I decided it couldn't
do any harm to pray for a miracle to make my father better. I still believed
strongly in God and Jesus. I remember it was around Easter because the
church was filled with potted white Easter lilies.

Having nowhere better to go, Gillis tagged along. Both of us really
didn't know what to do in a Roman Catholic church, so we drifted around
the edges and watched the faithful.

"You're not going to walk up the church steps on your knees, are
you?" Gillis asked.

"Do I look like I'm nuts? I'm just going to light a candle and say
a prayer." I crossed myself in front of a towering statue of St. Joseph,
dropped a dime in a container, and reached way up and lit a candle.

"Kneel down and say a prayer," I whispered to Gillis, who smiled
nervously and crouched down. As I prayed, my eyes began to water.
Then they began to sting. Gillis looked at me wide-eyed. His mouth was
twitching as he motioned at me wildly.

"You're . . . you're . . . you're on fire! Your arm is on fire. Your
sleeve," he sputtered.

"You're on fire!" a man yelled. A few people screamed. Frantically I
yanked my jacket off, threw it to the floor, and stomped the hell out of it.

"Do you believe this? My favorite jacket. I really loved that jacket." I
moaned. It was a genuine buckskin Davy Crockett jacket I'd ripped off
from a downtown department store. When I'd reached over to light the
candle, the fringe on my right sleeve had caught fire.

"Do you think somebody's trying to tell you something?" Gillis asked.

"Shut up. Let's get out of here," I said, looking up nervously at the statue of St. Joseph. A miracle just didn't seem to be in the cards.

"Your mother visited me last night," Dad said as Gillis and I strolled into the hospital ward.

"She did?"

"Fred is living with her now. She said Freddie was getting into a lot of trouble at Weredale. Why didn't you tell me he was getting into trouble?"

"I didn't want to worry you."

"She said that bastard Johnson tried to have him sent to training school. Your mother needs my permission to keep Fred with her and she'll have to stay home before the court will release any of you kids into her custody. She's also worried about you and Peter being left in the home without Fred to look after you. She wants the three of you back home together. So, we're going to try to make a go of it again."

I wasn't about to jump for joy. "What about your sentence? It's not over yet."

"The warden doesn't want me back. I'm too sick. I have to go back and forth for treatment and medication too many times a week, so he's recommending me for parole."

"How are we going to live? You can't work and you just said Mom won't be allowed to work if we go home."

"The Department of Veterans Affairs is going to give me a pension. We'll manage. I thought you'd be really happy. What the hell is with you?"

"No. I'm happy. Really," I said with a fake smile. Inside I was fighting to remain cool. Too many times before I had been told we'd be getting out. Too many times before I had psyched myself up to leave the boys' home and ended up crying myself to sleep when everything fell through. I would believe it only when it happened.

Peter and I were acutely jealous of Fred. While he watched television until all hours and got up late in the morning, Peter and I continued the numbing routine of Weredale life, counting the days when we would be free at last. While Fred ate Ukrainian cooking, pizzas, and Chinese food, we forced down creamed fish on Fridays, a thick slice of baloney on Thursdays, creamed corn on Wednesdays, and so on. And while Fred got rid of all his Weredale outfits and grew sideburns, we still had bean shaves and baggy pants.

My marks at school continued to nose-dive. I didn't understand how I could have dropped so low after scoring such high marks in grade six at Queen's School. I had given up, and my teachers couldn't have cared less. I juked most of my classes in the last quarter. No teacher asked for a note explaining my absence. In their eyes, I didn't matter, I was just another dumb boys' home kid. I knew I had failed my year and resigned myself to the fact that I would be revisiting grade seven. On the last day of school, my home-room teacher, Mr. Finch, proudly distributed the report cards and avoided my defiant glare as he handed me the bad news.

I walked back to Weredale along the out-of-bounds route. I didn't give a damn who saw me or whether I got caught by a prowling staff member. Occasionally I sneaked a peek at my report card, hoping the words "failed, must repeat grade seven" were an aberration. I glanced at the failing grades circled in red beside each subject. I recalled how a year earlier my name had been called out by the principal during the final school assembly for scoring one of the highest averages in the school. I remembered how proud I'd felt when the principal selected my composition as the best of the year and read it aloud.

Now I was just another Weredale dummy, flunking with the lowest marks in my class, a class in which I was the only boys' home kid. I would be fourteen in grade seven next year, while most of my classmates would be twelve or just turning thirteen. I feverishly hoped that I was really getting out of Weredale, because I didn't ever want to run into any of my former 7 MW classmates while trudging through the halls of Westmount High on my way to shop or metalwork classes. I knew that my music classes were finished. They were only for the brightest students. I would be demoted to general classes, classes packed with Weredale boys.

Until my mother had picked up Peter and me in a taxi and brought us home, I wouldn't let myself believe I was getting out of Weredale. Peter and I were waiting anxiously at the main entrance for her to arrive. It was a sunny morning on June 28, 1962. Three and a half years had gone by since my brothers and I first came through that door. She was already ten minutes late and my stomach was churning.

"She's coming! She's coming!" Peter shouted as he caught a glimpse of her in a taxi rounding the corner. He was jumping up and down, waving. I felt a surge of relief but I still wouldn't let myself relax until we finally were on our way home. After all, she might just say, "Wouldn't it be better if you boys went to camp just for this summer? Then you could come home in time to start school!"

She was smiling warmly as she climbed up the outside stairs. Peter rushed into her arms as the door opened.

"Hi, Mommy! How's Freddie?" Peter asked.

"He's fine. Are you all packed to go?"

"Yup!" Peter chirped.

"You, Victor?"

"I'm ready. How's Dad?"

"He's fine. He's anxious to have you home. Where's Mr. Johnson? I want to say goodbye and thank him —"

"For what?" I interjected. "Let's go! I hope I never see him or this place ever again. He never did anything for us, so why should you have to thank him. For three and a half miserable years? Come on, Mom!"

"Oh, there he is!" My mother waved to Johnson through the window of the door separating the general and inner offices. He came over.

"Hello, Mrs. Malarek," he said with that ever-familiar plastic smile. "Are you boys all ready?"

"Yes, sir!" we replied in unison. I held back saying what I really felt.

"Good! How's your husband, Mrs. Malarek?"

"He's feeling much better."

"And is Freddie being a good boy?"

"Oh, yes! He's staying at home and keeping out of trouble."

"Good . . . good. Well, I wish you all the best. Be a good boy, Peter, and I hope you do better in school next year, Victor," he said, adding a pinch of salt to my fresh wound.

The taxi came to a stop twenty minutes later outside our new home, a low-rent apartment complex on Barclay Street in the Côte des Neiges district.

"I can't believe it," I whispered to myself. I had a lump in my throat. "Thank you, God!"

It was difficult adjusting to life at home: the peace and quiet, sleeping in my very own room, not having to wake up at 7:30 a.m. or go to bed at 8:30 p.m. Even taking showers alone felt odd. I vowed never to eat porridge, cream of wheat, greasy pork sausages, baloney, or creamed fish again. I let my hair grow longer, and for the first time I had sideburns down to the middle of my ears instead of an inch above them. My mother took us out and bought us a complete wardrobe of our own choosing. I got a new pair of penny loafers (the pair Robillard had lifted for me were in turn swiped from my locker a few days later), a brown suit and casual slacks with no cuffs on the pants, a V-neck sweater, tab-collar shirts, a couple of skinny ties, and white socks. I threw every piece of Weredale clothing bearing the black indelible inscription 158 into the garbage.

After having had my life so regimented for the previous three summers, I was at a loss for things to do to occupy my time. The hours seemed to crawl by. I sometimes even wished school would start. During the days, my brothers and I would prowl the streets aimlessly. At night, we would saturate ourselves with late shows on television.

My mother had to take on a part-time afternoon job as a waitress, in defiance of the welfare department, to supplement my father's meagre pension. My father, being eager to help out as much as he could, took over most of the domestic duties. I stuck around to help him out. We would prepare the lunches and suppers together. I would peel the spuds and clean the vegetables, and while the food was cooking, we'd pass the time playing cards and shooting the breeze. Fred and Peter stayed out most of the time, usually until they were sure my mother had finished work and was home. They still hadn't grown any closer to my father and felt uneasy around him. My father never said anything about this, but I knew it bothered him. He hoped the barrier between them would eventually crumble.

Whatever the problems at home, none of us really complained. After Weredale, home was better than any place in the world.

Coronation School was a two-storey beige L-shaped building whose students were predominantly middle-class Jewish kids plus a pocketful of semi-slum-dwellers from Barclay Street. But what the school looked like or who went there didn't interest me. I didn't expect to stay long. My only concern was to get promoted to grade eight "on condition". However, the principal didn't believe my story of having been a victim of circumstances at Westmount and delivered me a soppy lecture on the fruits of hard study. I resolved at that point to breeze through, doing the minimum. After all, they didn't flunk students twice in the same grade and I had nothing to gain by scoring high marks.

By late fall, rumors were going about that I had been in a boys' home. The kids assumed that I had been sentenced to the home by the court for committing some sinister crime. Some eyed me strangely at first, while others thought I was definitely cool. I ignored them all. I wasn't about to offer those ginks any explanation as to why I was put in the home.

My being in the boys' home really seemed to get to one of my classmates, Brian McDowell, the resident hardrock. He never came straight out and mentioned my stint in Weredale, but it was obvious it bugged him. He wanted the reputation of being the toughest kid in the school, and he knew a lot of the kids thought I was tough because I'd done time in a boys' home. He had to prove he was king of the hill.

McDowell swaggered around the schoolyard. He kept his black curly hair greased with Brylcreem and his large mouth stuffed with Bazooka gum. He was the only kid in the neighborhood who wore a black leather jacket and motorcycle boots even though he didn't have a motorbike. He did have a bicycle with deer's antlers on the handlebars, which I admired. McDowell had a reputation for being a mean street fighter, although no one could ever swear to having seen him in actual combat because he was also new to the district. But his fawning younger brother could always tell you about the time when . . .

McDowell made it a point to bump into me in the schoolyard, just to show he wasn't chicken and to remind me that anytime was all right with him. I had resolved that as long as he didn't get too pushy, I'd let him go on thinking he was cool. Although I never admitted it to anyone, I was a little scared of him.

It didn't take too long before the inevitable happened. We squared off in the schoolyard right after school. McDowell came charging out of the building and bumped me a little too roughly. I would have ignored it except he shoved me in front of the wrong audience, a bunch of girls. He stood facing me with a sneer on his face and his legs spread wide apart. He was just waiting for me to try something. I let fly a well-aimed boot and he doubled over and staggered away wailing. I figured he had learned his lesson and would leave me alone from then on.

A strange transformation was beginning to affect my life. I was becoming aware of girls. In the classroom or in the schoolyard I would while away the time gazing starry-eyed at the luscious assortment of budding female bodies in the seventh grade. Most of the girls were shy and innocent. But there was one who was bolder, a sparkly-eyed blonde, with a real nice compact body. My only problem was how to meet her. She was in the other grade seven class.

One afternoon after school, I decided to follow her home at a discreet distance. To my surprise, she took the exact same route I did and strolled into the apartment building across the street from mine. I caught her peering out the corner of the door as I casually waltzed by pretending to take no notice of her.

That evening I devised a hundred plans to bump into her by accident. At precisely 8:10 the following morning, twenty minutes earlier than I normally left for school, I happened to walk onto the street just as she did. We practically bumped into each other.

"Hi!" I began cheerfully, trying to stifle a quiver in my voice.

"Hi!" she replied ever so sweetly.

"Mind if I walk with you to school, seeing we're going in the same direction?"

"I don't mind. Your name is Victor?"

"Yeah. How did you know?"

"A lot of the girls at school talk about you."

"They do?" I asked, beaming. "I didn't know that. What do they say?"

"I'm not going to tell you," she giggled. "But they think you're cute!"

"What's your name?" I asked.

"Linda."

"You lived on Barclay long?"

"Two years. Since my father left Mom."

"Oh!" I felt a little uneasy by the suddenness of her last remark. "I moved here this summer."

"I know. You were in a —"

"In what?"

"Nothing," she answered nervously.

"No, tell me."

"Some of the girls told me you were sent to a boys' home."

"So what?"

"Don't you have to get in trouble to be sent to a place like that?"

"No!" I snapped. "Does it bother you that I was in a boys' home?"

"Oh, no! I don't care. I like you." She blushed.

During recess and lunch, Linda and I kept our distance. My teacher really peeved me when she kept the class for an extra five minutes after the final bell sounded. I was dying to walk Linda home. When the teacher finally dismissed us, I bolted out of the building hoping to catch up to Linda somewhere along Barclay. Instead, I found her lingering by the school gate.

"Hi!" I called out, slowing down to a casual walk. "Waiting for someone?"

"I thought that since we live near each other, we could walk home together."

We strolled along Barclay chatting idly about anything that cropped up.

"You got any sisters or brothers?" I asked.

"An older brother. He's in the army."

"He must be old!"

"Twenty. He should be home on leave sometime next month."

"Do you get along with him?''

"I hate him. He thinks he owns me ever since my father left. He's a creep! Let's not talk about him.''

Our love affair began to blossom. We were the chatter of giggly school-yard girls, and I was the awe and admiration of a troop of envious pubes-cent boys. As for Linda, she turned out to be a great necker and had no qualms about petting and grinding. We got along terrific but her mother didn't like me. She had heard the same rumor – that I had been put in Weredale for some crime – and she thought I wasn't good enough for her daughter. Linda told me of the arguments she and her mother had because of me, always adding that her mother would come around, and if she didn't, she would still continue seeing me. Then her big brother came home.

"Are you Victor?'' a tall, lanky guy with close-cropped hair demanded as I entered Linda's apartment building.

"Yeah! Why?'' I answered defensively.

"I'm Linda's brother,'' he said, examining me closely through grey-rimmed glasses.

"Oh, hi! I'm just going up to –''

"You're not going anywhere. Linda doesn't want to see you!'' His face contorted. Without warning, his long arm shot out and grabbed the front of my shirt, ripping it as he shoved me against the wall. "What's the idea of you going around saying you busted my sister's cherry?''

"What! That's a lie! I would never say anything like that about her or any girl.''

"You calling me a liar?''

"Why don't you call Linda down here and I'll prove it.''

"I ought to mash your head through the wall, you little punk.''

"Bug off, man. Go pick on someone your own size and your own age!''

"A tough kid from the boys' home! You're supposed to be tough, punk,'' he taunted, tightening his grip on my shirt.

"You better not touch me or else.''

"Or else what?'' he demanded, jabbing his wiry index finger into the side of my neck.

"Take off!'' I said, swatting his hand away. "Or else I'll get the cops. That's what. You're over eighteen and I'm a minor.''

Linda's brother suddenly snapped and lunged at me like a madman, slapping, punching, and kicking. Every time I tried to get away, he dragged me back and continued the beating. I crumpled to the floor and huddled into a ball, poking my head out sporadically to scream for help. My cries finally brought his mother running frantically down the stairwell.

"Ralph . . . Ralph! Leave him alone. He's only a boy! You could get into trouble! Leave him alone. Get back upstairs!"

"I'll kill the little hardrock!"

"I asked you to talk to him," she cried, "not beat him up!" She managed to subdue him into a corner.

"He's going to get it for this," I said, groping to my feet.

"You little . . ." Again Linda's brother charged at me. I dropped to the floor, covering my head with my arms.

"Ralph, please! He's a boy! Come upstairs. You go home and I don't want to see you bothering Linda again. Is that clear?" the heavy-set woman ordered. "I don't like your type."

I scrambled out of the apartment building and ran home, more scared than hurt. Apart from a badly torn shirt, I had a bleeding lip and nose and a swollen left eye.

"Daddy, Victor's been in a fight!" Peter shouted as I tried to sneak into the house.

The family converged in the passageway.

"Who did this?" my father asked.

"Linda's brother! He made up some lie that I said something rotten about his sister and started beating me up."

"Did you say anything bad about his sister?" my mother asked nervously, wiping my face with a cold, damp facecloth.

"No! I like Linda. You know that!"

"I'll fix that jerk!" Fred said, heading for the door.

"No, don't! He's over six foot and he's in the army. The guy's twenty years old."

"I don't give a shit!" Fred charged out before anyone could stop him.

"Fred . . . Fred, get back in here," my mother yelled down the staircase.

"Let him go, Jennie," my father urged. He was proud that Fred was handling the situation the way he would have, had he been healthy.

"Mike, he'll get hurt!"

"I don't think so. I taught him how to look after himself. Victor, go after him and help out! Cripple the son of a bitch who beat you up if you have to!"

"Mike! They're only kids. Victor!" she shouted as I shot out the door.

"I'll go too!" Peter offered.

"You stay here!" Mom said, latching onto his arm before he had a chance to rush out.

Fred was having one heck of a nasty shouting match on the staircase with Linda's brother when I slipped through the door.

"Who the fuck do you think you are, you lanky cock-sucker. Victor's half your size!" I laughed inwardly: Freddie was two inches smaller and at least fifteen pounds lighter than me.

"So what the fuck you going to do about it?" the army boy smirked.

"This, jerk!" Fred fired a crushing punch square into the soldier's neck, He moved swiftly and with crippling accuracy. Before I could gather my first move, my brother had dug his fingers into his immobilized victim's eye sockets.

"Don't stand there gawking!" Fred yelled. "Put the boots to him. Boot the crap out of him. Move it!"

I laid in. The only thought on my mind was to get even. I got away two boots. Fred tripped him onto the floor and started kicking away much harder than I had the nerve to. He showed no mercy, no holding back. He was out to teach this guy a lesson for picking on his younger brother. The guy would think twice about coming back for more.

Linda's mother suddenly materialized on the staircase brandishing a rolling pin. She was screaming hysterically. We managed to scramble for the exit, leaving her son crawling on all fours.

Unfortunately Linda's brother had a thick skull. He wasn't about to let bygones be bygones. The following morning, which was a Saturday, Peter burst into the apartment. He was sheet white.

"He's down there! He's got two really big guys with him. He said he's going to send you and Victor to the hospital," Peter said.

"Who? What are you talking about?" Fred asked.

"The guy you beat up yesterday, Victor's girlfriend's brother. The one from the army. They're sitting on the railing downstairs. They told me to call an ambulance."

Fred and I tiptoed onto the balcony to take a peek. Peter wasn't kidding. Linda's brother and two brawny soldier types with crew cuts sat perched on the black steel railing below.

Linda's brother spotted us. "Come down here, you little sucks," he muttered through clenched teeth. His face contorted and turned beet red. He had two very black, very bloodshot eyes.

"Up you!" Fred replied, giving him the finger.

"We got all the time in the world!" one of the army types said.

"Then this is for you. Shove it!" Fred gave him the arm.

"What are we going to do?" I asked nervously, backing into the living room. "What if they come up here to get us? Dad's too sick to fight. He could get killed if they nail him in the face and Mom's at work."

Fred thought a moment. "I'm going to call Weredale and get some guys down here."

"They won't come down here to help me!"

"They will for me! I'll get Plager and some of the seniors. We'll see how tough those jerks are." Fred grabbed the phone and dialled. "Could I speak to Robert Plager? Thank you." A long minute passed. "Plager? Malarek! How the hell are you? How's jerk-face Johnson? Ha! I'm okay. It's great to be out. Listen, I need your help. Victor got beaten up last night by some guy in the army. I beat the crap out of the turkey and now he's out here with two of his army buddies wanting another scrap. Yeah! Could you and a few guys . . .? Good! Great! 4080 Barclay, apartment 5. Take a taxi. My father will pay you back when you get here."

Twenty minutes later, Plager, Robillard, Daniels, and the two Mekov brothers poured out of the taxi. They were the best street fighters the home had to offer and they were raring for a beef.

"That's them!" Fred yelled from the balcony. Plager waded into Linda's brother without a second's hesitation. The others ploughed into his buddies. Fred and I raced down to help out.

"Fix them good!" Daniels shouted. "We'll teach them to mess with Weredale!"

Plager drove his heel down full weight, crushing his victim's nose. Fred immobilized one of the soldiers by drilling his index fingers into the guy's eye sockets. The younger Mekov brother and I helped out, laying a flurry of boots and punches into a squirming, helpless body. Daniels and the older Mekov easily took care of the third soldier. Within minutes, one of the wildest street fights I had ever been involved in was over. The army limped away. Among the Weredale contingent, there were congratulations all around and well-deserved slaps on the back. We proudly strutted up to the apartment to celebrate and recount over and over again our glorious victory.

"I really want to thank you guys," I repeated for the umpteenth time.

"Look, Malarek, you know Weredale guys stick together. We're like brothers," the older Mekov said.

"That's right! We may scrap and even hate each other's guts in the Home, but outside we stick together. Nobody lays a finger on us. We're family. Sometimes we're the only family we got," Plager added.

"Don't worry, Malarek. You're all right. Maybe we didn't get along in the Home. That's just the way it goes. You handled yourself real cool! You're okay!" Daniels said, slapping me on the back.

For the first time, I felt really proud of having been in Weredale. I was moved by what these guys had said. I had never thought about it before, but what they said was true. Weredale boys do stick together! We are brothers. I finally felt accepted by some of the coolest guys in the Home.

About a week after the scrap, my parents received a registered letter summoning me to appear with them in Social Welfare Court the following Wednesday. They questioned me for the better part of the evening, trying to pry out of me whatever it was that I might have done wrong. They were looking for a confession, but for the life of me I couldn't figure it out. Unless the court had got wind of the street fight with Linda's brother, I was clean. I was sure the army boys would have been too embarrassed to press charges against juveniles.

When the court date arrived, I had no fingernails left to chew on. I stood quaking before a silver-haired judge in a black robe who sat bent over some papers in his private chambers. Each minute was nerve-wracking. When the judge finally glanced up, he stared at me for a moment, then over at my mother and motioned her to sit in one of the large black leather chairs to his left. The judge cleared his throat and began in a friendly, fatherly tone.

"How are you today, Victor?"

"Fine, sir, thank you."

"Tell me. Do you know a boy by the name of Brian McDowell?"

The mention of McDowell's name threw me for a loop. "Yes, sir."

"Then tell me, Victor. Why do you keep picking on him?"

"Picking? Sir, I'm not picking on him."

"Brian's mother seems to think you are. She came to see me last week and claims that you had beaten Brian up. She also says you are continually picking on him in the schoolyard and that everyone in the school is afraid of you because you were in Weredale House."

"Sir, that's not true. Man, this is unreal. I can't believe it. McDowell is the hardrock. Not me. He started the scrap, and he's the guy who's always pushing kids around. He's been pushing for a fight with me since school started. He's the guy with the black leather jacket and motorcycle boots."

"That hardly fits the description Mrs. McDowell gave me. It seems her boy had pneumonia when he was a child and he is not a strong lad."

"So what? I had pneumonia when I was a baby also!"

"We'll have none of your sarcasm, young man!"

"Your honor," my mother interrupted.

"Yes, Mrs. Malarek."

"Your honor, Victor came home so many times complaining about this McDowell boy always trying to start fights with him. Several children in the neighborhood told me about this boy picking on the kids, especially Jewish kids. It's funny that after one boy stands up to him, he ends up having to go to court."

"Well, Mrs. Malarek, there have been a lot of fights reported in that neighborhood of late, and your son has been implicated in many of them."

"I haven't been in any fights!" I yelled.

"Hush! Don't you raise your voice in this chamber." The judge studied some papers in an orange file folder for a few minutes. He looked up and gave me this fatherly "I'm doing this for your own good" look.

"I feel it would be better if Victor was to see a probation officer from time to time. Someone for him to talk to and give him a little guidance. It might do him some good. It certainly can't do him any harm. I've arranged that he see Mr. Gold after he leaves my chambers. I've asked Mr. Gold to talk to Victor. The court clerk will show you how to get to Mr. Gold's office from here. He's expecting you. Good morning, and I hope I don't have to see you here again, Victor."

With that, we left the judge's chambers and sought out the probation officer's office on the top floor of the old courthouse.

Some trial, I thought. I'm the victim, McDowell is the aggressor and I'm the guilty one! I knew the judge didn't believe me. His mind was made up before I entered the courtroom and I knew why. It was on my court record that I had been in Weredale, and Weredale boys had a reputation as street fighters and troublemakers.

Gold appeared to be a friendly sort. He was a small, pale man with a loud, resonating voice. He wore suspenders, starched white shirts, and stained ties. What amused me was he tried so hard to look important sitting behind a small wooden desk, one-third the size of the judge's but laden with three times as many documents, forms, and folders. A framed Bachelor of Arts degree with his name scrolled in Old English lettering hung on the wall behind him. To his right was a filing cabinet cluttered on top with coffee-making apparatus.

"Sit here, Mrs. Malarek," he said with a friendly smile. "You, Victor . . . it is Victor?" he asked, looking down at a form on his desk. "That's right. Victor, you sit next to your mother. Good. Now, I want you to understand that you are not here because you're in trouble with the law, or that you're a juvenile delinquent, or anything like that. You're simply here at the request of the judge, who, in his wisdom, sometimes feels that certain children may be heading into troubled waters and it is better to catch them in midstream before they reach the stronger current of the river."

Puke, I thought.

His sermon over, the probation officer proceeded to ask my mother a series of form questions, which took the better part of an hour, and then dismissed us by saying that he would be in touch. I could hardly wait.

After school one day in early February, I found a registered letter addressed to me on the kitchen table. The return address read Social Welfare Court – Quebec. I tore open the envelope and saw all sorts of red type underlined twice covering the paper. It was from my probation officer, Gold, and it looked all very official. At the top of the letter, typed in red capitals and underlined twice, were the words RE: COURT APPEARANCE. Then the letter ordering me, Victor Malarek, in red, underlined twice, to be in court the following Tuesday and date, in red, underlined twice, at 4:00 p.m., in red, underlined twice. Signed, Mr. Gold, probation officer, B.A.

I wasn't unduly worried because I hadn't been in any fights or any trouble since I had first seen him three months earlier. I figured my appearance was merely routine. Yet there was something about Gold's letter with its vicious underlinings that seemed to ooze anger.

On Tuesday, I took the bus down to the court building. I arrived ten minutes early and sat down outside Gold's office. He came by fifteen minutes later.

"Ah, Malarek!" he said, loudly pronouncing every syllable in my last name. He glared at me for an instant and disappeared into his office. I sat and waited.

"Get in here, Malarek!" he boomed from behind his desk half an hour later.

I got up and walked in.

"Sit down! No . . . stand up, you little punk!"

I stood up. I began to boil. Who the hell did this jerk think he was, calling me a punk?

"So you think you're pretty tough, eh? Well, what do you have to say for yourself?"

"Sir?" I said, wondering what he was talking about. "I don't know what you mean. I haven't done anything wrong."

"Don't play stupid with me, Mr. Tough Guy! I could take you and break you into little pieces! Do you know I could have you put in detention?

All I have to do is pick up this phone and call the judge. Whatever I say goes. Maybe I will. I think three days in detention will do you good."

"Sir, I don't –"

"Don't you interrupt me! Punk! Or are you going to beat me up too? You'd like to, wouldn't you? But I could break you into little pieces. I hate punks like you. You don't dare fight with anyone your own size. You beat up cripples."

"What?" I asked, stunned by the last comment. "What are you talking about?"

"Don't play stupid with me, Malarek! You know damn well what I'm talking about. You beat up a young Jewish lad last week. A lad whose left leg was crippled by polio when he was nine."

"I did not! I haven't been in any fights. I don't know what you're talking about."

"Don't use that tone with me, lad, or I'll call the judge this minute! You little punk! I detest punks."

"Sir," I continued, trying ever so hard to keep calm, "I haven't been in a fight in over three months, since the time you saw me for McDowell. And I didn't beat up any cripple. I don't go around beating up cripples."

"You don't know a boy named Katz? He's a grade eight boy in Northmount High." His face was inches from mine.

"I don't even go to Northmount High."

"I know that!" Gold snapped back. "He was beaten up on Victoria Street near your school," he said, eyeballing me for a confession.

"I don't even know what you're talking about."

"You're a little liar. Don't you lie to me! I'll have you put in detention."

"I don't know the guy."

"His mother called me last week. He may have to have an operation on his eye. The one you punched or kicked. Does that make you feel tough, Malarek? That may cost her a lot of money. Do you know who is going to end up paying the hospital bill? You! She is thinking seriously of bringing charges against you in court and suing your family for the cost of her son's operation. As a matter of fact, she's calling her lawyer today."

"I didn't touch the kid. She won't get a penny out of me or my family."

"Shut up, you little liar! Speak only when I give you permission. Don't interrupt me ever again. Now as I was saying –"

"You're not going to get me to admit to something I didn't do. You can forget that. If you're so sure it's me who beat the kid up, why don't you bring him here to identify me? That'll prove I never touched the guy."

Gold was caught off guard. He pursed his lips together tightly and stared intently at a report on his desk. "Sit down outside my office and don't move until I call you. I have work to do. I'll speak to you later. I detest punks. Get out!"

"Don't call me that. I'm not a punk."

"Get out. Don't you dare use that tone with me. Get out and sit out there until I call for you."

It was about 4:30 p.m. After a few minutes Gold left his office and disappeared down a stairwell. An hour later he reappeared with a boy wearing a pale-pink plastic patch over his left eye. Both of them stared at me momentarily and went into the office. There was some mumbling, a long pause, and some more mumbling. Then the boy left.

"Malarek!" Gold called out gruffly. "You can go home now. Just keep out of trouble or else."

I wasn't about to let the matter drop that easily. I walked into his office.

"What about this kid I was supposed to have beat up?"

"Just stay out of trouble. You can leave now. I'll let you know when I'll see you again." Gold refused to look up from the desk. I knew he knew he had the wrong guy and he was too proud to admit he'd screwed up.

"Mr. Gold, I want to know about the kid —"

"Get out of my office! Now! You better understand this, I can have you placed in detention. All I have to do is pick up this phone and call the judge. He listens to me. What I say goes. Now enough of your lip. Go home."

I stood firm for a moment and then left.

The tone for our relationship had been set on that afternoon. I detested Gold, but I knew I would have to endure him until I turned eighteen. I realized that afternoon that I would have to watch myself around him, that I'd have to walk on eggshells. He had his mind made up about me. I was a punk and he was going to break me. He would simply wait for me to screw up and then he'd come down on me like a sledgehammer. He claimed he could ruin my life by picking up the telephone, and it was true. Gold could have me sent to training school.

13

*A*s spring approached, my mother announced we were moving out of the neighborhood. The district was causing too many hardships for the family. Fred had quit high school. By a strange twist of fate, his principal had turned out to be the camp director, Armstrong. His warning to the teachers was: "Watch out for that boy! He's trouble." It was like a self-fulfilling prophecy. The teachers caught Freddie getting into trouble regularly, and just as regularly my brother was strapped or suspended. Since his return home, Fred had inched to a wiry five feet, seven inches, and had become extremely fast and agile. He excelled in sports and powered all his energies into them. He decided he had had enough of school and enrolled in a night course to study electronics while working in the day as a shipper in a clothing factory.

Peter also had difficulties at school. His teacher harbored the notion that he was an unsavory character, a juvenile delinquent, because he had been in a boys' home. She repeatedly singled him out for any number of minor infractions, dishing out more punishments than were required. There had to be a snapping point and it came one March morning. Peter was caught whispering to a friend during class and the teacher exploded. She exiled Peter to the cloakroom and all but ordered the class to stay away from him. Peter peered out of the cloakroom and asked her what she meant by her remarks. She screamed at him to get out of her sight. Peter stood his ground, telling her he would hang around with anyone he chose to. "And if you don't like it, you can lump it," he added.

Indignant, she slapped him across the face. Her nails caught Peter's cheek and drew blood. My brother retaliated by kicking her in the shins and slapping her right back before making a mad scramble out of the school. After hearing the teacher's one-sided account of what had taken place, the principal had Peter transferred to another school, where a harshly worded record of the event was sent.

The incident caused a dramatic change in Peter. He decided he would no longer stand for any more crap from power-tripping teachers. Confident in his solid, five-foot five-inch, stocky frame, he determined to handle situations more physically from that point on.

I, in turn, requested a transfer from Coronation School in protest against Peter's unfair treatment and completed my year at Edward VII School. It was in an old, rundown building on Esplanade Street, a few blocks over from our latest two-bedroom flat on Park Avenue in the city's north-central semi-slums. Edward VII was a far cry from the clean, new insti-tution we had just left. The school stood in the shadows of cockroach-infested, three-storey row-tenement dwellings. The laneway behind the asphalt schoolyard was a dismal scene of rickety old sheds, garbage oozing out of waterlogged cardboard boxes, and liberal sprinklings of bald tires, broken glass, bedsprings, boards, and beams. Inside, the school creaked with old age. Even the new coat of paint seemed as if it had been applied years ago. The classrooms were rundown and furnished with carved-up lid-top desks that were bolted to the floor. Having only two months to go before summer vacation, I decided to keep to myself as much as possible.

During my brief stint at Edward VII, I didn't have time to make any lasting friends. The cliques were already formed. And I didn't have any friends worth a forty-minute bus ride to my old neighborhood on Barclay Street. For me, the summer months looked as if they were going to drag on. Peter had so many side-kicks that he was hardly ever home. Fred was also busy with his friends, one of whom was Lloyd Roussel, an easygoing Gaspesian with black curly hair who had recently moved to the city with his mother, father, and seven siblings.

One evening in early July, Lloyd showed up to meet Fred with a buddy in tow. His name was Lorne Furtner, a Jew, although I didn't think he looked Jewish. He was the son of Lloyd's landlord. Lorne was about a month younger than me, about two inches shorter, and well built. It was obvious he lifted weights. His close-cropped hair was sandy and wavy. Faded freckles dotted his entire body and his complexion was slightly pale. He was dressed three years out of style and acted as if it didn't bother him. This guy would fit well in Weredale, I thought scornfully.

Needless to say, I couldn't stand Lorne and he couldn't stand me either. Whenever Lloyd came around to meet my brother, he'd have Lorne in tow. There were no words between us those first couple of weeks, only an uneasy tension. Poor Lloyd: he liked us both and tried every trick in his arsenal of friendliness to keep us from getting into a scrap, while Lorne and I would circle each other like distrustful alley cats.

"He's really okay. Honest," Lloyd would say. "Come on, try to be friends."

"Man, Fred can't even take the jerk. Lloyd, he even makes *you* look cool."

Lloyd giggled. "Yeah, but he's really okay. Honest. Come on, try to be friends."

One warm July evening, Lloyd and Fred took off together. Neither said where they were going and I didn't bother to ask. The doorbell rang sometime around seven. It was Lorne.

"Yeah?" I said, making damn sure I wasted no words with him.

"Is Fred or Lloyd here?" Lorne asked.

"No."

"Do you know where they are?"

"Nope."

"Could I stay on the verandah and wait for them in case they come back soon?"

"I guess." I slammed the door and went to watch television. After an hour, I decided to go for a walk up Park Avenue. Lorne was still sitting on the steps when I came out. "I guess I'll go and look for them. No use sitting here," he said, as I locked the door.

"Yeah."

"Do you have any idea where they might be?"

"Nope."

I grimaced when I saw he was heading in the same direction. I wanted to cross the street or head back home with an excuse that I had forgotten something.

"I wonder if they're at the Rialto pool hall?" Lorne said.

"Probably. I don't know. They didn't tell me where they were going."

"Want to see if they're there?"

I tagged along reluctantly. When we got to the pool hall, it was empty except for a few Greeks.

I still can't figure out how the rest came about. Lorne and I walked for hours. We started out looking for Fred and Lloyd but we ended up having the time of our lives. Our walk took us up Park Avenue, over Mount Royal, along busy downtown St. Catherine Street, to the pool halls on St. Lawrence, where we stopped for some steamed hot dogs and winked at a couple of transvestites who wiggled by with their tight-panted fag boyfriends. At first our conversation was sporadic and forced, but somewhere along the way we relaxed and the talk flowed easily between us. We talked about everything. We talked about our dreams, what we had done, what we wanted to do, and our home life. We joked and made passes at girls. We pretended to be drunk and sang a couple of songs marching with arms slung over each other's shoulders. By the time we parted, at three o'clock in the morning, we'd become best of friends. I felt fantastic.

When I walked through the main entrance of Montreal High School, I felt as if I had at last accomplished something in my life: I had officially made it to a real high school, not one that started with grade seven. At the general office, a secretary directed me down to the boys' gymnasium, where the rolls for grade eight classes were being hollered out. I leaned against the monkey bars at the back waiting for my name to be called. After quite some time had passed, I began wondering if someone had forgotten to add my name to the school's register or if I had missed hearing it shouted out. The once swollen crowd had rapidly dwindled to a motley lot as each class from 8-A to 8-E lined up and marched out to the classrooms above.

"Class 8-F," the man who had been calling out the names continued in a loud, monotonous monotone. Again he began to read off a list of names in alphabetical order.

"Malarek, Victor!"

Shaking my head, I pushed myself off the wall and joined my new class. A hodgepodge of every ethnic origin you could think of, 8-F was Montreal High's answer to multiculturalism. We had a smattering of Chinese, Poles, Jews, Ukrainians, Germans, Armenians, Canadian Blacks, Greeks, a Russian, a French Canadian, an Italian, a Scot, a Lithuanian, an East Indian, a couple of West Indians, a Turk , and a Mexican. A good half were recent immigrants who spoke hardly any English. There was also a large contingent of repeaters and a dose of those the school authorities had labelled low-achievers or troublemakers. I had been marked for the latter.

Montreal High was segregated by sex. There were no females on our side of the building. The massive white brick structure, built in the shape of an H, was divided down the middle. The boys' section was called the High School of Montreal. The other half was the High School for Girls. Through the heart of the four-storey complex ran an imaginary borderline, and no student was permitted to cross it without official permission.

The 8-F classroom was in a remote corner at the back end of the building on the top fourth floor. I took a desk in the third row, second from the back. Behind me sat a skinny braggart of a Ukrainian named John Sawchuk. He didn't know we were of the same nationality. His buddy, George Fararian, an oily-haired, acne-scarred Armenian, sat beside him in row two. Once the class had settled down, the teacher, a mild-mannered

Englishman, scrawled his name on the blackboard: Mr. Stevens. He was our home room, English, and history instructor. Stevens wore a faded green corduroy jacket with gaping pockets and beige corduroy slacks, a white shirt, his British school tie, and brown Hush Puppies. He spoke softly and sounded as if he didn't mind being stuck with us.

Class elections were held on the second day of school. I knew two nominees vaguely from Edward VII. The rest were total strangers orginating from half a dozen public schools in the high school's sweeping boundaries. The elections meant little to me or anyone else. We went mainly on looks and a few dumb sentences by those who volunteered themselves to run.

"I want to be president because I do good job. I am man for the job. I will do good." With that, a rangy Greek called Steve Mederis got the top job. Michael Schmidt, a lanky, blond German boy, was elected vice-president.

My resolve was to keep my nose clean and get out of 8-F. I was sure I deserved better. My other resolve was not to take any crap. No more of what had happened to me at Westmount High. If the teachers wanted to vent their frustrations on someone, it wouldn't be me.

Since leaving Weredale, I had put on fifteen pounds and had shot up four inches. I was now around five feet nine inches tall and weighed 110 pounds. My hair was longish, and I dressed in the latest fashions: stovepipe pants, high-collar shirts, and black suede boots with silver buckles.

I was also changing inside. I was becoming more and more high-strung and tense. I would snap at the slightest provocation. I knew a lot of my irritability had to do with the deteriorating situation at home. My parents were arguing again. My father was back to starting fights whenever he could. He was picking on me incessantly and I was going nuts trying to cope. When high school started, my father slapped a 9 p.m. curfew on me on weekdays and, to make matters worse, he ordered me in by 11 p.m. on weekends. When he'd been drinking heavily and popping painkillers, he would sometimes order me to stay at home altogether.

I tried to keep my problems out of school but it became increasingly difficult. After a seemingly endless night of fighting with my father or listening to my parents argue, I'd be in no mood for horsing around. One morning, my father and I had a heated exchange over his wanting me home twenty minutes after school finished. When I arrived at school I plunked myself at my desk and sat there fuming. It was still quite early in the school year. Sawchuk was being his usual obnoxious self, muttering obscenities in Ukrainian. He thought no one understood what he was saying. Although I knew little Ukrainian, I still remembered some choice curses.

"Why don't you shut your head?" I threatened, turning to Sawchuk, who was whispering a translation to his Armenian side-kick.

Sawchuk mouthed a Ukrainian obscenity at me.

"Keep it up and I'll knock your teeth down your throat," I shot back.

"You touch him, you touch me," Fararian interjected.

"Big deal, zit face. Watch me shake." I turned around and saw my name written on the blackboard, signalling a detention. "Where's those guys' names, man?" I shouted at Mederis, the class president, who responded by placing a large asterisk beside my name.

The next period was French, and the French teacher was a fanatic. He was strict and ran his class like an army platoon. Any name on the board meant writing out four pages of the vocabulary at the back of the French textbook after class. Each asterisk added two additional pages to the punishment. All that was required was the president's word. No questions asked, no excuses accepted.

I shouted a Greek obscenity at Mederis. "*Malaka!*"

He put another asterisk beside my name. Sawchuk muttered another Ukrainian curse. Fararian broke up.

"Put their names on the board!" I demanded. Instead, I received a third star. "You keep it up, Sawchuk, and you're dead." Sawchuk leaned against the wall grinning.

"Touch him and —" Fararian began.

That was enough. I swung around and smacked Sawchuk with a flying open right hand. He fell off his chair, holding a bleeding lip. Fararian jumped up and was doubled up by a punch to the groin. The vice-president crept up from behind and tackled me to the floor. He had me pinned but I managed to free my right arm, slip off my loafer, and club him on the side of the head. He tumbled off screeching. I scrambled to my feet, barely dodging a chair Mederis winged at me. Just what I needed, a crazy Greek, I muttered to myself as I charged forward. I had Mederis pinned against the blackboard with my fingers digging into his throat when the class shouting suddenly died down. Mr. Mohamed, our math teacher, had come in from a neighboring classroom to investigate the ruckus. When he realized what was happening, he rushed over, spun me around, and slapped me across the mouth with the back of his hand. I turned to retaliate but froze in my tracks when I saw who it was. He grabbed me by my arm and hauled me over to a corner.

"Stay there and don't you move," he commanded. "Now what on

earth has been going on here?'' Mohamed asked in an East Indian accent. ''Tell me! I want to know!''

''Those . . . those four guys all . . . all tried to take on dat guy,'' a stuttering member of the class offered.

''Yeah. The president kept putting his name on the board for talking and fooling when he wasn't. It was those guys sitting behind him and just because they're Steve's friends, they get off,'' another explained.

I was surprised that the class came out in support of me.

''They started the scrap!'' still another classmate charged.

''Yeah,'' the majority of the class added. ''It was those guys.''

I heard Mohamed's footsteps behind me.

''Turn around, boy!'' He gasped when he saw my face. Blood was trickling from my mouth. I had munched on it a little to make it look worse than it really was just in case I had to appear in front of the principal.

''Did they do that to you?'' he asked.

''No! You did when you whacked me!''

Mohamed's eyes popped wide open. He bit his lower lip and rubbed his hands together. ''I . . . I guess I got a little carried away, man. I'm truly sorry. I am. Please, go to the washroom and clean up. I'm very sorry.''

''Yeah, sure. I got a bleeding lip and you're sorry.''

''Man, you should see the class I got stuck in,'' I complained to Lorne after school. ''What a bunch of turkeys! I got into a scrap with a couple of them today and then the teacher belted me in the head. Can you believe it?''

''The teacher punched you?'' Lorne asked.

''He nailed me with a backhand across the mouth 'cause I got into a fight with the president and vice-president and a couple of other guys.''

Lorne laughed. ''What were you doing, taking on the whole class?''

''I just got pissed off at this one jerk and belted him. Before I knew it, I was in a scrap with one guy after another. I don't think these guys ever expected anyone to be so dirty. I nailed a guy a shot in the nuts.''

''You kicked him?''

''No. I punched him in the nuts.''

He cracked up. Lorne was in grade eight as well, but he went to Outremont High, a predominantly Jewish school in the more affluent area of Outremont where his father owned a couple of three-storey houses. He hated his school because it was filled to capacity with ginks who were all trying to suck up to the teachers.

"I'd love to go to Montreal High. It's got a cool reputation."

"Yeah? Tell me about it."

"I hear a lot of the girls go," Lorne winked.

"Yeah, sure. By the way, guess who got elected new class president this afternoon?"

"Not . . . not you?"

We both fell over in a fit of laughter.

Just after Christmas, my father was forced into the hospital for detoxification and dehydration. He had gained too much weight from the several quarts of beer he drank daily, swelling from 165 pounds to over 235 pounds. He was also addicted to pain-killers. He was popping 292s, 293s, Secanols, and a variety of tranquillizers. His dresser looked like a pharmacy counter. His doctors also had detected new traces of cancerous tissue and wanted to start cobalt radiation therapy rather than risk a third operation.

My father lapsed into a depression in the hospital. He was lonely. His only visitors were my mother, Fred, Peter, myself, and a few of my friends. None of my father's old friends bothered to visit him. On a rare occasion one of his two brothers showed up. His afternoon visiting hour was almost a write-off. My mother had to work until four. Peter didn't finish school until 3:15 p.m. and he was too far from the hospital to make it in time. Fred had to work until 5 p.m. The only one he could count on was me and I made sure I got there as often as I could.

School ended at 2:30 p.m., giving me enough time to catch the bus up to the Veterans' Hospital. I had the bus schedule down pat. If I was thirty seconds late, the whole thing would be thrown off and I would lose at least twenty minutes from the visiting hour. I kept to a tight routine. My home-room teacher never held us back once the 2:30 bell rang, unlike some tight-assed teachers at that school. I would run full speed down the corridor and, if no teachers were around, shoot down the up stairwell, shaving an extra second, out the door, down University Street just in time to catch the Number 4 bus heading west along Sherbrooke. I would stand close to the front door, jump off at Guy, and catch the 65 bus up Côte des Neiges at 2:45 p.m. It never took more than fifteen minutes to get to the hospital, and visiting started at 3:00.

One December afternoon, I raced past Mr. Kotelis's class, 8-A, where all the brains were supposed to be. At 2:30 he usually closed his door to avoid the clatter and noise of other students being freed from their classrooms. He never let his class out until at least 2:35 or 2:40. This day, his door happened to be open when I bolted by. I was just about to shoot down the stairwell when Kotelis's voice boomed behind me.

"You! Where do you think you're going?"

"Who me?" I shouted back, pointing at myself.

"Yes, you! Come here!" Students began to mill about.

"You don't mean me, sir?" I figured as long as he was going to aggravate me, I might as well piss him off good.

"Yes, you! Come here!"

"You can't mean *me*, sir?" A few students laughed.

"I said come here! Now!"

Pretending to be totally bewildered, I looked straight at the red-faced teacher, then behind me and back at Kotelis. I slowly stretched my arm and pointed a finger at myself, at the same time mouthing, "Who me?"

"I said get over here! Now!"

Again I looked inquisitively at the teacher, who suddenly tore down the hall after me, latched onto my arm, and hauled me into his classroom, slamming the door behind him.

"Wipe that expression off your face!"

"It's my face. If you don't like it, don't look at it."

"Don't get smart with me, lad! I have ways of dealing with smart alecs like you."

"Yeah, I'm sure you do."

Someone in his class snickered.

"Do you think this is funny, Charles? Do you? We'll see if you find this funny. You have a one-hour detention for three days after school. Now everyone sit up!" The class sat at attention, hands cupped neatly on the tops of their desks. What a bunch of ginks, I thought.

"Now, where do you think you were going to? A fire?"

"I had to go somewhere."

"Well, we'll see if we can't slow you up a little. You will come here every day after school for two weeks for one hour. What's your name?"

"No I won't."

"What?" he asked, in disbelief.

"I won't come here every day for two weeks for one hour."

"Did you ever get the strap, my young man?"

"Yeah!"

"Yes, sir, when you're talking to me! Idiots say yeah."

"Yes, sir. Idiots say yeah," I mumbled.

Someone giggled. "Harold, detention. One hour for three days," Kotelis said without turning around.

"Well, young man! You've never gotten the strap from me, have you?"

"No."

"Don't take my detention and you will. You'll beg to get a month of detentions rather than get the strap from me."

"Ha! You'll never see me beg."

"Ha? You dare to *ha* at me! You dare!"

"Are you finished with me?" I asked. "I have somewhere to go."

"What?" The teacher's face turned crimson red. "Get downstairs and wait for me in front of the vice-principal's office. Move! And when I get there, you'd better be standing at attention!"

You really did it this time, Victor, I said to myself on the way down the stairs. You're going to be suspended for sure.

I was leaning against the wall outside the vice-principal's office when Kotelis appeared in the corridor.

"I said at attention!" he bellowed.

"This is not the army!"

He stomped into the vice-principal's office. He wasn't in.

"Come with me."

We walked over to the principal's office, which was a little further down the hall.

"Now we'll see how tough you are, you little imbecile. Wait out here!"

"Don't call me an imbecile."

The teacher glared at me and entered the general office area. A second later, he disappeared into the principal's office. I could hear him yelling, "He laughed at me! Me, Mr. Kotelis!" A moment later, the principal's secretary tiptoed out.

"Mr. Wright wants to see you. Come this way."

I pushed myself from the wall and followed her.

"Here he is, Mr. Wright," she said.

The principal, a bald, skinny man, stared at me without saying a word. He was sitting behind his desk holding a pipe to his lips. Even though he was sitting, I could tell he was quite tall. His expression was serious and pensive.

"What's your name, son?" he asked in a low, quiet voice.

"Victor Malarek, sir," I replied nervously.

"What class are you in?"

"8-F, sir."

He stared at me a moment longer.

"Is what Mr. Kotelis tells me true?"

"If he says so," I mumbled.

"That is not an answer, young man. Is what he tells me true?"

"Yes, sir."

"Then I have no alternative but to give Mr. Kotelis permission to strap you."

"Yes, sir." I wasn't terribly worried. The strappings I got at school could never top the beatings I'd had at Weredale.

Mr. Wright pulled open the bottom left-hand drawer of his desk and retrieved a black book with a fifteen-inch leather strap wedged in the centre.

"How do you spell your last name?" the principal asked.

"M-a-l-a-r-e-k."

Kotelis took out the strap, flexed it a few times for effect, and motioned me to the centre of the room.

"Put your left hand out and with your right hand hold the sleeve of your shirt down near your wrists."

I did as I was instructed.

Whack! It didn't hurt. I got six on that hand, not counting two tips, which stung more than the ones that connected.

"The other hand now!" the teacher commanded.

Getting my face out of view of the principal, I gave the teacher a cocky smirk which really enraged him. He swung at my hand like a madman. I pulled it away and the blow hit his leg.

"You'll get three extra for that."

I got nine on my right hand, not counting one tip.

"Let's hope this teaches you a lesson, Victor. Do you have anything to say to Mr. Kotelis?"

"No, sir."

"How about 'I'm sorry, sir'," the principal suggested.

I didn't reply. Damned if I was going to apologize after this guy just strapped me.

"Obviously the strap wasn't enough! I'm going to suspend you for three days. When you return to school, come back with either your mother or your father and see me. I want to have a talk with them."

Wright filled in the suspension form and told me to leave the school immediately. I figured a three-day suspension was better than two weeks of detention. I would still be able to visit Dad in the hospital.

My mother was upset when I told her I'd been suspended.

"I don't want you to get into trouble in school. I want you to get an education, Victor. You're a smart boy."

"Look, Mom, that teacher is nothing but a jerk. I'm not going to let this guy think he can push me around just because he's got a mean streak. I took enough of that in Weredale. His job is to teach. Mine is to learn. Whatever else is none of his business. All I did was run down the hallway. No one was in the hall. Then he comes out and gives me two weeks of detentions after school. I've got to see Dad after school. You know that.''

''Well, talk to him. Talk to the teacher. Tell him where you have to go after school. I'm sure he will understand once you explain.''

''Mom, this guy is on a power trip. He doesn't care a hoot about me or my problems.''

''Will you please try to speak to him? You could be wrong. At least try.''

''Yeah, okay.''

I loathed the thought of spilling my guts out to strangers, especially teachers and social workers. I preferred to keep my life private. What was inside stayed there, simmering. I relied heavily on my keenly honed instincts in my dealings with adults. I judged the world around me by what I had learned on the streets and what Weredale had drilled into my skull: Don't drop your guard for an instant. Maybe I was wrong in my outlook. That thought drifted through my mind on occasion back then but I had become jaded. It seemed easier to be detached and indifferent, though inside I was screaming and primed to explode. At my mother's insistence, I grudgingly resolved to at least broach the subject with the principal.

I came back to school three days later without my mother. She had to work and couldn't get the time off. Wright, to my surprise, was very sympathetic when I explained the circumstances.

''My father is in the hospital. He has cancer,'' I said, staring down at the floor.

''Cancer?''

''Yes, sir. I go to see him after school as often as I can. My mother has to work until four and can't get to see him during the afternoon visiting hour. Then my mother has to go home and cook supper for my two brothers and me.''

''Well, Victor, I'll permit you back to your classes. I hope you've learned a lesson from all this and I hope you'll stay out of trouble.''

''Thank you, sir.''

I felt good about our brief chat. Wright really seemed to care. He had a gentle, almost priestly way about him. And he didn't yell.

At 2:30 p.m., I was walking fast down the hall, only to be ambushed by Kotelis as I passed his classroom.

"Get in here, you!"

"Sir, I've got to go somewhere."

"I don't care where you've got to go. You've got two weeks of detentions after school with me to serve first."

I sat at a desk fuming and waited until he dismissed his grinning class. Nine boys from his home room remained behind to serve their detentions. Another twelve boys arrived from other classes. What a 10-karat bastard, I thought, thrusting my hand into the air.

Kotelis ignored me. After a minute, I cleared my throat loudly to catch his attention. He looked up, grimaced, and resumed marking class papers.

"Sir? Sir?"

"Will you be quiet! I have work to do. Don't you have any homework?"

"Sir, can I speak to you?"

"Make it snappy. What is it?"

"Sir, can I speak to you outside in private?" I didn't want the other boys to hear what I had to say about my father.

"Speak to me here. I'm not going anywhere."

"Sir, I can't take —"

"Speak up! Don't mumble."

"I can't take the detentions. I have to go somewhere after school. It's important and —"

"I have somewhere I'd like to go after school as well. Do you think I like staying behind after school?"

"Sir, I have to visit my father. He's in the hospital and —"

"Sonny, you should have thought about that before getting into trouble."

I was at my wits' end with his sermonizing interruptions. I took a deep breath. My hands were trembling. "Sir, I've been punished for that. I was strapped and suspended."

"And now you're serving your detention. Now go back to your seat and quit your whining."

"Sir, I can't. You don't understand. I have to —"

"Sit down and shut up! I've heard enough from you. If you don't want to be here, then I suggest you stay out of trouble from now on. And then maybe I won't have to waste my time after school with the likes of you."

"If you don't want to be here, then why do you give out so many detentions?" I snapped back.

"Three weeks! After school for one hour. That includes the two weeks you have now. Where are you going? Get back in here and sit down!"

"I'm not taking this crap! I'm going."

Kotelis charged down the hallway and grabbed my arm. "Get in that classroom and sit!"

I pulled away. "Keep your hands off me. I mean it. Don't you touch me again."

"Get back here. I'm going to have you kicked out of this school," the teacher screamed as I headed down the stairwell.

Promptly at 9 a.m. the next morning the intercom beeped. "Is Vic Malarek there?"

"Yes, he's here," Stevens replied.

"Would you please send him to Mr. Wright's office."

"Yes, I will. You heard the word, Malarek. Off you go."

"Yes, sir." My stomach was in knots as I entered the principal's office. I figured I was out for at least two weeks. I knew I didn't stand a chance against a teacher.

Wright sat grim-faced at his desk. He was examining my school records from the year before. Kotelis stood near the window, leering at me.

"What do you have to say for yourself?" Wright finally asked.

I could never find an answer for that question. "Nothing, sir."

"You're a bright lad. You got a high passing grade last year. Your first term marks so far are in the high 80s and 90s. I can't understand your rude behavior. Mr. Kotelis tells me you simply marched out of his class after he gave you a detention. He also tells me you were quite rude and impertinent."

"Sir, I already got punished. I was strapped and then suspended. After I got back to school, he decides that I still have to do the two weeks' detention he gave me. I told him I had to see my father. I told him that but he didn't want to listen."

From the expression on Wright's face, I could tell that Kotelis hadn't told him the whole story. "Go stand in the hallway. I'll speak to you in a moment."

About ten minutes later, Kotelis emerged in the general office red-faced and upset. He avoided me by leaving through a second exit further on down the hall.

The secretary motioned for me to come in. Wright was puffing on a pipe.

"I think I've straightened this mess up," he began, taking a deep breath and letting it out slowly. "You've served your punishment. You don't have to take the detentions. Now I don't want you thinking of this as a victory of sorts. It was simply a misunderstanding. I want you to stay out of trouble and keep a lid on your rude mouth. Understood?"

"Yes, sir, and thank you." Wright's fairness flabbergasted me. It didn't fit with my view of the world, in which ego-tripping teachers got away with everything. I was afraid to admit I might occasionally be wrong about people, and pushed the unwelcome thought to the back of my mind.

That spring, my lustful attentions zeroed in on a gorgeous grade 11 student with flowing auburn hair. I was head over heels in love, but there was no chance for me to meet her. She didn't show up at any school dances and she didn't hang around the schoolyard during recess or lunch, or after school. She was into the arts. Drama, painting, and music appreciation. So I did the next best thing.

"I joined the drama club."

"You did what? Come on. You're kidding," Lorne said.

"No, I'm not. You remember that chick I told you about. Alice, the one in grade 11. She's in the drama club and is working on the play the school is putting on this year."

"Man, she's not going to bother with you. You're in grade 8."

"Yeah, but I would be in grade 10 if I hadn't been screwed around when I was in the boys' home."

"Are you going to act in the play?"

"No. Are you nuts? I'll work backstage."

The play was a comedy called *My Three Angels* and was about three convicts in an Australian penal colony. I did everything to catch Alice's attention, but she seemed taken by the actors and actresses rather than by the stagehands. Part way through rehearsals, one of the actors took a tantrum and quit. He was playing the role of Paul, a despicable wimp who got to do a passionate love scene with the leading lady. I stood in for the afternoon rehearsal just to read the lines while some of the drama members scoured the school for a new Paul.

"If you only knew how much I ache for you, how much I desire you," I said flatly.

"Oh, for Christ's sake, give me a break!" the director yelled. "If you had a girlfriend would you talk to her like that? 'If you only knew how much I ache for you . . .' Sounds like you need to go to the toilet. Give it some feeling. I want feeling."

"Sir, I'm just filling in."

"I don't care. Make it real. Pretend she's someone you want, someone you desire."

I caught Alice smiling at me from behind the curtain. My heart fluttered and I poured my soul and youthful passion into the lines. "If you only knew how much I ache for you . . ." (I stressed "ache" and looked over towards Alice.) "If you only knew how much I desire you." (I put special emphasis on "desire".)

"That's it. That's it. You're Paul. We've got our Paul." The cast applauded. I couldn't believe what I had gotten myself into.

On the afternoon of the dress rehearsal, the grade eights and nines got to see the play for free. The first three rows were filled with pockets of rogues from the boys' side who had come to catcall my love scene. They had all heard that I had to kiss this gorgeous grade 11 girl passionately on stage. I was nervous as hell. Alice did my make-up and gave me a good-luck kiss on the cheek. It was all worth it, I thought.

The love scene was a triumph. I put everything I had into it and the guys gave me a standing ovation. In another scene I was supposed to read a will left by my recently deceased actor uncle, and someone in the cast had drawn a funny caricature of a nude woman on the make-believe document. I crushed the paper, slamming my hands together to stop myself from bursting out laughing on this supposedly sad occasion. In another scene I was supposedly bitten by a poisonous snake and was calling out for one of the three convicts to help me when everyone in the cast went blank.

"What are you staring at?" I ad-libbed. "I need help. I'm dying." I threw myself at the boy who had the next lines. "Say something, you fool. I've been bitten by a snake."

His lines suddenly came back to him. The play was a hit, but the party afterwards almost broke my heart. Alice, it turned out, had a boyfriend in first-year university.

CHAPTER

14

I passed out of grade 8 with marks in the eighties. I had proved I was no dummy and was promoted from 8-F to 9-C. My father was discharged from hospital in time for the summer break. I knew he would be okay for at least a month after the drying-out period and then things would get progressively unbearable. His intake of beer and pills would increase and the atmosphere at home would once again become tense. The mindless, angry confrontations between my father and me were what I dreaded most. Alone in my room, seized by vicious attacks of anxiety, I would close my eyes, grit my teeth, and wish to God he would drop dead and leave me alone. When I calmed down a tidal wave of guilt would leave me despondent for days. A typical scene between the two of us went like this:

"Victor! Get in here," my father yelled from the kitchen.

I dashed into the kitchen.

"What is it, Dad?"

"Wash the dishes."

"Lorne's here. I was just going out."

"I said wash the dishes."

"But I did them yesterday and the day before. What about Freddie or Peter?"

"Did you hear me or are you deaf? Wash the goddamn dishes! Or are you too smart now to wash dishes?"

"I'll go tell Lorne to wait."

"Do them now!" He slammed his fist on the table, knocking over a glass of beer.

"I'll wait for you outside," Lorne whispered from the doorway.

I turned and gripped the faucets tightly. I felt my father's cold stare piercing my back as I poured the detergent into the sink.

"I'm finished," I said, putting the last of the pots in the cupboard.

"Get me a beer."

"Dad, don't you think you should get some sleep?"

"Get me a beer!"

"Yes, Dad."

"Where are you going?" he asked as I placed the bottle in front of him. His eyes suddenly saddened. I knew he felt guilty for yelling at me. We had gone through the same scene so many times before.

"Out for a walk with Lorne."

"Don't come back late and don't get into trouble," he said calmly.

"Yes, Dad."

"Victor," he called as I was about to leave.

"Yes, Dad?"

"Don't you kiss your father goodbye any more when you go out?" he asked, smiling sadly. His eyes were glistening. Returning his smile, I leaned over and kissed him on the cheek.

"You know," Lorne said one day while we were sitting on a cement abutment atop the lookout on Mount Royal, "we'll be friends until we die."

"At least!" I replied. "You know, my grandfather's best friend made a pact with him when they were young Cossack soldiers in Ukraine that whoever died first, the other would dig his grave. My grandfather was eighty-nine when he died this year. I went to the cemetery after the funeral and this real old guy was standing near the grave covered in dirt and mud. My mother told me that old guy had spent the past three days digging my grandfather's grave. They both came over to Canada after the Russian Revolution and remained best friends for a long time. They hadn't seen each other in years, ever since my grandfather went into an old age home five or six years ago."

Lorne sat pensively for a moment. "That's really something. Let's make the same pact. Whoever dies first, the other will dig his grave."

Our pledge was sealed in a solemn handshake. Afterwards we strode along the streets as had become our custom, chatting about anything that crossed our minds.

"Ever make it with a girl?" Lorne asked.

"You?" I didn't want to show my hand first.

"No."

"Me neither. I came close though, but I blew it. Was I ever embarrassed."

"What happened?" Lorne asked, his curiosity piqued.

"Promise you won't tell anybody."

"I promise. I swear."

"And don't laugh."

"I promise. Come on. What happened? Tell me."

"You know that French chick who lives across the street. The blonde one. The fifteen-year-old one."

"No."

"You know her. Her name is Colette. The cock-teaser!"

"Oh, yeah."

"I was up in her house one afternoon this summer when her parents weren't home and we started necking. I was feeling her off and she didn't stop me when I started taking off her clothes. She didn't stop me when I took off my pants."

"What happened then?" Lorne's eyes were wide.

"I . . . ah . . . well, I came."

"What?"

"I came just as I pulled down my underwear. Man, was I embarrassed."

Lorne burst out laughing.

"Come on. It's not funny." Although I too was laughing.

"Man, would I ever like to get laid," Lorne said. "I'm tired of necking and petting and then going home and –"

"Whacking off," I added.

"I've got to find a girl who goes."

"Me too! Everyone I know grinds. They're always saving themselves for someone else."

On a crisp Saturday afternoon in November, I decided I wanted to be a star. Not a big star, just a local one. I thought I could dance pretty well. I got my mother to teach me rock-and-roll steps and I watched television dance shows to pick up the latest dance crazes like the Monkey, the Jerk, the Continental Shuffle, the Heat Wave, and so on. Lorne dug only the slow dances and had mastered the Grind.

"Lorne, let's ask Susan and Linda if they want to go with us to 'Like Young'." "Like Young" was a popular live weekly television dance show for teenagers.

"Are you crazy? I can't dance."

"So what? You can sit in the audience. I want to get on TV. I can dance better than half those turkeys."

"Naw. Let's go down to the pool hall."

"Come on. It'll be fun. Afterwards we'll go to the dance at Rialto Halls."

"What dance?"

"They're having a dance for the two goofs who do 'Like Young'. You know that turkey guy and that snob chick. It's free. We'll have fun.''

"All right. But I'm not going on the floor at 'Like Young'.''

Susan and I managed to make more than just a fleeting bid at local stardom. I'd figured we'd get caught by the roving camera a few times, so I'd told my parents to watch. I'm sure they were as surprised as I was when we won the dance contest.

"What's your names?'' a beaming hostess asked.

"Susan!''

I stared at the camera. "Ah . . . ah . . .''

"Victor!'' Susan said.

"And what high schools do you both attend?''

"Northmount High,'' my date said.

"Montreal High. I'm in grade nine.''

I was flying higher than a kite when the four of us left the CFCF television studios. We decided to walk home and save the bus fare. Lorne and I told our dates that we loved walking, which was true. Not too far ahead of us was a rough-looking gang of nine guys in their mid-teens. I knew at least five of them, so I gave them no thought. As we entered a railway underpass, I noticed four of them scale the wall. The other five stopped at the exit of the tunnel.

"Let's turn back, Lorne. I smell trouble,'' I said.

"The other guys are behind us, Victor,'' Susan said.

"Man, can you believe this?'' I said angrily.

"What's going on? What's happening?'' Lorne's date asked.

"Those jerks set us up. That's what's happening,'' I said.

"There's nine of them. What are we going to do? I'm scared. Are we going to get beaten up?'' Susan cried.

"There's nine, Victor,'' Lorne said, ripping off a fingernail.

"I can count. I swear if those guys try to take us, I'll go for the leader and tear his face apart. I swear it.''

"We're in for it, Victor,'' Lorne said.

Lorne really wasn't a fighter but he wasn't a chicken either. He simply avoided scraps by using diplomacy to get out of tight situations.

"Let the girls go by. We only want those two clowns,'' the burly, acne-covered leader commanded.

"Look, man, we don't want any trouble,'' Lorne said.

"Well you've got it! You two think you're so friggin' cool, eh? Well, we're going to find out just how cool you are,'' the leader snarled, combing back his greasy black hair.

"You guys know me. What's this all about?" I said, turning to four of the gang standing in front of us.

"You know how it goes, man," one of them said, shrugging his shoulders. He avoided my eyes.

"Well, I've got a proposition for you," I said, squaring off in front of the leader. "Back off or I swear I'll fix each and every one of you one by one. I'm not kidding. If it's a gang war you want, I'll make your gang look like a bunch of fairies. As for you, if you want a scrap, one onto one, that's okay by me, but as soon as any of your guys go in to help out, I'll scrap to kill you."

"Who the fuck do you think you are, King Kong?" The gang leader laughed, shoving me backwards a little.

"No. I'm Victor Malarek. That's who, and I'll be fucked if I'm going to let you push me or my friend around."

Two of the guys who knew me from the neighborhood pulled the testy leader to one side and whispered some words into his ear.

"Hey, man!" he called out in a wide grin, holding his hand out. "Why didn't you tell me you were in Weredale. Hey, you're cool with us, man. I guess we had you two mixed up with some other guys."

"Yeah, sure," I said, ignoring the outstretched palm. A path broke open to set us free.

"Man, that was close!" Lorne said, wiping his sweaty hands on his pant legs.

"You see those guys? The ones that we know from the neighborhood?"

"Yeah."

"I'm going to get even with every one of them. I hate double-crossing slime like that."

"Ah, leave it be, Victor. It's not worth the hassle."

The girls were frazzled and went home. We didn't even get to neck.

"I should get a baseball bat and go after those bastards," I said as we sat down on the front porch.

"Forget it, Victor. Let's get ready for the dance at the Rialto Halls. It should be starting soon."

"Man, I almost forgot about it."

The joint certainly wasn't hopping when we came through the door. There were barely thirty kids in the cavernous hall. Most of them looked like ginks, just the kind of kids who would be fan club members of those two goofy "Like Young" hosts.

"Let's go, Lorne."

"Naw. Stay a few minutes. You never know what might come in the door."

"Will you take a peek at those chicks coming in right now. Don't gawk! Act cool! Watch this, Lorne!"

I strolled over to a shy-looking girl with long, flowing brown hair. I blocked her path with my arm against the door. "Hi. You here alone?"

"No. My sister and her friend are with me," she said with a warm smile. "Can I get by?"

"Only if you promise to save a dance for me."

"Okay." She laughed and joined her sister.

It was just like in the movies. I heard bells and rockets going off in my ears. I was in love. Lorne told me I was nuts. When the first slow dance came on, I rushed over and asked the girl to dance.

"What's your name?"

"Anna."

"I'm Victor." My heart was pounding. My hands were sweaty. I was a nervous wreck.

"You want to hear something silly?" I said.

"I don't know. What?"

"I'm going to marry you one day."

Anna laughed. She didn't stay long. She was just passing by when she noticed the "Like Young" hosts getting out of a car outside and entering the hall. Anna was an Italian Catholic and she had a curfew, an early curfew.

"Do you want a milk shake or soda or something? I mean, your sister could join us. We'll go to the restaurant on the corner." I needed time to get up the courage to ask for her phone number.

"I'll ask my sister. But I can't stay out much longer. My parents are expecting us home by nine."

I was a little hungry so I ordered french fries and a Pepsi. She ordered a milk shake. I could have died when I threw a few chips into my mouth. They were hard and crunchy. The chewing noise was blowing my cool.

In the next months Anna and I dated on the rare occasion. Her sister, Angie, who was my age, tagged along. After all, Anna was only fourteen, although she looked and acted more mature. I was also the first boy she had ever dated. And we saw each other from time to time on the bus on the way to school. She went to D'Arcy McGee, a Catholic high school, which was a few bus stops away from where I got off for school.

"Man, do you believe this?"

"What?" Lorne asked.

"I'm going to have to wait at least four or five years before I can marry her."

"What?"

"I swear, Lorne, I'm going to marry her and you'll be my best man. Okay?"

"Fine with me. But I'm not going to get married until I'm forty."

My father's dictatorial whims, bolstered by pills and booze, continued to drive me crazy. One of his more peculiar orders was that the whole family attend church for the Ukrainian Orthodox Easter mass which began at 11 p.m. on Saturday and ended at dawn the following morning.

"I don't want to go," I argued with my mother. "What the heck for? Why does Dad want to go? He's not religious. He's just doing this to bug us."

"Your father wants to go to church. He wants us to go. Just be quiet and do it for him. It won't hurt. I just don't want to hear any more fighting," my mother begged.

"Jesus, Mom! You know I've got no use for churches and priests."

"Victor, do it for him. Fred and Peter have agreed to go. It will make him happy and it will keep him off your back."

"But Mom, you know how much I hate those hypocrites. Where was the church when we needed them? Where was the Ukrainian community? They stiffed us, Mom. They pretended we didn't exist. They turned their backs on you and they're still turning their backs on us. Look at us. The English give us welfare and the Salvation Army gives us a free turkey at Christmas. Come on, Mom. I don't want to hear all those hypocrite Ukrainian women talking about you behind your back. That's all they ever do. Let them find someone else to gossip about."

My mother's pleading eyes cut through me. "Okay, I'll go. But I'm going to stay at the back of the church."

"It'll be fun. We'll make a nice Easter basket for the priest to bless like we did when you boys were little children. Remember? We'll even color some Easter eggs. After church we'll come home and have a nice meal together."

The one thing I remember about the Ukrainian Orthodox church on 6th Avenue in Lachine is the smell. The air inside was steeped with the haunting fragrance of incense. I can still bring back that smell by simply closing my eyes and thinking about the church. A half-dozen chairs for elderly parishioners lined the walls of the quaint, tiny building. Everyone else had to stand. The altar was covered with old icons. It was here that my parents were married and my brothers and I were baptized. It was where the funerals were held for my grandparents and my mother's godfather.

My father's oldest brother, my uncle George, a short, fat man who loved sucking back beer from quart bottles, sat at the back of the church selling candles. Although I hardly ever saw him, I liked him. He was a heavy drinker who cried at the drop of a hat.

On this particular night, my uncle was in a silly mood. He kept snickering every time he looked over at me. I couldn't figure out why. I went to the washroom in the hall next door to check in the mirror to see if anything was wrong with my face. It was all right. When I returned, Uncle George broke into a muffled fit of laughter. He turned beet red trying to suppress it so as not to disrupt the service. I thought he'd choke himself to death. Then the answer came.

"Victor Malarek," a thickly accented voice summoned from the altar. I looked up and the priest, dressed in a heavy gold robe, motioned me to come to him. I didn't know what to do. I made a beeline for my mother.

"What's going on?" I whispered. I was frantic.

"Your father and your uncle George arranged for you to go to confession."

"What?" my voice squeaked. "I'm leaving!"

"The priest is waiting. Don't upset your father, Victor!"

"I'm going nuts, Mom. You know that? I'm going out of my mind!" I trudged over to the left of the altar where the priest was waiting. I didn't know what I was supposed to do. My eyes scanned the tiny room searching for the booth to confess in. There was none. The priest approached and asked me to kneel. As my knees touched the floor, he dropped down before me, throwing his robe over my head. Had I been aware that confession was heard in this manner in the Ukrainian Orthodox church, I would have ignored my mother's pleas and left.

"Victor, I have not seen you since you were little boy," he began.

"Me too! I mean, yes. I'm sorry about that."

"You should come to church. You keep God's commandments?"

"Some of them." I was sweating. His breath was heavy with the smell of garlic and it was turning my stomach.

"You have sinned?"

"Yeah . . . I guess so. From time to time."

"How have you broken God's commandments?"

"How? Yes . . . well . . . I get into fights. Things like that. You know." The priest gazed solemnly into my eyes, waiting for me to say more. Hesitantly, I continued. "And I, uh, mess around a bit . . . you know, with girls. But, I, uh, won't do it again!" Somehow, that sounded really stupid. I hoped the priest wouldn't ask for details.

"Victor, you should come to church on Sunday. It is only one hour for God. That is not too much to ask. You must try to obey His commandments. They are to guide you. I want you to stay here on your knees and pray to God to forgive your sins. Ask Him to give you strength . . . guidance."

"Yes, sir — father." Sensing that it was all over, I pressed two dollars into his hand. "My mother told me to give you this."

As soon as the priest disappeared behind the altar to prepare for communion, I inched my way to the back of the church, keeping my head glued to the floor.

"Big joke!" I muttered to my uncle, who began chortling when he saw the vivid color of my cheeks.

The service ended several hours later. But, as I had feared, we didn't go straight home. My father wanted to talk to his brother and my mother got herself cornered by the local chatterboxes. I kept a safe distance to wait it out.

"Victor," my mother called. I went over to her.

"Yes?"

"You remember Mrs. Hanchuk and Mrs. Koshyk?"

"No." Mrs. Hanchuk and Mrs. Koshyk looked surprised and a little hurt that I didn't remember them. Why the hell should I, I wondered. They meant absolutely nothing to me. They certainly had never even sent our family so much as a Christmas card or an invitation to anything since we'd left Lachine in 1956.

"I remember when you were so high," Mrs. Hanchuk said, bringing her hand down to her knees. "You and your brothers were so adorable, so cute."

"Yeah, I know," I said blandly.

"What are you doing now?" Mrs. Koshyk asked, looking down the bridge of her beak-like nose at me.

"Victor is —" my mother began.

"I'm just finishing off first year at McGill. I'm majoring in biochemistry and physics." Their mouths dropped. I knew they were impressed. After all, where did a Malarek get so much brains? I decided to embellish my standing a little more. Anyway, why not have some fun at their hypocritical expense? "I was awarded two scholarships last year. All my expenses are paid for because I scored the highest marks in my matrics in chemistry and trigonometry."

"My, my. You must be smart boy!" Mrs. Hanchuk said.

"Yeah, I study hard but I must admit science does come rather easy for me. I guess I have my mother's brains as well as her good looks. Mom, did you tell them I'm being considered to go into medicine next year?" She didn't answer. She just stood there smiling passively. I could tell from her eyes she was confused and annoyed. "I wanted to go into electronics like my older brother, Fred. But one electronic technician in the family is enough. Well, nice to have met you. Dad's calling for us to go, Mom, and you know I have my biology exams this week."

The women scanned each other's Easter baskets to see what booty lay in them. They were looking to see who had the most colorful and artistic Ukrainian Easter eggs. My mother blushed. All she had in her basket were bland, dyed eggs we had dipped in red coloring. Mrs. Hanchuk and Mrs. Koshyk exchanged a pair of exquisite eggs. They acted as if my mother wasn't even there. After all, she didn't have anything of equal value to exchange. I knew she was hurt but I bit my tongue for her sake. As we got into the taxi, I glanced over at the cross in the churchyard. Families my parents had known for years were inviting each other over to their homes to break bread. We didn't get one invitation. Not even from my uncles.

15

Lorne couldn't understand why I was so reluctant to go up north to his family's rented summer cottage in the Laurentians. I hadn't gotten Camp Weredale out of my system and the north didn't hold much allure for me.

"We'll have fun," Lorne coaxed. "Come on. Let's go. My parents don't mind. They invited you."

"Lorne, I spent years having so-called fun up north," I said acidly. "Forget it."

"No, I mean real fun. There are lots of horny chicks up there."

"Girls? There's *girls* up there?" It had never dawned on me that there were anything but boys' camps in the Laurentians.

"What did you think I was going up there for? To swim? I'm going up there to have fun."

That Friday evening, after hitchhiking and getting a ride up in a Montreal *Gazette* newspaper delivery truck, we swaggered into a dusty soda-pop shop in a small Laurentian hick town to meet a couple of chicks Lorne had set us up with. He introduced me to Tina and Sharon, and the four of us went to Tina's cottage. Lorne got Tina, a well-developed sixteen-year-old blonde with bedroom eyes. She was a gentile. I got Sharon, a very cute fifteen-year-old blonde, who was Jewish. I spent all evening trying to talk her into going beyond necking and the odd feel while Lorne was in the adjoining room getting a hand job.

"Tomorrow we leave," I said, frustrated and a little jealous.

"Have I got good news for you. Let's go for a walk." As we got out of earshot of Tina's cottage, he said, "Tina goes."

"Lucky you. Mine grinds and that's it. Thanks. You take the best. You call yourself a friend."

"I *am* your friend. Tina's got another friend that goes. Her name is Elaine. She goes to your school."

"So what!"

"So what? So Tina's going to set it all up for next Friday night. That's what. We're going to get laid!"

"Far out!"

I doused lots of Jade East all over my face, chest, and armpits. I even rubbed some on my underwear. I wanted to smell good. I was so excited I had trouble walking.

"You ready, Victor?" Lorne asked, poking his grinning face into the washroom.

"Yep!"

"Fuck! You smell like a whorehouse."

"Drop dead! It's Jade East. That stuff's cool. Girls love it."

"Tina's got her place for tonight until eleven when her mother gets home from work. Come on, let's move."

"Where's her father?"

"He's dead. Come on."

"I hope this Elaine broad goes."

"Yeah, she goes. Tina told me she does."

"What if she doesn't with me?"

"She will. She will. Come on. Is something bugging you?"

"Well, remember what I told you about when I blew it with that French chick?"

"What are you talking about?"

"I might come before I get in."

Lorne laughed. "You're crazy. Anyway, I got a remedy for that. A guy told me to drink a glass of Crisco Oil and you won't come for hours."

"Bullshit."

"No. It's true. I drank a cup before I left home."

Before leaving the house, I took two gulps of Crisco Oil from the pantry. I almost vomited.

"It better work, Lorne," I said, gagging.

Lorne giggled. "It will. It will."

Elaine looked like she went. She had just turned seventeen and she had brown frizzy hair, dark eyes, and big boobs. She wore a tight red mini-skirt and a tight white tee-shirt. Her smile said yes and I could hardly wait.

At Tina's house we all chatted for exactly twenty-two minutes. Beatles music played in the background. Then, as planned, Lorne took Tina by the hand, winked at me, and disappeared into her bedroom.

"You want to dance?" I asked as a slow song came on.

"Sure." Elaine rubbed her thighs into mine. I thought I would blow it right there. I almost came instantly.

We were into passionate necking and wild petting before the song was half over. I pulled her to the floor with my hands up the back of her tee-shirt fumbling for the clasp of her bra. I couldn't find it.

"It's on the front," she whispered.

"What?"

"You undo it from the front."

"Oh . . . yeah . . . I knew that." My ice-cold hands fondled her big breasts.

"Oooh, they're cold."

"I'll warm them up," I panted, removing my hands and rubbing them briskly together.

She giggled and began to peel out of her clothes. I almost blew it again when she undid my zipper. Damn, I cursed to myself, that oil isn't going to work. I'll kill Lorne.

We were both naked. I hurriedly dove on top of her. In and out four times, and it was over. I was in ecstasy. I had finally made it. I was no longer a virgin. Elaine was pissed off.

Forty-five minutes later, Lorne and Tina tiptoed into the room. Elaine and I had just completed another more successful engagement.

"Well . . . well . . . what do you say?" Lorne asked as we bounced along the sidewalk.

"You turkey. Crisco Oil doesn't work."

"I know," Lorne shot back and took off down the street roaring.

After just one month in grade ten, Lorne and I talked ourselves into being totally fed up with school, teachers, and the system. We struck on a better idea. Drop out and join the U.S. Marine Corps. We hopped a Greyhound bus to Plattsburg, New York, and marched into a recruiting office. We'd seen *Iwo Jima* and were eager to emulate John Wayne. I thought that the recruiting sergeant was definitely cool in his uniform, but I wasn't too keen on the Weredale-style crew cut. Lorne went prepared. He'd had his locks sheared in order to make the best possible impression. I never played my bets until I knew what the score was, so I'd kept my hair long.

I got as far as filling out the application and getting fingerprinted before my mother intervened with a vengeance. She flatly and irrevocably refused to sign the consent form. Lorne and I were both seventeen and we needed our parents' signatures.

"I'll shoot you myself before I let you go to war," my mother said.

"I'm not going to go to war. I'm just joining the Marines."

"What the heck do you think is happening in Vietnam? That's a war, and if you're in the Marines, you'll get sent there. You're not going. Get that out of your head, and you tell that friend of yours to stop putting stupid ideas in your head. Look what the war did to your father. Ask him about the army and war. He'll tell you about it. Go and ask him. As far as I'm concerned, you're not going."

Lorne's will was far more resolute than mine. He was relentless in his quest. He threatened, argued, cajoled, pulled tirades, and ran away from time to time. His haggard and heartbroken parents couldn't take any more and finally signed the documents. A few weeks later, their only son was packing his bags.

I never believed Lorne would go without me. I tried to persuade him to drop the whole thing, but he was determined. I felt desperate at losing my best friend.

"Come on, Lorne. You'll get sent to Vietnam. Man, you could get killed."

"I want to go, Victor. I have to go."

"You don't *have* to go. Don't give me that patriotic shit. You're Canadian."

"It's not that. You know what I mean."

"Lorne, wait till I turn eighteen in June. We'll go together. My mother won't sign and she told my father if he did, she'd leave him for good. Come on, man. It's only eight months the most."

"I can't wait. I got my papers for boot camp. Anyway, who knows what will happen by then. I really want to go, Victor."

"Doesn't our friendship mean anything? You're my best friend. The only really best friend I ever had. I don't want to lose that friendship. It's important to me."

"It's important to me, too. You'll always be my best friend. We'll be best friends forever. I know that. It's just that I got to do this. I can't wait."

I hated Lorne at that moment. I felt our friendship would end once he got on the bus. He would find new buddies in boot camp and I would be left alone in Montreal. I was seething with jealousy, envy, and anger.

Before Lorne left, I threw a farewell bash in his honor. He didn't have many friends, so I invited the in crowd at Montreal High and everyone I knew in the neighbourhood. The word went around that this would be a party to remember. Sixty-odd people showed up toting bottles of booze and cases of beer. A few guys brought some marijuana.

The party was talked about for months and I garnished a reputation for throwing the greatest parties in the entire high school. My mother managed to get my father out of the house that evening so we could have the place entirely to ourselves for at least five to six hours. Fred played disc jockey with his impressive collection of rhythm and blues 45s, and I spent the evening drifting from girl to girl trying to determine who would go. A little after 1 a.m., my parents returned, and within seconds my father was hollering for me. I was busy in Peter's room, grinding and breathing heavy. I fell off the bed when I heard my father's voice outside the door.

"Victor! I can understand kids wanting to neck and feel each other up, or do whatever the hell they want to do at your age. I don't mind finding couples in the closets and I didn't even mind that there were kids in my bedroom. I don't even care that there was a couple in the pantry. But when I need a leak I draw the line! Could you get the couple in the toilet out of there for a few minutes so I could have a leak?"

Thank God, he's in a good mood, I thought. The problem this time was my mother. She didn't say anything in front of the kids, but if looks could kill, I knew I was in for a sound lecture the following morning.

Next day, Lorne and I gripped each other's hands at the bus terminal. We hugged. The lumps in our throats kept the conversation to a few grunts. A part of me tore out of my chest when the Greyhound coach roared out of the parking area on that cold, wet November morning.

Occasionally I was summoned to see Gold, the probation officer, by either a phone call or a letter. He was a zealot in his job and a glutton for handing out tedious sermons. He had me labelled as a bully and never let up reminding me that one day some little kid would teach me a lesson. I could never understand where Gold ever got the idea I was a bully. The scraps I got into were never with weak kids. I wasn't a hardrock and I certainly didn't walk around the schoolyard looking for fights. A lot of guys in Montreal High thought they were tough and wanted to prove it. If they tried to prove it on me, I'd fight back, no matter what their reputation was. I made sure everyone knew I wasn't to be picked on no matter what.

Gold got on my nerves because he never talked to me. Instead, he growled, yelled, threatened, snarled, and raved. After each and every unsettling encounter I would complain to my mother.

"Just listen to him, Victor, and don't get angry."

"But Mom, he's driving me crazy. I can't stand when he yells at me. I get enough of that from Dad and from some of those stupid teachers at school. He's on a power trip."

"Victor, just listen and for God's sake don't blow up at him. It's not for long." My mother was afraid of rocking the boat. She was afraid of the authorities; she had lost us twice before and she believed they held the power to take us away again.

Sometimes I found myself counting my lucky stars that Gold was my probation officer when I saw what some of the other guys got stuck with. I knew one probation officer was definitely a predatory homosexual. I swore if I ever got that queer on my case I'd kill him. I knew he probably wouldn't try anything with me because I was too old and I had a reputation as a street fighter. There was another who was usually piss-drunk by lunch time. A third read proverbs from the Bible to his bored charges. These were the front line of the juvenile-care system.

"Malarek!" Gold shouted as I waited one day in the anteroom to his office.

I jumped up and glared at him. I hated when he sneaked up behind me and shouted into my ear.

"Get into my office."

I followed him in and sat down in front of his cluttered desk.

"Stand up! Where do you think you are? At home? Well, you're not at home. You are in my office. Show some respect. Get up! Wait until you're asked to take a seat."

I deliberately got up as slowly as I possibly could, refusing to meet his leering stare or play his silly game. Gold sat down and continued eyeballing me. I didn't flinch. I was used to his tactics, and although his bug eyes annoyed me, there was no way I was going to let him know he was getting to me.

"Fighting again, eh, Malarek? Mr. Tough Guy is at it again. Aren't you? I told you, one more fight and I would put you in detention. Didn't I? As a matter of fact I am going to put you into detention. How does three days sound? I could do it with a flick of my finger," he said, snapping his fingers. "All I have to do is pick up the phone and call the judge. What I say goes. The judge listens to me. Whatever I recommend goes. You realize that, don't you?" He paused for a second and leaned over his desk towards me. "Do you have anything to say for yourself, Malarek?"

"No," I answered calmly. I didn't know what to say for myself. I didn't have a clue of what he was talking about. Anyway, I was positive he was playing another one of his games because I hadn't been in a fight for quite some time.

"Sir, damn it! Sir when you address me," he ordered, tossing a thick file on his desk.

"Sir," I muttered.

"I used to break hardrocks like you in half when I was your age. Bullies we used to call them then. You are a bully, Malarek. You pick on little kids. You prey on weaker boys. You are a bully. But you don't scare me. Try to bully me. Go ahead. Try. I'll break you in half. I'll throw you in detention. Well, Mr. Bully, don't you have anything to a say or are you going to try and bully me?"

My stomach was churning acid.

"Can you give me any reason why I shouldn't put you in detention for three days?"

I didn't answer. There was a long pause. Reaching for the file folder, Gold said, "I'm going to give you a test, Mr. Bully Malarek, and if you pass it, and it's going to be a tough one, I won't put you in detention. Sit down!"

I sat down.

"Stand up!"

Before I was on my feet, he ordered me to sit down again.

"Stand up!"

Again I stood up, and again he ordered me to sit down. I didn't budge on his last command.

"I said, sit down!"

I hesitated and sat down. Gold got up slowly, glaring right into my face.

"Do you see that kettle on the filing cabinet?" he snarled.

I nodded.

"Plug it in."

I obeyed.

"Now sit down." Gold didn't say a word until the water started to boil. He just sat at his desk acting as if he was writing important notes on some forms.

"The water is boiling."

"Yes, sir."

"So unplug the kettle!"

Again I obeyed.

"There is a cup beside the kettle. Place one teaspoon of coffee in it, one teaspoon of sugar, and a little Carnation milk. That's right. Now, pour in the water."

I placed the cup in front of him and sat down. Gold cleared his throat.

"Well?" he asked.

"Well, what, sir?"

"Do you leave the jar covers off at home?"

I took a deep breath and corrected my blunder.

"Well, Malarek, you passed, but barely. You're very lucky. Had you failed, I would have had no other alternative but to send you to detention for three days. You can go home now. I'll see you in a few months. And stay out of fights!"

"Victor! Victor! Wake up," my mother screamed.

"What . . . what is it, Mom?" I said, leaping out of bed. My heart was racing.

"Your father! He fell on a glass. He cut himself badly. He's on the kitchen floor bleeding."

I was in the kitchen before she finished. "Dad . . . Dad! Mom, call the cops! Just dial zero. Hurry! God, look at all the blood. Dad! Christ, he's going to die."

I rolled my father onto his back. His eyes were fogged. He was unconscious and barely breathing. His skin was cold, damp, and sickly pale. A jagged piece of glass was buried deep into his wrist. Blood was gushing from a severed artery.

"Oh God, why? Why the hell does he have to drink so much and take all those friggin' pills?" I looked up. Gillis, who had run away from Weredale and had been living with us for a while, was standing petrified in the doorway. "Don't just stand there, Gillis! Get me a towel. Move!"

He bolted down the passage to the closet and scrambled back with a bundle of white towels. Fred knelt down and tied a tourniquet tightly around my father's wrist to stop the bleeding.

"Mom, are the cops coming?"

"Yes, Victor. They're coming."

Peter was staring wide-eyed from the kitchen doorway as my mother threw down towels to soak up all the blood on the floor.

"Gillis, get out and get the cops in here fast. Christ, where the hell are those bastards when you need them?" I shouted.

Tires screeched outside. Two policemen, dragging a stretcher behind them, rushed into the house.

"We got to get him to the hospital quick. Please hurry!" I pleaded.

The older-looking police officer knelt over my father.

"The stretcher . . . the stretcher," he signalled to his partner.

"Take him to the Veterans' Hospital. They know his case there," my mother instructed. "Victor, you go with them."

While they eased my father onto the stretcher, I raced into my room and tugged on my jeans. Grabbing a shirt, I shot into the street and hopped into the back of the ambulance. Gillis followed frantically behind, pulling up his pants over his pyjamas. The ambulance squealed off, sirens blaring. Two attendants in white met the ambulance at the hospital ramp and pulled the stretcher through the emergency doors. An elderly nurse stopped me at the entrance.

"Are you related to the patient?" she asked calmly.

"Yeah . . . yes, he's my father."

"I'll need some information from you then."

"In a minute. I've got to see how he is."

"He'll be fine. The doctors will take care of him. There's nothing you could do for the moment except give me the information I need."

"He's lost a lot of blood! He needs help."

"He'll be all right. He's in good hands now. Now come with me for a few minutes."

After ten minutes of answering questions while she typed the answers on an admittance form, I joined Gillis in the waiting room.

"Any word? Anybody come out of there yet?"

"No," Gillis replied nervously.

"Take it easy, Gillis. He'll be okay. He's not ready to die yet," I said, trying to reassure myself.

I started pacing up and down the corridor. An hour passed and still no word. My hands were shaking and I was sweaty. My fingernails were chewed and ripped to shreds. An orderly appeared in the centre of the waiting room.

"Are you Victor?"

"Yes!"

"Your father is asking for you. Come with me."

I went with the solemn-looking orderly, trying to quicken his pace as we marched through the corridors. Suddenly his words hit me! What did he mean by my father is asking for me? My heart raced. My God, he's dying. Don't let him die, I prayed. The orderly drew back a long white curtain as we entered a small room. My father, his skin almost grey, lay on a narrow examining bed. A bottle of blood hung over him feeding the dark red fluid into his arm.

"Dad . . . Dad," I whispered, tiptoeing to his side.

He slowly opened his eyes and stared curiously at me.

"Victor?"

"Yes, Dad. Are you okay?" My voice was trembling.

"I'm fine. The doctor said I have to stay here for a little while. Will you visit me?"

"Sure, Dad. You know I will. Every day, I promise." His eyelids closed. He was out cold. I kissed his cool cheek and turned to the orderly.

"Where's the doctor?"

"Right here," he said, coming into the room. "He'll be all right. A minute or two longer and it might have been a different story. That was a bad cut. He lost a lot of blood. We'll be keeping him in the hospital for a few weeks to dehydrate him. I see he's been drinking a lot again."

I looked over at my father. He was lying very still, but breathing evenly. His face was contorted and wet. He looked troubled and sad. His right hand, buried in a thick gauze bandage, lay motionless across his chest. A lump choked my throat. Goddamn, rotten, son-of-a-bitch life, I cursed.

My father was home for Christmas, and soon after, he was back to heavy pill-popping and beer-drinking. All our nerves were raw. My mother talked in whispers to Fred, Peter, and myself about leaving him again. She said we were old enough to make our own decisions about what we wanted to do. She was afraid of my father's violent, uncontrollable outbursts when he was smashed.

"I don't know what he's going to do one day. I'm afraid for you boys," my mother tried to explain to me.

"I know, Mom. But I can't leave him alone. He'll kill himself."

Fred managed to steer clear of my father by leaving early and coming home relatively late. On weekends, he was rarely around. His television and radio electronics night course had finally paid off. He got a job at Northern Electric and was earning good bucks. Peter played hooky a lot and ran away from home on occasion. Once he ended up in Halifax and other times in Quebec City, Winnipeg, Calgary, Vancouver, and twice in Toronto, surfacing when he was destitute, very hungry, and homesick for my mother. On his flight to Quebec City, he decided to return home in style in a taxi. He and a Weredale runaway faked a call home to satisfy the sceptical cab driver that the fare would be paid. Three hours later, my father told the ranting cabbie where he could shove the $65 fare.

I tried to handle the verbal abuse my father dished out the best I could. I was his vent, his frustration valve, and no matter how upset and tense he was, I remained loyal. For me the hardest thing was having no one to talk to. At least when Lorne was around I could bounce my frustrations off on him. Now I felt very alone.

16

*M*y new friend Steven Miller was full of himself. He bragged incessantly about his exploits with the opposite sex. Girls swooned over him, or at least that's what he kept telling me. I didn't believe most of what he said. He had this curious habit of glancing upwards whenever he recounted an adventure, which confirmed my suspicions that he was more brag than action. We had met through our mothers, who in turn had met while shopping. They thought it would be nice if we became friends. Miller was okay, someone to hang out with while Lorne was away. We both liked going to dances and he was a bit of a zany character.

"Hey, man, what you up to?" Miller asked as he swaggered into my bedroom.

"Not much."

"Hey, there's a dance at Querbes Academy. Maybe we'll meet a couple of broads. You know how horny those French broads are."

"Is that all you ever have on your mind? Can't you ever just go for a simple walk?"

He thought for a second, pursed his lips, and replied jokingly, "Sure, let's get a couple of chicks and go for a walk up to Mount Royal tonight."

"And feel them off. Right?"

"I don't only feel them, man, I lay them," he said, gazing up towards the ceiling.

"Sure you do, Steven. You're so full of it."

"Yeah, well, you want to go or not?"

"Where?"

"To the dance, dummy."

"I don't know. I'm not in a very good mood."

"Well, the dance will get you in a good mood. Think of the chicks, man. Come on, your brother Fred's already gone there. I met him with Lloyd on the street about ten minutes ago. They said there were three chicks to every guy."

"All right, let's go."

The dance had regressed to a grinders' pit by the time we got there and paid our fifty cents. There were plenty of girls.

"Malarek! Come here. Come here! Listen to this line. Bonjour chérie! Voulez-vous danser avec un beau jeune homme comme moi? If not, you'll be missing out on the chance of a lifetime." Steven winked lasciviously.

"Quoi?" a petite brunette asked.

"You're nuts, Steven," I said, shaking my head and wondering why I tagged along with him.

The slow dances switched abruptly to rock and upbeat rhythm and blues. After a couple of numbers, I joined in with a group doing the latest craze, the Monkey, which I was pretty good at. During the dance, I noticed a cute French girl staring at me, and when I smiled, she giggled. Next set of slows, I mused.

"Allo! Veux-tu danser avec moi?"

"Eh, you speak French?"

"Un peu. You speak English?"

"A little."

"What's your name?"

"Marie."

"Mine's Victor."

"I like that name."

"Yeah, well I like you." What a stupid line, I thought, but she seemed to like it.

We danced, and after the record finished, she disappeared into the crowd. Steven came running up to me.

"Hey, Victor! Man, did my broad ever grind! I'm sure she goes."

"With you, man, every broad goes."

"Listen, can I bring her to your home later? My father's probably smashed by now and you know what a prick he's like when he's drunk."

"I don't know about bringing her to my place. My father's in a weird mood."

"Say, where's that sharp broad you were dancing with?"

"Over there talking to those two guys."

"She looks like a real cock-teaser. Hey! Dylan, 'Like a Rolling Stone'. Now that's the kind of long slow I like. See you." Steven darted off in search of a grind.

I walked up to Marie and tapped her on the shoulder.

"Marie?" She wore a teasing smile.

We danced very close but I felt somehow that she wasn't really into it. She was probably winking away to her friends and thinking she was too much, I thought. Still, I was getting turned on to the way she pushed her thighs into mine.

Someone bumped into me but I paid no attention. I was too involved in Marie. I was bumped a second time, then again. Three times! I had learned that that was where coincidence ends and trouble begins. I spun around just in time to block a flying fist.

I kicked my assailant between the legs. He dropped to the floor shrieking and holding his crotch. One of his friends rushed to his rescue and Fred rushed to mine. The unfortunate teenager careened to the floor, cupping a bleeding nose.

"Let's get out of here, Vic!" Fred shouted.

"Yeah, I guess so!" I said. "I think I've been set up. Steven, let's go!"

Five guys blocked the path outside the school. I was right. The fight was a set-up. I felt a surge of intense hate and anger boil violently inside me. The only thing I could think of was fixing all those bastards blocking my getaway, fixing them good.

"Get out of the way, pepsi!" I demanded.

"Quoi?"

"You don't understand English? Move!"

"Hey, Vic! There's only five. We could take them!" Steven said.

"Yeah, sure, stupid, and about a dozen more behind us, you jerk!"

"I'll take the rock with the suede jacket," Fred yelled, singling out the leader of the pack.

The fight began. I hit my first target as hard as I could, landing a vicious blow smack on his nose. I felt it snap under my knuckles. He fell to the sidewalk. One guy tried to kick me but lost his balance on the ice and fell. I went wild and started to kick at his head with my boots.

"Vic, look out!" Lloyd screamed.

I swung around. Three guys inched their way towards me, each with a makeshift club in his right hand.

"Vic! Watch it!" my brother yelled. I ducked and looked up a split second later to see a bloodied head crumple to the pavement. I knew right away that the boy was badly hurt. Sirens echoed up the street.

"The cops! Run!"

I tore off down the street but didn't get far. After a harried chase, a panting cop cornered me in a laneway. For all the exercise I gave him, he repaid me with a few slaps in the face before dragging me to a waiting squad car.

"Wipe off that smug expression, punk! You might be up for murder!" a detective ordered as I was being led into a nearby police station.

I felt my stomach turn to acid. My knees went weak.

"You're lying!" I countered defiantly.

"Oh, I'm lying? Tell him, sergeant. Tell the punk all about it."

"We brought a boy to the hospital. He wasn't breathing. His face was green. His skull was fractured," the sergeant said.

"Why did you hit him over the head with a bottle?" the detective asked in a harsh voice.

"I didn't hit anybody with a bottle!"

"If you didn't, punk, then who did?"

"I don't know!"

"Bad memory, eh? Who was with you?"

"No one!"

"We were told you came in with a gang of at least ten guys to break up that dance."

"That's a lot of bull! I was alone."

"You know, if the kid dies, you'll be charged with manslaughter."

I was terrified, but I wouldn't stool. I couldn't stool. Weredale had taught me not to squeal on my friends. My father had taught me never to squeal on my brothers.

"Put him in the cell for now," the detective told a constable.

I was escorted to the back of the building where the holding cells were. The constable opened the main door and led me into a small room housing three cells. He put me in the first one and locked the door. About half an hour had passed when I was ordered to accompany another cop. He led me to the same room where I had been questioned earlier. I was shocked to see Steven there.

"What are you doing here?"

"I didn't want to see you take the rap alone. So I gave myself up. I stick with my pals."

"You're a friggin' nut, you know that?"

"Shut up!" the cop shouted.

The detective who had questioned me earlier walked in. "Well, he won't die. He's regained consciousness but the doctors still don't know if he'll not suffer from some sort of brain damage."

"Who won't die?" Steven asked, his eyes riveting on me for some kind of a clue.

I felt relieved but still very weak inside.

"His parents, and I agree they should, are thinking of pressing attempted murder charges. Now, once again, if you didn't hit the boy with the soft-drink bottle, who did?"

"Look, I don't know! Honest. I was too busy fighting with some other guy and watching out for my own head. There were three or four of them coming at me with clubs in their hands. I don't know who hit that kid. I swear."

"Did you do it?" the detective asked, turning to Steven.

"No, sir. Honest, sir. I didn't do it, sir. I didn't. Honest! I swear."

"All right, shut up. I guess you don't know who did it either?"

"No, sir. Honest. I swear. I don't know. Honest!"

"What are you? A broken record?" The detective stared coldly at me. I refused to squirm.

"Your mother is here," he said after a while. "She's in my office. She told me your father's dying of cancer. He's a veteran. Is that right?"

"Yes." I stared at the floor.

"You should be ashamed of yourself. I spoke to your mother. She's a fine lady. You don't deserve her. Tomorrow you go to juvenile court for assault and disturbing the peace. I'm going to let you go home with your mother, only because she's a nice woman and your father's sick. Otherwise I'd have you locked up in the juvenile detention centre. You'd better think about the guy you're protecting. You're in enough trouble yourself without that on your hands. You broke one boy's nose, another boy's jaw is broken, and someone else has six stitches on the side of the face. If their parents sue, your parents will have a lot of money to pay!"

"They won't get one cent out of them! Those frogs started the fight and they got what they deserved. Let them try and collect."

My mother, looking completely devastated, was waiting at the front desk. Her eyes were swollen and glassy. I felt terrible. We walked home quietly, neither one of us saying a word. When I got home, I locked myself in my room and lay down on the bed, forcing every thought out of my head.

The next morning, I left home for juvenile court and went directly to my probation officer's office.

"Mr. Gold?"

"Why, hello, Victor. Do you have an appointment with me today?" he asked cheerfully.

"No, sir."

"Then what are you here for?"

I hesitated. "I got into a fight over the weekend and have to appear in court this morning."

"Another fight!" he snapped angrily. "Well, obviously, you weren't beaten up. Who did you beat up?"

"A few guys. Some of them got hurt pretty badly. I didn't start it."

"You never start it," Gold added caustically.

"I didn't start this one, sir." I recounted the story to him and as I talked, he grew angrier and angrier.

"I'm afraid we're going to have to do something about you. Maybe a few days in detention is what you need. I cannot permit this to go on any longer. What time do you appear before the judge?"

"At ten."

"I'll see you in court. Now, get out of my office."

I was seething. I knew then I should never have tried to explain anything to Gold. He never listened to me. He had his mind made up about me long ago and nothing I could ever say would change it.

I sat in the waiting room outside the judge's chambers for about an hour before my name was called out. I entered the courtroom with my head slightly bowed and avoided looking into the judge's eyes.

"Well, Victor. It seems you were a busy boy over the weekend, what with smashing a few heads about. What do you have to say for yourself?"

The matter-of-fact question caught me off guard. What do I say? I thought. I was confused. "Well, sir. I didn't start it and I didn't want anyone to get hurt. It just happened that way," I blurted out.

"Where are the boys he fought with?" the judge asked the court clerk.

"They're not here, your honor."

"They should be. Have them here for next week."

"Yes, your honor."

"I don't know what to do with you until then, Victor. Put you in detention or let you go home? You've gotten yourself in pretty serious trouble this time. Mr. Gold has recommended I put you in detention for three days. What do you think, Victor?"

"Your honor, I have exams this week at school and if I miss them I'll flunk my year. I promise I won't get into any trouble."

The judge gazed thoughtfully at me from his pulpit. "Very well. Stay out of trouble and I'll see you here next Tuesday morning at ten o'clock."

I left the courtroom feeling convinced that Gold would push to have me sent to training school. On my way home I decided to stop in at the Balfour pool hall on St. Laurent Boulevard and shoot a couple of games to settle my nerves. I was just about to break up the balls when a guy came up to me.

"Hey, aren't you Malarek?" a lanky, tough-looking guy with black greasy hair asked.

"Why? What's it to you?" I knew the guy from somewhere but I couldn't place him. I wondered if at some point we had fought and he was out for revenge.

"Weren't you in Weredale?"

"Yeah. Why?"

"Right! Man, you ever grow! I'm Marino."

"What do you say?" I said, grabbing his outstretched hand.

Marino had a reputation in the boys' home of being a damn good street fighter, as well as a master locker thief. His deep, sunken, shifty eyes and pale complexion gave him a distrustful appearance. In the boys' home Marino had never bothered with me, or even once said hello to me. Now, four years later, it was as if we were long-lost buddies. Here he was, slapping me on the back and jokingly reminiscing about the good old days at Weredale.

"How's your brothers?"

"They're both okay. Hey, why don't you come over to my place? I bet Fred would like to see you."

"No, man. Not today. I'm trying to get some bread together. I want to split Montreal. Give me your address and maybe I'll drop by before I split."

I skipped school the next day and headed back to St. Laurent Boulevard to watch three movies at the Empire Theatre. When I got home, I went straight to my room. The only thought that tormented my mind was that I was going to be put away, sent to training school. I didn't want to be put away again. Three and a half years in Weredale were enough. The whole evening I was haunted by visions of being sent away until I was eighteen. Even though that was only a few months off, I knew I couldn't take being away from home again. I was sure my father would die while I was away. I buried my head in my pillow.

My mother woke me up around 8:30 p.m. "Victor, there's someone here to see you." She didn't seem too pleased. She had good instincts about people and she didn't like this visitor.

"Hi, man!"

It was Marino.

"Hi!" I said, rubbing my eyes. I hadn't really expected him to drop over. Frankly I hadn't cared if I ever saw him again.

"You want to go for a walk?" he asked. "I want to talk to you about an idea I got."

"Okay, I need some fresh air." I was still groggy.

"Where are you going, Victor?" my mother asked as I got to the door.

"For a walk, Mom."

"Stay out of trouble, do you hear me?"

"Yes, Mom."

As we walked the streets around Park Avenue and Bernard, I recounted the fight and my certainty at being put away. Marino listened intently.

"Man, you're in trouble! Big trouble. There's no doubt about it. That probation officer you got is out to put you away. You should get some money and split town until you're eighteen. When are you going to be eighteen?"

"In a few months. In June."

"You should take off until then. Then when you come back, they won't bother you. You won't be a juvenile any more. They won't give a crap about you."

"I don't get it."

"Look. I know a couple of guys who did the same thing. They were in worse trouble than you are with the juvenile court. They split and came back when they were eighteen. They're okay now. No one's bugging them. I did the same thing two years ago when I got nailed for shoplifting."

"Yeah, well I don't have any money to get out of town."

"Ever pull a score?"

"No, and I never will. So forget it!" I said bluntly.

"It's easy, man. It's over in a few seconds. It takes at least five to ten minutes for the cops to arrive. By that time, you're long gone."

"Forget it! I'm not into that."

"Think about it. I'll do it with you and we'll split the bread. I need a little bread to leave town."

"No. There's no way, Marino! Forget it!"

"Think about it. It's either being put away for sure or getting away for sure."

We walked in silence for a few blocks. My mind was numb. Marino glanced at me a couple of times, flashing a phony reassuring smile. When we got to Fairmount Street, he stopped.

"I need a package of cigarettes." We strolled down Fairmount to a variety store on the corner of Jeanne Mance. The rest happened in a few seconds. All I could remember vividly was Marino holding a knife to the terrified store owner's throat and yelling, "Get the cash, get the cash!" I was so scared I started to laugh and couldn't stop.

"Get the cash, you stupid idiot! Get the cash!"

I went to push the button to open the cash register and suddenly yanked my hand back. I hit the button with my elbow. "Fingerprints! I mustn't leave fingerprints," I thought. I scooped out all the bills and silver coins. Quarters, nickels, and dimes jangled across the wooden floor.

"Let's get out of here!" he shouted. He threw the trembling elderly Jewish shopkeeper bodily onto the floor and raced out. I was at his heels. We ran down Fairmount to St. Viateur and back to the safety of the crowds on Park Avenue.

"We'll stop at the Rialto pool hall and split the cash in the washroom."

"Marino, you're nuts! You're crazy!" I was pouring sweat. My heart was hammering in my chest.

"See how easy it was?" he cackled.

We went to the washroom in the pool hall and locked the door in the back stall, and I emptied my pockets. He began to count out the loot, slipping a few one- and two-dollar bills up his sweater sleeve when he thought I wasn't looking.

"Relax, man! We're in the clear," Marino said, handing me seventy-six dollars.

That evening and the rest of the next day were sheer horror for me. I went home and nervously put the stolen loot into the bottom drawer of my dresser and refused to have anything to do with it. I was sure that only bad could come out of spending stolen money. Every time the door-bell rang, or the intercom sounded in any one of my classes, I jumped up with a jolt, sure it was the police. During recess, I spotted a police cruiser outside the school and blanched. I was sure a fingerprint had been lifted from the cash register or a fallen coin and had been traced to me by now, or that my photograph had been taken by a hidden camera.

By Friday evening, I was ready to give myself up, confess, and turn in my share of the loot. But I couldn't. That would mean stooling on Marino and I couldn't do that. It wasn't in me, and if I did, I was sure he'd kill me. I wanted so desperately to talk to somebody, but I had no one. Lorne was away in the Marines. I couldn't tell my brothers; they might get pissed off at me one day and tell Mom.

"What do you say, Vic?" Steven asked, bursting into my room.

"Not much! What did the judge say to you in court?"

"Oh, I have to appear next Tuesday when the French guys go in to tell their side of the story."

"Did he ask you any questions?" I asked.

"Just if I knew who hit the guy with the bottle."

"What did you tell him?"

"I said I didn't know. I told him I was sure it wasn't you. I said you were too busy taking on three or four guys. I told him you didn't start the fight, that some little French cock-teaser set it up because you were English. I'm sure the judge believed me."

"Thank you, lawyer." I laughed nervously. Maybe he wasn't such a bad guy after all, I thought.

"Look man. Close the door. I want to talk to you about something."

He shut the door and sat down on the bed beside me. I spilled out the whole story about meeting Marino after my court appearance on Monday to the robbery on Wednesday. All Steven could say was, "Wow, how much did you get?" I knew at that point I'd made a big mistake in opening up to him.

My father knocked on the door.

"Victor."

"Yes, Dad."

"Your friend is here," he said, pushing open the door.

"Who?" He didn't have to answer. Marino was standing right beside him with a wide grin plastered on his face.

"Thank you, Mr. Malarek. We should go out together for a beer one day. I'll buy. You're really an okay guy."

"Sure. I'd like that." My father smiled and left.

"What do you want, Marino?" He knew by the sound of my voice that I was pissed off. I certainly hadn't expected or wanted to see him again.

"Hey, you're the guy who did the job with Vic!" Steven blurted out.

"What did you tell him for? Are you nuts or something?" Marino scolded. "You should learn to keep your trap shut."

"He won't stool. What do you want?"

"I need a little extra bread to leave town."

"You got your share. What the hell else do you want?"

"Hey, listen, man. I don't want your share. I was just thinking. I know this Greek who runs a store on St. Viateur just up the street on Hutchison. He takes in quite a lot of bread over the week and brings it home on Friday. He doesn't believe in banks."

"Forget it, man. That was my first and last job. That's it! No way!"

"Will it be easy?" Steven asked. I shot him a dirty look.

"Simple, man. But I need two guys. One as a lookout and one to grab the bread out of the cash register while I take care of the owner and get his wallet."

"How much money do you think you'll get?" Steven continued.

"Knock it off, jerk," I said, growing more and more impatient.

"A couple grand if not a little more. That's split three ways. What do you say, man?"

"I said forget it, Marino! I'm going to the dance at Devil's Hideaway tonight. Robbery is not my line."

"Go up to the Devil's Hideaway after the job. You'll have a good alibi, man. Everybody knows you up there. Your friend could be a lookout."

"Come on, Vic. I could use the bread for a motorcycle."

"Steven, are you nuts? Do you know how dangerous this is?" Marino then played his trump card.

"Well, I'm going to do it and if I get caught I'll be made to spill my guts out about the other job. You know then what will happen to you. You'll get sent to training school for sure or maybe even prison. Man, that would just break your parents' hearts."

"You wouldn't do that!"

"When the man wants you to sing, he makes you sing whether you want to or not. Like I said, I need two guys. Your buddy here is willing to be lookout. Now, how about it?"

"Come on, Vic!" Steven urged.

"Look, Marino, this is absolutely the last job! I'm not going to do any more and I mean it. Now this is it! After that, I don't want you to come around here any more. I mean it!"

"Yeah, man, I won't need any more bread after this. I'll leave town. You'll be cool, don't worry! I cased this place for the past three days."

Marino explained what we had to do. The store was only one block away from my house. He would go in first and get the owner out of the way. I was to walk in after counting to ten.

"He's a Greek. He won't be any trouble! You run in and hit the cash register. You, man," he said pointing at Steven, "keep watch across the street. If you see or hear any cops, hammer on the window and keep walking. Don't run! Walk!"

It was 8:30 p.m. and very dark out. When we got to the corner, Marino took a deep breath and nonchalantly entered the store. I felt like taking off and leaving him there but I knew he'd get back at me if I did.

"You're a real prick, Steven!" I said. I took a deep breath and walked in.

Marino was sitting at the counter drinking a Coke. All of a sudden, he lunged at the unsuspecting owner, grabbed him by the collar, and punched him in the head.

"You slimy Greek," he yelled. "You tried to feel up my sister when she came in here for a bottle of milk yesterday!" Marino jumped over the counter and pulled out a knife. The owner turned sheet white and started to wail like a foghorn. Marino went to kick him but slipped and fell when the chubby middle-aged Greek jumped out of the way. The Greek scrambled for the door, throwing containers of empty milk bottles in Marino's path to slow him down.

"Stop him, man!" Marino shouted.

I laid into the terrified Greek with every ounce of energy I had. He fell to the floor dazed. Marino rushed to him, put the knife to his throat, and dragged him into the back.

"Get the cash! Move it!"

I did as I was told. As I was scooping the money out of the till, Marino rushed out from the back room. There was something strange about his eyes. They were deathly cold.

"I got the wallet!" he said and bolted out the door.

I stood there frozen for a second and made for the door, leaving money scattered all over the floor. When I hit the street I could hear sirens. A police car was headed straight at me. I darted down Hutchison Street towards Fairmount. Then I heard someone yell, "Stop, police! Stop or I'll shoot!"

Two loud bangs like firecrackers exploded behind me.

"I can't let them catch me, I can't! Let them shoot me. I'll be better off dead!" I muttered to myself. I was terror-stricken. I reached Fairmount and headed towards Park Avenue. An unmarked car cut me off. A detective jumped out and tackled me. I looked up into my captor's face. It was the same detective who had interrogated me for the fight.

"You!" he said. "Your parents don't deserve an animal like you!" He pulled me up by the front of my shirt and threw me to the side of the car.

"Hands over the top and spread your legs, punk! Move!" He searched me, twisted my arms behind my back, and put handcuffs on my wrists. All energy drained out of me when I heard the clicking of the cold steel cuffs. It was the end of the line.

"They're too tight," I winced.

"Too bad, punk!" the detective replied, pushing me into the back seat of the car.

His partner started up the car and they sped with sirens blaring to the hold-up scene. The car screeched to a halt outside the store. A constable ran over to the detective, rattled off something in French, and darted back into the store.

"Did you have the knife, punk?"

"No. I don't know what you're talking about!"

"Don't tell me you're going to play stupid?" He turned sharply and smacked me across the face. "Who was the guy with the knife? I'm not talking bottles any more. I'm talking about a knife. The owner was stabbed, or are you going to protect this guy too? Was it the same guy with the bottle? How many were you? Speak up!" He smacked me again across the face.

"I was by myself!" I screamed.

"Pull into the lane," the detective instructed his partner.

"Now punk, who was with you? How many were you? Start talking!"

I didn't speak. The detective got out of the car, opened the back door, and dragged me out by the hair.

"Gee, he's trying to escape," he said to his partner and punched me in the mouth. I dropped to the ground and was kicked in the ribs. My mouth was oozing blood.

"Get up!" The detective hauled me up by the hair.

"Who was with you? Speak! I haven't got all fucking night, you little bastard. Who was with you?"

"I don't know their names. Honest! I don't know!" He smacked me again. My nose started to bleed.

"Oh, so there were more than two of you? Was it that guy who was in the fight with you? The guy who gave himself up?" The detective jumped into the car and radioed the police station for the name of the boy who was with me in the fight last Sunday.

"Steven Miller, residing at 630 Querbes, apartment 11," came the reply.

"Let's go!" he shouted to his partner and shoved me into the back seat. The car rounded the corner of Hutchison and Lajoie when the detective yelled, "There he is! Pull up alongside the punk."

The detective rolled down his window. "You, come here!" he called over to Steven.

Steven obeyed. He wore an innocent, curious expression.

"Yes, sir?" he asked calmly. "Oh, hi, Vic! What are you doing in there?"

"Were you with him tonight?"

"No, sir. Why?"

"That's funny. We have a signed confession by him that you committed an armed robbery with him and another fellow this evening.''

''I didn't pull no robbery, honest! I was just the lookout! I swear, sir!''

The detective hopped out of the car and placed my accomplice in the front seat.

''Who was the third guy, punk?'' the detective said, leering at me. I didn't answer and received an elbow in the chest.

''Who was he?'' Again I said nothing and was punched solidly in my stomach. I tumbled onto the floor trying desperately to catch my breath. Steven started to moan.

''Tell them, Vic! Tell them, Christ! The guy's name is Marino. That's all I know about him. He was supposed to meet us at the Devil's Hideaway to split the money. That's all I know. I only met him this evening. He's Vic's friend. I couldn't even identify him if I saw him again. Honest, sir! Please don't hit me. I'm telling you the truth!''

''What does he look like?''

''He's about six feet two inches tall. He's skinny and has black hair and a lot of pimples on his face. That's all I know,'' Steven whimpered.

''How old is he?''

''I don't know, honest! Maybe about twenty.''

''That's the guy we want. Could he identify him?'' the detective said, pointing to me on the floor.

''Yes, sir! I'm sure he could.''

''Pass me the radio,'' he said to his partner. ''This is Detective Gauthier. Send a squad car to pick up robbery suspect at Lajoie and Bloomfield. Also send a backup unit car to assist and radio Montreal police for assistance at the Devil's Hideaway on Jean Talon and Waverley.''

The squad cars arrived in seconds. Steven was taken out and put into one. ''Take him to the station. I'll question him later,'' Detective Gauthier said to a uniformed policeman.

''Now, punk! Who is this guy Marino. Some wop?''

''I don't know his full name. He's from the Rosemount area. I met him in the Rialto pool hall on Park Avenue yesterday,'' I lied.

''Now that's more like it. See how easy it was!'' the detective said with a menacing grin. ''Let's go to the pool hall.''

On the way, the detective wiped the blood from my face with a handkerchief and melted snow from the roof on the car. I was pulled out of the car and into the pool hall, where everyone was ordered not to move. A few of my friends were shocked to see me in handcuffs.

''Another scrap, Malarek?'' one of them asked. I didn't answer.

''Is he here? Come on. Come on. Is he here?''

''No.''

"Are you sure?"

"Yeah."

"Let's go."

Once in the car the detective radioed the police station. "Has Montreal been notified?"

"Yes, sir. Three cars are waiting for you at Jeanne Mance and Jean Talon."

"Thank you."

The sirens blared and we arrived at the Devil's Hideaway within two minutes. The detective left the car for a moment to explain the situation to the Montreal police.

"Okay, let's go, punk!" he said opening the door. "Now listen, this guy Marino is the one we want. We're not interested in juveniles. You cooperate and I'll put in a good word about you to the judge. All right, let's go."

At the entrance to the dance hall, I pulled back.

"Could you take these off? I have a lot of friends up there and –"

"You don't have any friends. Up," he said, waving towards the stairs. All activity had come to a complete standstill. The lights were on and the boys and girls were lined up on opposite sides of the wall. I was led onto the dance floor, handcuffed, with a dozen police officers surrounding me. I heard my name called out a couple of times.

"It's Malarek!"

"It's Victor!"

"Hey, it's Malarek!"

"Hey, Fred. It's your brother!"

Oh God! My brother's here!

"What's wrong?" Fred asked.

"I'm in a lot of trouble, Fred. You'd better get home."

"What kind of trouble?"

"Who's he?" the detective asked.

"His brother!" Fred answered defiantly. "What's it to you?"

"Another punk! Great family! Say goodbye to your brother, punk! He's up for armed robbery with assault and maybe even attempted murder."

Fred's face went pale.

"Is he joking?"

"No," I said. My eyes were watering. "Go home and tell Mom before he does." The detective yanked me away.

"Walk up and down the centre of the floor. If your pal Marino is here, point him out."

"He'll kill me if I stool!"

"You'll get worse from me if you don't!"

I trudged up the centre of the floor. The place was dead silent. Everyone's eyes were riveted on me. I didn't once look towards the girls' side nor did I look into anyone's eyes while scanning the line of guys for my main accomplice. My heart started to pound on the way back. I noticed Marino behind a black guy slightly taller than him. I quickly regained my composure and kept walking.

"He's not here," I said in a hoarse voice.

"Once more for good measure! You better not be lying. Move it!" Detective Gauthier warned.

I walked up and down one more time at a quicker pace. The detective thanked the police officers and led me back to the patrol car. In the car, he looked me straight in the eyes.

"Are you sure he's not in there?"

"Yes, I'm sure."

"Back to the station."

At the police station, I was relieved of all the contents of my pockets — a comb, a wallet, a key chain, and $365.25 in bills and silver.

"God, kids get a pretty good allowance these days!" one constable joked as the money was counted out at the front desk.

I was taken to a tiny interrogation room where I was soundly grilled for three hours.

"How many other robberies have you pulled?"

"This was my first! Honest!"

"If you say honest one more time, I'll tear your balls off, punk. You fit the description of three recent robberies in my area."

God! I thought. They know about the other robbery? "This is my first robbery, honest!"

The detective smacked me across the mouth. "Next time, it's your balls. How many break and entries you pull around here?"

"I . . . I never pulled any. I swear."

"Sure you did! Liar! You pulled a B & E two nights ago, didn't you?"

"No, this was my only robbery. The first I was ever in! Hon —" I caught myself in time.

"We have a confession for you to sign admitting the robbery and implicating your two friends. It'll go easier on you in court if you sign it."

"Nothing will go easy on me in court. Forget it!"

"How about if I change that to say we'll go easy on you if you sign it?" he said, rapping a knuckle on the top of my head.

I signed.

A constable escorted me to the cells and Steven was led away for interrogation. Half an hour later I was taken to the front desk, hand-cuffed to Steven, and placed in the back of a police car. It was 1:30 a.m.

"Where are we going?" Steven asked nervously.

"We can't keep you here. It's against the law," one of the constables said. "We're taking you to St. Vallier Detention Centre for Boys."

CHAPTER

17

The patrol car sped through the streets, its red cherry top flashing and siren wailing. It screeched to a skidding stop some minutes later in a dark laneway off Bellechasse Street between St. Denis and St. Vallier streets. The detention centre was a gloomy, forbidding seven-storey institution. Thick wire mesh covered the windows on the ground floor and all was black inside. Outside the wind had picked up considerably, whipping gusts of stinging ice pellets in every direction. The narrow walkway was slippery and difficult to manoeuvre handcuffed to someone else. At the rear receiving entrance, a solitary light bulb, shielded under a rattling tin shade, cast eerie shadows around the bolted metal door.

One of the policemen pressed the brass buzzer. The faint buzzing from within summoned a pair of clacking footsteps. A narrow slit in the door opened and closed in two swift jerks, followed by the sound of rattling keys and tumbling locks.

Once inside, we were ushered into the reception office. The room was divided in two by a long counter. Three men wearing grey uniforms sat around a rundown metal government-surplus desk cluttered with empty soft-drink bottles, coffee containers, and pizza cartons. Two weathered wooden desks, each topped with a battered manual typewriter, and a row of beige metal filing cabinets against one wall completed the furnishings.

We were ordered to stand against the wall while the police explained the particulars of Stevens' and my arrest to the guard in charge. The other three listened attentively. At one point in the dialogue, the talking suddenly stopped and all eyes turned and focussed on us. I ignored their drilling pupils and continued staring at the paint peeling off the ceiling.

After the cops removed the handcuffs, we were led down a dark corridor and into a room at the far end by a beer-bellied guard who kept shoving us forward every two or three steps to show us who was in charge. The room was large. At one end was a wooden table. Behind it were four steel racks with rows of green overalls and shirts stacked in neat little piles. We were ordered to stand in front of the table. The guard shouted something to us in French. We didn't understand.

"What?" I asked.

"Maudit anglais! Strip!" he shouted.

Slowly, Steven and I removed our clothes, placing each garment in a pile on the table until we were down to our underwear. The guard then leered at us and again shouted, "Strip!" We did.

"You!" he said, pointing his thick finger in my face. "Stand over here and put your hands over your head."

I did as I was told. I could feel my blood starting to boil.

"Turn around! Stop! Bend over!"

The body search over, he ordered me to face him, cover my face with my hands, and bend slightly over towards him.

"What for?" I asked.

"Cover your face with your hands and bend over towards me! No talking! Do as I say!"

The guard then began to spray my head, armpits, and pubic hair with disinfectant.

"Turn around and bend over!" He then sprayed my backside.

"Take a shower!" he ordered, waving his hands towards the other end of the room.

I started to walk naked to the shower closets, which were about twenty feet away. Three guards sat opposite the shower stalls talking to each other. The stalls had no doors or curtains, so I turned my back to my audience and started to wash.

"Turn around!" a skinny, bald-headed guard yelled.

I ignored the order and kept soaping myself.

A second later, a searing open-handed slap stung my back. I turned sharply with one thought in mind, to beat the hell out of that bastard, but I backed off when the other guards jumped up.

"Turn around when I say turn around! We have to see you're washing properly. Here you do what you are told!"

I was stepping out of the shower when one of the guards, who wore thick-lensed glasses and what appeared to be a cheap black toupee, said, "You didn't wash your parts!" I gnashed my teeth and returned to the shower stall. A towel was thrown at me when I was finished, while Steven, who was aware of what had just transpired, wiggled into the shower. He turned and faced the guards, lifted the soap with two fingers, showed it to them, and with slow, round strokes began to wash his penis and testicles, occasionally lifting his leg like a dog to give his audience a better view.

The guards said nothing. They seemed amused by the performance. When we had finished drying ourselves, we were issued green uniforms. Our street clothes were taken away. Once dressed, we were ushered down the same passage but were ordered to halt in front of a door just short of the reception office. The guard unlocked it and we followed him inside.

In the dimly lit room were two short rows of jail cells at right angles to each other, about twelve cells in all.

"What's this? You're not going to put me in there!" Steven said.

The guard didn't answer. He walked down a narrow corridor and opened a cell door.

"Get in!" he said to me.

I cringed when he slammed the steel door behind me and locked it. Ignoring his protests, the guard placed Steven in another cell further down.

The cell consisted of bare green painted walls on three sides and a barred grey iron door. Attached to the walls was a thick wooden board with a crumpled grey blanket hanging off the edge.

I felt that something was missing and then it hit me. There was no mattress! By this time I was so tired and confused that I couldn't give a damn. I lay down on the board and pulled the blanket over me and realized the bench was too small for me to lie flat out. I cursed and threw the blanket on the cement floor. The lights went out and I lay motionless, staring into the total darkness.

"Vic! Vic!" Steven whispered.

"What do you want?"

"What's your cell like?"

"I have to sleep on the floor. I'm too tall for the bed. There's no mattress!"

"I've got one. All the cells on this side have one."

"Lucky you! I guess that's your reward for a great show. Why didn't you blow them off? Then they might have let you go home."

A few minutes of silence followed.

"What do you think is going to happen to us?" Steven asked.

"I don't know. I'm sure I'll get time."

"How much time do you think?"

"Look, Steven, I'm in no fuckin' mood to talk. So cool it!"

"What's with you, man? I'm in the same shit as you."

"You think so, eh? It's your first offence, turkey. I've been in court a dozen times. I'm the one who's in deep shit. Not you."

I didn't sleep that night. I tossed and turned, trying desperately to force myself not to think about the evening before, about my mother, my father, and how they were feeling at that moment. It must have been around 7 a.m. when the guard came in. Steven, myself, and two other guys were led out of the cells and into the passage outside.

"We're going up to the fifth floor," one of the two guys whispered.

"What's up there?" Steven asked.

"That's where we stay in detention. Everybody from fifteen to seventeen years old on the fifth and the younger boys on the fourth."

"Do we come back to the cell at night?" Steven asked.

"No. You stay in here only on your first night for a taste. If you get into any trouble upstairs, you come down here for three days straight."

"Shut up!" the guard shouted.

"We're going up for breakfast now," the same kid said.

"Good! I'm starved," Steven replied.

The guard opened the door which led to a stairwell and we marched five flights of steps up to the fifth floor. I was surprised to see so many boys on the floor. There must have been close to two hundred. They were packed into two sparsely furnished rooms across a corridor from each other. Inside, wooden benches lined the walls. There obviously were not enough because a lot of the boys either were sprawled out on the floor or remained standing. The windows were covered from the inside with iron slats and on the outside with thick black wire mesh. An emergency fire exit was bolted and locked. At one end of the corridor was the dining room packed with picnic tables and a washroom with two toilet partitions with the doors removed, four yellow, rust-stained urinals, and three grey, greasy sinks over which hung a faded metal mirror. At the other end of the corridor were two dormitories.

The guard waved us into one of the lounges.

"Hey, Malarek!" someone yelled as I walked through the entrance. I looked up and to my surprise two old Weredale boys, Dubois and Nicols, stood beaming in front of me.

"Hey, what's up? What are you doing here, Dubois?" I asked.

"I got nailed on a B & E," he said.

"What's with you, Nicols?"

Nicols had spent more than five years in the Home. He ran away repeatedly and got picked up a number of times for purse-snatching and shoplifting. Somewhere along the line, I'd heard his drunken father was killed in a car accident and, a little later, his mother deserted him and took off with some guy. A few weeks back, Nicols had been sentenced to

Shawbridge Boys' Training School on a charge of purse-snatching and had to stay there until he turned eighteen in another ten months.

"I broke from Shawbridge and got nailed shoplifting. The judge sentenced me here for a month. I get sent back to the training school next week."

"What are you in for?" Dubois asked. "Fighting?"

"Armed robbery."

"Come on! Cut the bullshit! Really, what are you up for?"

"Armed robbery."

"Are you kidding? That doesn't sound like you, man!"

"He ain't kidding, man! He's pulled a couple but last night went sour!" Steven boasted.

"Keep your mouth shut, jerk, or I'll ram my fist into it!" I threatened.

"Okay, okay!"

"You pulled other jobs?" Dubois asked.

"No, this jerk just likes to brag," I said, staring hard at Steven. I didn't want anyone to find out about the other robbery.

"Hey, there's a few other Weredale guys here," Dubois said.

Just then a guard came to the entrance and yelled something in French. Everyone got up and started to form six lines.

"What did he say?" I asked Dubois.

"Just get into line fast and don't be last!"

I rushed into the second row with Steven. The line stood still and at attention. Three guards were now at the door.

"You!" the guard said in French, pointing at some guy at the end of the row. "Up here!" A small skinny kid ran up, turned around, bent over, and received a solid boot in the ass for being last.

"They'll never do that to me!" I whispered into Dubois's ear.

"Me neither!"

We marched one line at a time into the dining area and filed six a side to each picnic table starting from the back of the room. Steven sat down as soon as he arrived at his place and dug in. A bad mistake. One of the guards bolted over and pulled him by the hair out of the room. He had to kneel at attention for one hour without breakfast for not waiting until grace was said. The centre was run by French Catholics.

I didn't feel like eating, so I gave my meal, except for a glass of milk, to a French kid sitting next to me who wolfed it down. After breakfast, we returned to the lounge. I stared out a window which offered a clear view of the district where I lived.

"Malarek . . . Malarek. Time to line up for lunch," Dubois said, tapping my shoulder.

"Huh?"

"You okay?" he asked, looking at me oddly.

"Yeah, sure, let's go."

Again I wasn't hungry and drank only a glass of milk. I returned to the same window after the meal. Steven came by and asked if I wanted to play cards. I brushed him off with a wave of my arm. A little later Nicols asked if I wanted to talk with some of the other old Weredale boys in detention. I didn't answer. He left and no one bothered me until line-up for supper. Hunger pangs were needling my stomach by then, but after a couple of slices of bread and a few chunks of meat out of a strange-smelling stew, I pushed my plate aside and gave my dessert to Dubois, who gulped it down in two disgusting slurps.

It was dusk outside when I returned to my perch. The wind had picked up and gusting snowdrifts created havoc for those making their way home from work on the streets below. My daydreams drifted to home. A vision of my father appeared before me. He was standing in the kitchen. An angry, almost vengeful look filled his dark eyes.

"You think you are so tough. Well, let's see how tough you are, big shot." An open hand stung the side of my face. I lunged out and grabbed his wrists. He squirmed, trying desperately to break my hold, but couldn't. He no longer had the strength he used to possess. I knew that bothered him immensely.

"Mike, leave him alone!" my mother screamed, jumping between us. I let go of his wrists and went to my room. Tears were streaming down my face.

"If you don't stop picking on him, Mike, I swear I'll leave and take the kids with me," I heard her threaten. A moment later, she was sitting on the edge of my bed, gently stroking my hair.

"Mom, why does he hate me so much? I thought I was his favorite."

"I don't know, Victor. I can't understand why that man keeps picking on you like he does. It's as though he almost wants you to hate him."

"Why? He knows I could never hate him."

"He knows he hasn't got long to live now. The pain is worse and he's taking too many pills. He knows how much you love him. Maybe he doesn't want you to suffer and miss him when he dies. This is his way of making sure. I don't know, Victor."

"Mom, I don't want him to die."

"He's getting worse, Victor."

"Mom, I don't want him to make me hate him. I can't hate him. Just tell him to stop picking on me. I can't take it any more."

"Get some rest, Victor. I'll talk to your father. Get some sleep."

The thunderous voice of a husky guard ordering us to line up snapped me back into reality. It was 8:30 p.m. Each boy's name was called out and in turn he was assigned a bed number in one of the two dormitories. I was assigned to dormitory A, bed 35, upper. Afterwards we were marched single file down the corridor to the rooms.

Dormitory A was a poorly lit room packed on either side with grey metal bunk beds. The hot, musky stench of urine was so terrible that I forced myself to hold my breath for the first minute or so to get used to it. Barely a foot separated each bunk – forty-nine in all – so that no matter which side you slept on, you had your neighbor breathing or farting in your face. The mattresses were about six inches thick, and from under the top bunks you could see they were all covered with large, rust-colored urine stains. Most of the beds sagged and looked very uncomfortable. I pulled myself up onto my bunk and discovered someone had pissed in it the night before.

"Guard!" I called out.

"Oui," an older man replied. He reeked of cheap whiskey.

"Someone pissed in this bed. The sheets haven't been changed."

"The sheets are changed on Monday."

"You don't expect me to sleep in someone else's piss?"

"Get ready for bed!"

I sat on the bunk fuming. I was just about to accept my fate when something inside me snapped.

"I am no fucking animal, frog! Sleep in it yourself!"

The old man squealed for assistance. Two guards who looked like retired night club bouncers came to his rescue.

"You sleep in the bed or in the cell. Take your pick!" one of the apes snarked. The other glared at me with a look as if he was daring me to try something.

"I'll take the cell, it's cleaner!"

I punched the cement wall as the cell door slammed.

"Don't break the wall," one of the guards taunted.

"Up you!"

He walked away chuckling to himself. A moment later, the lights went out. The darkness in the cell was complete. The silence was stupefying. I sat on the bench for what seemed a long while and unconsciously began talking to myself.

"Christ, you really did it this time! Didn't you? You couldn't tell them to drop dead. No! You had to be a hero. Mr. Big Shot strikes again. Man! You couldn't tell that bastard Marino to stick it. You stupid ass! You're a stupid ass! Do you know that? A stupid idiot! Who the hell are you trying to impress? Another bunch of stupid idiots who don't even give a damn about you. Yeah, they don't give a damn about you. Face it!

"Why the hell did I let myself get into this? Armed robbery! I can't believe it. And that fight at Querbes Academy! Christ, I hate fighting. And if fighting's not enough, I got to pull a robbery. Great going, man! You really did it, Victor. Man, did you ever do it. Now they're really going to put me away. How am I ever going to face Mom? She had so much faith in me and I go and let her down. You stupid, rotten bastard you! You rotten, slimy bastard! That's it, punch the wall! Break your goddamn hand. Idiot! God, Dad's going to die soon. You know he's going to die soon! You know he needs you! He's going to die all alone. This can't be happening. God, please . . . let me wake up and discover this was a bad dream. Please! Listen to me! I'll be good. I swear I'll be good.

"To hell with my friends. Christ! They're not even my friends. I don't have any friends. That bastard Lorne. Him and his goddamn Marines. My only friend in this whole rotten world and he fucks off to the Marines. Prick! Look at me. Mr. Idiot, jerk ass behind bars. For what? Shut up, man! You're beginning to sound like a nut. . . . Maybe I am nuts. God, I wish I was dead. Maybe I'd be better dead. Nobody would give two shits if I died anyway.

"This place is driving me crazy. . . . How the could anyone name this hole after a saint. Who the hell is this Saint Vallier? A jailer! Who cares? What a way to treat kids! Some fucking law! Cops handcuff you to a car and punch the shit out of you. You get thrown in a hole like this. A bunch of faggot guards watch you shower! Jesus! Rotten bastards. I hate this rotten world.

"That bastard Gold. Trying to talk to that arsehole of a probation officer is like trying to talk to a brick wall. Creep! All he ever does is yell and hand me bullshit stories about punching out bullies when he was my age. Guy couldn't punch his way out of a wet paper bag. You prick, Gold. What the hell do you know? Just as much as that judge. Screw all! Judge! Ha! What the hell does he know about my life? Man, what a hard life he must have had growing up in Westmount never-never land.

"Christ! I don't believe this is happening. I don't believe it! It can't be real. It can't be. Tell me it's a bad dream. It's all a rotten dream. My whole life is a nightmare. Come on, wake up. It's got to be a bad dream. It has to be! Come on!

"Fuck! No one better ever mess with me from now on. No one! I'll kill them! Do you hear me? I'll tear their eyes out! Just let them try to lay a finger on me. Let them try. I've got sweet nothing to lose now. Nothing!''

I kicked and punched the walls, cursing myself and everyone else. All alone in this dark, tiny prison I was free to vent my frustrations, a flood of confused emotions jammed inside me for years. I was bent on getting even with myself, with society, with the world.

That night was an eternity. The guards didn't come to take me to the fifth floor that morning. I spent Sunday in the cell. The only person I saw was the guard at mealtimes, when I didn't even bother to look to see what was on the tray. Before breakfast and after he took away the untouched supper tray, the guard opened the cell door and escorted me to the toilet at the other end of the cell enclosure. Throughout the day, I sat motionless on the bench bed. When the lights were turned off, I felt my way to the crumpled grey blanket on the floor and curled into a tight ball.

The next morning the door at the end of the cell block was flung open and crashed heavily against the wall. The lights flashed on. I covered my eyes from the sudden brightness pouring in through the spaces between the bars.

"Lève-toi!" the guard commanded as he approached my cell. "Ton déjeuner!"

"You know what you could do with it, eh?"

The guard put the tray on the floor and left as abruptly as he had come in. He returned half an hour later to collect the dishes. I hadn't touched a thing.

About another half-hour had passed when the door was whipped open again, smashing against the wall. I jumped up.

"Jesus Christ! Do you have to slam the fucking door open? You jerk!'' I yelled.

Two guards came towards me. Shit, they're going to fix my ass! You should have kept your big mouth shut, I thought to myself.

"Back up to the far end!" one ordered while the other opened the cell door. "Put your hands out in front of you."

A heavy set of black handcuffs was snapped around my wrists. I followed the guards out of the cell block. In the outside corridor about forty boys, all arrested over the weekend, were lined up for the bus ride to court. They looked ragged, dressed in faded green army work clothes that didn't fit any one of them properly. A guard at the front of the line was calling out each boy's name and sending him into a room next to the exit to be issued a dark blue nylon winter jacket before being escorted outside. I was taken a few yards behind the line, where I waited until everyone had been processed.

"Vic . . . Vic," Steven whispered as I passed by him. "You all right?" I didn't answer. The last boys were finally herded outside.

"Ton manteau," the guard said, pulling out a coat at random from a huge pile on a table behind him.

"How am I supposed to wear it?" I muttered, holding up my manacled hands.

The guard behind me draped it over my shoulders and led me outside. Four guards blocked the small space between the detention centre exit and a mud-brown school bus to ensure that no one made a break. Inside the vehicle, two guards sat beside the emergency exit at the rear. I was escorted aboard last and placed in the front seat opposite the driver. The handcuff on my right wrist was removed and latched onto the handrail in front of me.

In less than ten minutes, the bus came to a stop inside a small courtyard surrounded by a high cement wall. Single file, we were ushered into a cavernous waiting room in the basement of the courthouse. Once everyone was in the room, a heavy metal desk was moved in front of the doorway, securing the only possible escape route. The guards sat on the other side of the barrier smoking and talking. Every so often, one or two of them were called on to escort boys to the judges' chambers.

I had the jitters. I kept expecting to see Gold storm into the room for a yelling session, but he never showed up. It was late morning, about 11:30 a.m. Most of the boys had been seen by judges and were back in the waiting room. Some were crying. Some were laughing and cracking jokes. A few were red with anger. I was ready to snap.

"Miller, Steven! Malarek, Victor!"

Finally! Steven and I converged on the desk. He was taken out immediately. A burly guard, who looked like a crazed wrestler on television, ordered me to hold out my arms and locked my wrists together with a set of black handcuffs. He rammed his hand under my armpit and led me out. Trudging through the corridors of the courthouse, I kept my head bowed and my eyes riveted to the floor. A large pair of black Oxford shoes walked by, slowed down, turned, and stopped under my nose. My eyes inched up a pair of grey pants and then past a matching jacket, a white shirt, and a striped blue tie. My throat went dry. It was Johnson from Weredale.

"Malarek?"

"Yes, sir."

Johnson shook his head as his gaze fixed on the handcuffs. Jeez, of all the people to run into, I thought. Johnson was at court to retrieve two runaways who had been picked up by the cops over the weekend and put in St. Vallier.

"What did you do to deserve this?"

"I got into trouble . . . a lot of trouble," I whispered hoarsely.

"I can see that. What kind of trouble?"

"A bunch of fights and some other stuff."

"You Malareks will never learn, will you?"

"I got into trouble. Not Fred or Peter. Anyway, I don't feel like talking to you."

"Still with the smart mouth," Johnson said loudly.

The room went quiet. I bit my tongue. I was in enough trouble.

The first person I saw in the courtroom was my mother. She was sitting at the back of the room clutching a handkerchief and weeping. I avoided her eyes. Steven's mother was sitting beside her. She was busy mouthing something to her son, who was standing in front of the judge's bench. Gold was beside him fidgeting with some papers. He appeared to be quite upset. He didn't even look up when I was brought in, and he acted as if I wasn't there. "Up his," I mumbled to myself.

The court clerk appeared from the judge's private enclave and shouted, "All rise!"

Everyone stood up and the judge, looking very, very sombre, came in and sat down. The clerk began blurting out something about the Crown, the plaintiff, and the accused, and concluded by asking me, "How do you plead? Guilty or not guilty?"

"Guilty," I replied.

He began to read aloud from another document, but before he could finish, I pleaded guilty.

"He has not finished," the judge said.

The clerk resumed from where he had been interrupted.

"Guilty," I said, again interrupting him before he was through.

"The clerk has not finished," the judge repeated in a much harsher tone.

"So what?" I shouted. The outburst caught everyone by surprise. Gold glared at me. His eyes were screaming at me, calling me a punk. The clerk looked flabbergasted. The judge's face was beet red.

"I've had it!" I was burning. I moved towards the judge's bench, hurling a chair out of my path. The guard lunged forward and grabbed my shirt collar. A moment later, I was jostled, tugged, and shoved to a holding cell away from the waiting room. At St. Vallier, I was placed back in solitary confinement to cool down.

The guards transferred me back to the fifth floor the next morning. It was Tuesday. I passively welcomed the move. I didn't want to be alone any longer. My mind was driving me crazy. I wanted to keep from thinking about what was going to happen to me.

After lunch, Dubois and Nicols joined me on the lounge floor to shoot the breeze about old times in Wercdale. We had just found ourselves a comfortable niche when my name was called out. I was escorted up to a small, narrow room on the sixth floor.

"Go sit down over there," the guard instructed, pointing at two wooden chairs near the window. I clumped down as two tall, heavyset men came in. I rose to my feet.

"Is your name Victor Malarek?" asked the one with a brushcut.

"Why?"

"We'll ask the questions," he replied.

"You're cops!"

"Police officers. Detectives. Montreal Police."

"What do you want?"

"Do you know a guy called Marino?"

"No!"

"That's strange. He knows you."

"Well, I don't know him."

"Where were you on the night of February 9 at about 8:30 p.m.?"

"I don't remember."

"Last Wednesday, what were you doing last Wednesday evening?"

"How the hell should I know? I can't remember that far back."

"Were you around Fairmount and Jeanne Mance streets around 8:30 that night?"

"No!"

"That's funny. This guy Marino swears that you were with him at about that time on Wednesday." There was a pause. I could hear my heart crashing against my rib cage.

"He also said you helped him hold up the variety store on the corner of Jeanne Mance and Fairmount. We have a signed statement to that right here in this briefcase," the detective continued. "Now, where were you last Wednesday evening?"

I tore a chunk of fingernail off my right thumb. It started to bleed. They knew everything. Marino had stooled about the first robbery.

"If you cooperate, you'll make it easier on yourself. We'll tell the judge and it'll go in your favor."

"Cooperate! Christ, nothing can help me now," I said. My voice was hoarse and trembling. I cleared my throat and stared up at the bare light hanging from the ceiling, forcing myself to keep control. I was shaking.

"If you sign a confession admitting your part in the robbery with this guy Marino, we'll see what we can do."

"I'm not signing nothing."

The detective's partner, who had been silent until this time, suddenly spoke up. "You'll sign."

"Try and make me."

"You'll sign," he repeated with a cold grin.

"Give yourself a break, kid. We'll help you out. We don't want to see you go to jail. You're just a kid. All we want is to clear up this case as quickly and as easy as possible. Come on. Give yourself a break," the first detective said, shoving a pen in my hand and placing a sheet of paper in front of me.

I caved in. There was no use in fighting it any longer. I began writing what the detective dictated.

"At about 8:30 p.m., February 9, 1966, I, Victor Malarek, held up the variety store at 221 Fairmount Street with Tony Marino. While he had a knife at the owner's throat, I took $450.00 from the cash – "

"$450? Are you crazy? There was no $450 in that cash register!"

"The owner signed a statement saying he was robbed of $450 from the cash register and a wallet containing fifty dollars," the detective said.

"The son of a bitch. Christ, he's a worse crook than I am. You should lock him up. I don't give a shit what the hell he said. There was exactly $152 in that cash register and no more. We split the money down the middle. I can prove it. I didn't spend a penny of that rotten money. It's in my bottom bureau drawer at home. Go check for yourself."

The detectives didn't respond.

"Look, man. I'll sign your rotten confession. But I'm not signing anything to give that goddamn bastard anything extra. And that's that! And by the way, he only had a lousy two-dollar bill in his wallet. Not any fifty bucks! I saw Marino open that wallet in front of me. He never had a chance to stash any of that money before we counted it."

I completed the confession, inserting the correct amounts taken from the cash register and wallet, and signed it. The detective who had been buzzing me sat down to reread the statement. His partner launched into another round.

"Did you pull any other jobs?"

"What?" I asked.

"Have you committed any other armed robberies or break-ins that you would like to clear up?"

"No!"

"Come on, kid. We've got your description for at least half a dozen robberies around Montreal."

"This was my first robbery. Outremount was my second and my last. I didn't pull any others. So don't try and con me."

"It'll be harder on you if we find out later that you did. You have your chance now to come clean."

"I told you, I haven't pulled any other robberies."

"Okay, Victor," the first detective interrupted after putting my confession into his briefcase. "I'll tell the judge you cooperated with us and ask him to go easy on you."

"Yeah, sure you will."

The following morning after breakfast, my name was read out for court to face the second robbery charge. When I was summoned to the courtroom, I found myself being taken into another judge's chambers. I went cold when Judge Long, who wasn't the judge I had before, walked in. Long had a reputation for being the meanest, toughest judge on the English side. He was a Catholic, and like all Catholic judges he meted out stiff punishments for even the most inane delinquencies.

The charge was read out by the court clerk. I didn't listen to a word. I stared blankly at the floor, wondering why my judge had been switched. There was a minor commotion at the back of the room. I winced when I heard that familiar cough. It was my father.

"Is any member of your family here? Your mother or your father?" the judge asked.

"Yes, I'm here. I'm his father."

I turned slowly and watched in disbelief as my father stumbled out of a chair. I could tell by his eyes that he was flying high on pills. My heart began to pound. I didn't know what he was going to do but I knew he was going to do something. I could feel it.

"Mr. Malarek, your son Victor has been brought to this court this morning to —"

"I know what he's here for," my father shouted angrily. He pushed aside a few chairs and marched up to Judge Long's desk. "Let me tell you this, you dried-out old bastard, you're not going to put my son away. Try it and I'll —"

"Order! Order! Do you know who you're talking to? I'll hold you in contempt," the judge boomed.

"Hold me whatever you want. You're not putting my boy away. He's my son. What the hell do you know about kids, you old jerk. Look at you sitting on your pompous ass —"

"Order! Order! Guard! Remove this man. I'm holding you in contempt! Clear this court. There will be a fifteen-minute recess."

"Don't worry, Victor. I won't let them put you away," my father shouted as he barrelled past the guard and stormed out of the building.

I couldn't believe what had just occurred. As if my luck wasn't bad enough. I was escorted back to the waiting room.

"Sir, could I use your phone for a just a minute? I have to call my mother. It's important. I have to call her."

The guard read the urgency in my eyes and let me use the phone even though it was against regulations.

"Mom . . . Mom, Dad's going to get me put away for good," I blurted out as she came to the phone. "He came to court this morning and threatened the judge. He called him names. I'm going to get the book thrown at me. The judge is going to fix me for that. Mom, don't let Dad come back here. Please! Tell him to stay home."

"Victor, calm down. Jesus, I can't leave your father alone for a moment. I shouldn't have told him you were being brought to court this morning. The police and Mr. Gold told me it was only a formality, an arraignment. I'll call Mr. Gold and see what I can do. I can't leave work right now, Victor. The lunch rush is just starting."

"I know that, Mom. All I'm asking is don't let Dad come back here. He'll end up in jail with his mouth and I'll end up in more trouble."

After lunch, I was called back to court. Gold was talking with the judge when I entered. I stared nervously at the floor, shifting my weight from one leg to the other. I wished I had gone to the toilet.

Judge Long cleared his throat and Gold trotted off to one side. "Judge Gammell is away today," the white-haired man behind a leather-topped oak desk began. "This is an arraignment. It's a matter of formality. You will not be having your case before me, especially now after the outburst this morning. You will be having your hearing before Judge Gammell. All you are here for today is to enter a plea to the charges that will be read out. Do you understand?"

"Yes, sir."

The court clerk was given a nod and read out the particulars.

"Guilty," I replied. Judge Long and Gold shook their heads.

I was sure that after hearing what my father did in court, Judge Gammell would turn my case over to the adult court with a recommendation to put me in the penitentiary for a few years. Steven tried to cheer me up when I arrived back on the fifth floor later in the afternoon.

"Look, Vic, it's no use getting down. I'm sure everything will work out okay. My mother told me —"

"What the fuck do you know, eh? You're just a jerk. You're getting off. It's your first offence. I'm the one who's in a lot of trouble. Not you. So why don't you just take off and leave me alone!"

Steven frowned and returned to a group of boys he was talking with when I arrived. I slumped down on a bench to wallow in self-pity. I realized right then I had to keep myself from thinking. My mind couldn't hack it any more. I felt I was losing my grip on reality. Nothing was making sense any more. There was too much confusion.

I looked over at Steven, who was playing a stand-up comic to the delight of the English guys.

A slight smile cracked at the corners of my mouth. Steven caught it and rallied with another dumb crack.

"What does a horny frog say? Rub it . . . rub it . . . rub it . . ."

I broke up.

"Ha ha ha! Look at the turkey. Laugh, man! Ha ha ha!" a voice behind me heckled.

I glanced up at a loud-mouth with sunken, shifty dark eyes glaring down at me. He was a hardrock who was forever bragging about all the tough guys he knew. He was constantly picking on the weaker guys. I knew I could take the jerk but decided to ignore him. I was in enough trouble. I didn't need to get into another fight.

"What's with you, man?" one of my Weredale buddies asked, shoving him up against the wall.

"Leave him alone, Dubois. He's an asshole," I said.

But the hardrock wouldn't leave it alone. "You think you're so cool, eh, Malarek? Big man. Well, I hear you'll be going to training school and let me tell you this. You ever hear of Brian White? Well, he's my cousin and I'm going to get word to him about how tough you think you are. When they send you up to Shawbridge, he'll be waiting for you. He'll kick your head in."

"What's with you, jerk?" I snapped. I was beginning to boil.

"Don't try to suck up to me, Malarek. My cousin doesn't like brown-nosers. My cousin —"

Before he could complete the sentence, he was on the floor cupping a fat lip.

The normal punishment for fighting in the detention centre was three days' solitary confinement in the cells. Instead, the guard made us kneel at attention with our pants rolled above the knees facing the wall near the exit. After about ten minutes, what I had thought was a rather light punishment had become an increasingly painful torture. My knees burned. My back ached tremendously, forcing me to slouch for relief. The guard sneaked up from behind and booted me in the small of my back. I keeled over onto the floor writhing in pain. A crowd of gawking boys gathered around. There was no way I would let myself be seen as a weakling or a coward in front of them. Taking a deep, deliberate breath, I scrambled to my feet and tore after my assailant.

"I'll fix you, you slimy frog!" I yelled. I tackled the surprised guard to the floor and rammed his head into the concrete. My eyes suddenly focused on the guy who had started it all. He was leaning up against the wall grinning. I charged over, pushing a few bodies out of my path, and grabbed him by his shirt. All I saw was red! I wanted to kill him. Smash him out. Rip him to pieces. He pulled away and made a desperate dash for the exit. I kicked out my foot, tripped him, and threw myself onto his squirming body. He began to scream for help.

"Get off! Leave me alone! Help! Someone help! Guard! Guard!"

I didn't want to hear the sound of his voice. I went for his throat, digging my fingers into his neck. Beneath me, I felt the straining muscles, the tenseness, the fear. His terror-filled eyes bulged as if they might pop out. He was gasping frantically for air, spitting and frothing at the mouth as my fingers dug harder into his neck.

Two bouncer-like guards bulldozed a path through the cheering crowd of delinquent teenagers. A dull, heavy blow on the back of my neck stunned me. I was dragged to the main floor and sentenced to solitary confinement. Before I was heaved into the cell, a couple of the guards made certain I would think twice about ever touching one of them again.

I crumpled to the floor of the cell. I didn't move the whole night. I didn't cry. I didn't think. I didn't dream. My mind was a black pit. I just lay there like a heap of dirty laundry. I didn't care whether I lived or died.

Three days passed. I ate very little. The meals in the cells had no taste. They served weak tea and plain bread in the morning, milk and a stale baloney or cheese sandwich for lunch, and the regular main course without dessert for supper. I was very weak. My throat was starting to swell and I was feeling hot and dizzy. My head was throbbing.

"Guard! Guard!"

The door opened at the end of the corridor.

"Quoi?" the guard asked from the doorway.

"I feel sick."

"Merde!" he grunted and slammed the door.

"Drop dead, you slimy frog! Pepsi!"

My fever got worse and my throat swelled up to a point where I couldn't even swallow. I was sweating, but out of sheer obstinancy I refused to call for help. For all I cared, they could find me dead.

18

"**W**here am I?"

"You're in the clinic on the seventh floor," a matronly nurse answered.

"Then it wasn't a bad dream. I'm still here."

"What did you say?"

"Nothing. What day is it?"

"Sunday morning. The guards carried you up here Friday afternoon. You were very ill. The doctor gave you an injection. You'll be all right now."

"Who cares?"

The nurse ignored the last comment. "Roll over and pull up your nightgown. I have to give you an injection."

I drifted into a deep, undisturbed sleep.

A rattling key in the door woke me a few hours later.

"You have a visitor!" an aging guard said. He was carrying a robe and a pair of paper slippers. "You'll have to go downstairs."

Sunday was visiting day in St. Vallier. The day that I had dreaded had finally arrived. I knew my mother was downstairs. Now I would have to face her. I put on the flimsy, faded orange robe over my white hospital tunic and followed the guard. We were both too weak to walk down seven flights of stairs, so he called down for the elevator.

The visiting room was hideous. No tables, just dozens of benches and steel chairs scattered around a spacious room packed with detainees and their grief-stricken parents. A half-dozen guards were placed at strategic locations, two at the doorway and the rest roving about to ensure that no contraband was smuggled to the boys. My mother was sitting on a bench towards the centre of the room. She forced a sad smile when she saw me. I half-heartedly returned it.

"They wouldn't let Peter or Freddie in. They said only parents can visit. How are you?"

"I'm fine, I guess. I don't know."

"How come you're dressed like that?"

"Oh, I was a little sick. Nothing serious. I've been staying in the hospital upstairs but I'm okay now. How's Dad? Is he mad at me?"

"He's all right. He hasn't said much. He can't believe what you did. He misses you. I brought you some chocolate bars but they said I couldn't give you anything. Do they treat you okay here?"

"Nobody bothers me."

"You're not getting into any fights, are you?"

"No. I'm staying out of trouble."

"Do you eat good?"

"The food's crap but it's okay. I got good training for it in Weredale."

There was an uncomfortably long pause. The idle chit-chat was over. I couldn't think of anything to say. I began chewing on the remains of my fingernails and watching the other guys and their parents. Most of the people were talking in embarrassed whispers. A few mothers wept. One stern-looking father scolded his delinquent son. Most of the boys seemed to pay little or no attention to what their parents were saying. They were either staring at the floor or flashing sign language and winks to their buddies. Then I noticed Steven talking with his mother a few benches over. He was sobbing.

"I spoke with Mr. Gold on Friday. He's very upset with you."

"Who cares?"

"He said the judge won't be able to let you go this time. He said the judge is thinking of sending your case to adult court with a recommendation to send you to a minimum federal penitentiary." Tears started to roll down her cheeks.

"They can't do that! I'm still a juvenile!"

"Apparently they can. Mr. Gold said the court has the power to do that."

"Gold is a real bastard. I wonder why the hell he ever became a probation officer. He hates my guts. He never liked me."

My mother quickly changed the subject. "Freddie and Peter miss you. Freddie is very upset. He doesn't know how you got caught up in such a mess. He feels responsible."

There was another long pause. I picked at a piece of hanging fingernail.

"Victor, why? Why did you do it? It's not like you to steal. I know you've had your problems with fighting. But stealing? Armed robbery? Why did you do it?"

"I don't know, Mom." I couldn't think of what to say to her without bursting into tears. I bit into my lip. We sat there quietly, not knowing what more to say to each other. A guard tapped me on the shoulder.

"What?" I asked.

"Time!"

"Time? She just got here!"

"There are others who would like to visit. We don't have much room."

"What the . . . I don't believe this place."

"It's all right, Victor. I have to go to work. Don't lose your temper. You're in enough trouble without making these men angry at you."

"This dump is worse than an adult prison. At least there you get an hour visiting time."

"Stay out of trouble and control your temper," my mother repeated as she kissed me on the cheek. "I'll say a prayer for you and light a candle at St. Joseph's Oratory."

I was ushered into the same room in which I had been forced to strip when I first arrived at St. Vallier. There, along with half a dozen other boys, I was ordered to put my hands up against the wall and spread my legs. After a quick hand search, a husky guard told me to drop my pants and bend over. Once that search was over, I was taken back to my room. An hour later, the same old guard unlocked my door and brought in my lunch.

"Do you know whether I could go down to the fifth floor? I'm going nuts here. I'm not sick any more," I said calmly.

"I'll go check."

When the guard returned, he tossed me a pair of green pants and a shirt. I got dressed and went downstairs.

"Hey, Malarek," Dubois shouted out, running over to me with a broad smile across his face. "How you been?"

"Not too good but I'm okay now."

"You look awful!"

"That's 'cause I was sick, dummy."

"Vic, what's happening?"

"Everything's okay, Steven. I saw you with your mother during visiting. What did she have to say?"

"Oh, not too much. She said my father's really pissed off at me. He wouldn't come to visit me. He said he's going to disown me. Like I give a shit whether he disowns me. He doesn't have anything to give me. How about you? What did your mother say?"

"Not too much. She's very upset."

"Hey, listen, Vic, I was thinking —"

"Look, turkey, I told you a dozen times I hate being called Vic. My name is Victor. If my mother wanted a son called Vic, she would have called me Vic. If you can't understand that, then take off."

"Look man, I . . ."

"Look, do me and yourself a favor. Take off. You're getting on my nerves and you're liable to get hurt."

Steven mumbled something under his breath and disappeared into the crowd. Good riddance, I thought.

"Say, Malarek, you going to church?" Nicols asked.

"Are you nuts?"

"You get seven cigarettes for going."

"So what, man? I don't smoke."

"Yeah, but you could use them to buy desserts. It beats eating that other shit. Or you could use them to get guys to do you favors. The French Catholic priest only gives the frogs three cigarettes each, so they're always willing to do just about anything for an extra smoke. You could get a blow job for two cigarettes."

"Just what I need, Nicols, a blow job. Why do they get only three cigarettes and we get seven?"

"There's too many of them. The English guys go to the Protestant service. The priest there gives us more smokes because the guards don't force us to attend like the frogs. He's got to get our souls somehow."

I laughed. "So he has to bribe us to go to church."

"Yeah!" Dubois scoffed.

"Hey, Nicols, aren't you a Catholic? I thought you went to St. Leo's Catholic School when you were in Weredale."

"Not so loud. The guards here think all the English are Protestants. That's cool with me. That way there I don't have to go to confession or communion or any of that crap and I get more cigarettes. Let's go! The guys are starting to line up for church."

The service was short. Three hymns, a stern lecture on the evils of coveting thy neighbor's stuff, and it was over. Afterwards, the minister issued us our cigarette quota and a "God bless you" for attending. The rest of the afternoon was spent either puffing or making deals for cigarettes and butts. I sat down in a corner with Nicols and two other former Weredale boys, Taylor and Cowan, to shoot the breeze about old times. Both Taylor and Cowan were a year younger than me, and although they were in the boys' home at about the same time I was, I only knew them by sight.

"What are those guys doing over there?" I asked Cowan.

"Making tattoos. There's a French guy over there who makes real good ones. You want one?"

"Are you out of your mind? No way do I want any of that crap on my arms."

Dubois emerged from the group looking proud as a peacock.

"Hey, Malarek! Look at these cool tattoos," he said, shoving the backs of his hands in my face. Over the knuckles of his right hand were the letters LOVE; HATE was etched into the knuckles of his left hand.

"Cool, eh?"

"Yeah, real cool. Dubois, I'm finally convinced you're playing with half a deck!" I said jokingly.

"Hey, my mother passed me a message from my brother," Cowan said to Dubois.

"You mean the guards didn't dig it out of your ass and confiscate it?" Taylor interjected.

We all laughed.

"No. Come on. You know what she told me?"

"Your girlfriend has syph," Dubois replied.

"Come on. You remember Chapman?"

"Who can forget Chapman," I said. The only thing I could remember about Chapman was him blowing off a staff counsellor in the woods at camp.

"He's dead! Shot by a cop."

"What?" we all asked, staring at Cowan in disbelief.

"Yeah. It's true. He was shot stealing a car."

"You're bullshitting," I said.

"No. It's in the newspaper. Some cop shot him. The cop said he saw a silver object, thought it was a gun, and shot in self-defence."

"Chapman had a gun?" Taylor asked.

"Naa! The newspaper said there was no silver object within a hundred feet of his body."

"You guys heard about Harris, eh?" I asked.

"You better believe it! I was still in Weredale when he got out," Nicols said. "Man, I can't believe that guy strangled his sister. I knew he was weird. Someone told me he got life."

"I think he's in the nuthouse," Taylor added. "I never trusted that guy. Real strange."

"No. He's in maximum at St. Vincent de Paul," Dubois said.

"You guys remember Gray?" Cowan asked.

"Sure. He showed me around Weredale when I first came in," I said.

"He's dead too!"

"Bullshit!"

"No. It's true. He was killed in Vietnam."

"Where's Vietnam?" Nicols asked.

"You're a jerk," Cowan replied.

"How the hell am I supposed to know where Vietnam is?" Nicols protested.

"What the hell was Gray doing there?" Dubois asked.

"He joined the U.S. Marines," said Cowan.

"Man, it's weird what's happened to some of the guys," I said, shaking my head. I thought about Lorne at boot camp in South Carolina. How I wished he hadn't left!

"You better believe it. I ran into Boucher. You remember that jerk? He deserted from the Navy over some broad. And Daniels, Smith, and Plager are all in the pen for robbery. It's too bad for them. They're over eighteen. The ball game is over for them," Dubois said.

"Plager's in the pen? Wait till Fred hears about that," I said. It was odd, I thought, Plager was following in his father's footsteps. He had been sent to the same prison where his father had slit his throat.

"Man, there are at least as many ex-Weredale guys in Shawbridge," Nicols said. "Carter, Page, Brunet, Russell, Doyle, Dubois . . ."

"I'm here, stupid!" Dubois said, jabbing Nicols playfully in the ribs.

"Oh, yeah. Sorry!" Nicols apologized. "It's just that it's so hard to notice you, you fat slob."

We burst out laughing.

"Hey, did you say Brunet is in Shawbridge?" I asked, thinking back to the time we ran away from Camp Weredale together and got lost in the forest.

"Yeah! He's a real thief, that guy. Wait, by the time he's eighteen, he'll be in the pen. Mark my words. The guy's habitual. One day he's going to get life or some cop will shoot him," Dubois said.

"Boy, look at all the guys Weredale screwed up," Cowan said, shaking his head in disbelief.

"You better believe it," I added.

Yet I knew deep down that even though Weredale had played a significant role in our lives, it couldn't be held totally to blame for what had happened to us. Most of these guys had had their courses charted for them long before they reached the Home. Weredale simply ensured that the course was maintained. I would have liked to blame Weredale for everything that had happened to me. It would have been an easy way out. Dubois, Taylor, Nicols, and Cowan surely did. And maybe they had good cause. Our situations were different. They had spent several more years in the Home than I had. They had had a lot more time to learn to hate, cheat, con, and steal. They had never had the chance to escape to a real family, even if that family was less than perfect. At Weredale, they were just numbers. No one had ever asked them with any real interest how they felt. No one had ever put their arms around them and told them that they loved them. After a while they had come to feel that they had nothing to lose. Nobody cared about them, so why should they care about anyone.

I got a bit of a jolt the following evening just as we were finishing supper. Two guards came over to my table and ordered me to follow them. We here heading for the main floor. I figured I must have done something wrong and was being returned to the cells for the night. I wasn't. At least not right away. I was led to the admission office, where the two Outremont detectives who had arrested me during the hold-up were waiting.

"Where are you taking me?" I asked as Detective Gauthier snapped a set of handcuffs around my wrists.

"To court. Municipal court to testify," the detective replied. "You're going to testify against the other guys who were charged in the fight you were in at Querbes Academy. Four of them are over eighteen years of age. We charged them with disturbing the peace."

"Big deal!"

"Yeah, it's a big deal and you better treat it as such," Detective Gauthier's bad-guy partner said as he stuffed me into the back seat of an unmarked car.

"Are you allowed to do this? Do you have a warrant?"

"Shut your face!"

In a dimly lit room for prisoners behind the courtroom, Detective Gauthier played nice guy, trying to persuade me to cooperate so he could get top marks for solving yet another dastardly crime.

"Listen, Malarek, between you and me, who was it with the bottle? Just between you and me. Come on, tell me."

"I don't know. I told you that when I was first arrested."

"Come on, Malarek. Who used the bottle? We know you didn't. Those French kids told us it was some big blond guy. Who was he?"

"I told you, I don't know. I was busy fighting."

"Who was it? Don't fart around with us," his tough-guy partner snarled.

I didn't say another word.

More than two hours passed before I was called to testify. I didn't have a clue what was going on in the courtroom. After I was sworn in, the prosecutor asked me my name.

"Victor Malarek."

"Your address?"

"I don't know."

My answer drew a round of snickers from the packed courtroom.

"Order," the magistrate called out.

"I'll ask you again and let's not have any smart-mouth answers. Where do you live?"

"And like I told you before, I don't know."

"You don't know where you live?" the magistrate interjected angrily.

"I was brought there late one night in handcuffs by the cops. No one bothered to tell me the address."

My response drew a chorus of chuckles.

"Your honor, if I may, he is being held at St. Vallier Detention Centre for Boys," Detective Gauthier said.

"Fine."

"Occupation?"

"Juvenile prisoner."

"That will be enough," the magistrate shouted to the roaring courtroom. "You, answer the questions properly or I'll hold you in contempt."

I looked down, trying hard not to laugh.

"If you're finished with the wisecracks, maybe you could tell me where you were on Sunday afternoon two weekends ago?" the prosecutor asked.

"At what time?"

"Your honor?" the prosecutor interjected.

"You cut that out, young man. You're treading on thin ice. And if there is one more outburst I'll clear the court," the magistrate bellowed.

"Were you at the Querbes Academy on that Sunday in question?" the prosecutor asked gruffly.

"Yeah."

"You will answer with a yes or no. Is that understood?" the magistrate instructed.

I nodded.

"Is that a yes?" the irate prosecutor asked.

"Yes!"

"Were you involved in an altercation?"

"A what?"

"A fight?"

"Yes."

"Do you recognize anyone in the court as being one or more of the boys involved in the fight?"

I gazed at the line of Querbes boys who had snapped to attention in their seats when the question was asked. Inside I was seething. Here I was charged with assault and all these guys got nailed with was a misdemeanor, disturbing the peace. Now I was being grilled as if I were the one on trial by an idiot playing Perry Mason. I wasn't going to point the finger at anyone.

"Well?" the prosecutor asked a few long minutes.

"Could you repeat the question?"

"Look, you –"

"I'm not fooling around. I don't remember exactly what you asked. My mind was somewhere else."

"Do you recognize anyone in the court as being one or more of the boys involved in the fight?"

"You don't have to shout at me."

"Just answer the question and keep your comments to yourself," the magistrate warned.

"I don't recognize anyone."

"What do you mean you don't recognize anyone?"

"I was busy protecting myself. I wasn't interested in what anyone looked like. It all happened so fast."

"Do you know the person with the bottle?"

"Who has a bottle?" I asked, looking around the room.

Taking a deep breath, the prosecutor rephrased his question. "Who was the person who was with you that used a bottle to hit another boy during the fight?"

"I haven't a clue. Like I said, I was busy looking after myself."

The exasperated prosecutor winced. He stared angrily at his notes. After a minute or so, the magistrate cleared his throat loudly.

"I have no more questions," the prosecutor said.

"You're dismissed," the clerk said.

Detective Gauthier escorted me out. "Well, that's finished," he chirped as he clipped the handcuffs on my wrist. "Come on, why don't you tell me who the guy with the bottle was? The trial is over. No one can get charged now. I just want to know for my own curiosity."

He must have thought I was born yesterday to fall for that scam. "I don't know. I told you that. And even if I did, I would never tell you."

"You'd better tell me, you little punk," his partner threatened.

"I doubt it."

Detective Gauthier, his partner, and the victimized Greek store owner were leaving Judge Gammell's chambers as I was being led in for my trial. It was Wednesday afternoon, February 23, 1966.

"You should be thankful, son. We put in a good word for you," Detective Gauthier said. "We got the guy we wanted. He pleaded guilty this morning and got five years."

I went white. "Marino got five years? Five years?"

"That's right! He'll have a lot of time to think about life in St. Vincent de Paul," his partner said.

The fat, balding Greek we robbed paced nervously a few feet away. He obviously didn't want to be around me and I didn't want to be around him.

"I go now, yes? I have business to run. I go?" he said, tapping Detective Gauthier on the shoulder.

The courtroom was still. I noticed a man with a briefcase on his lap sitting beside my mother. What the hell did she go out and get a lawyer for, I asked myself. He can't help me. Man, he's going to soak her and for what? I knew there was nothing he could do for me. I was finished. Gold avoided me. He pretended to be busy reading some documents on the table before him. The judge was also studying some papers. The guard stood with me in the centre of the room. My right hand was handcuffed to his wrist. Finally, the judge looked up, cleared his throat, and spoke.

"Victor, we've been studying this case carefully. We've talked to a lot of people about you. Do you have anything to say for yourself?"

"No, sir," I said, almost whispering. "Except that I'm sorry for all the trouble I caused. I didn't mean to. It just happened. I'm sorry for the misery I'm putting my mother and father through."

Judge Gammell wrote something on a sheet of paper and passed it to the clerk.

"I'm going to postpone judgment until Friday, February 25. I've ordered an assessment from our clinic upstairs. You may go now."

After the hearing, I was taken back down to the waiting room until the remainder of the court cases were concluded before being returned to St. Vallier. I felt terribly low. I kept seeing my mother before me in the courtroom, her eyes swollen and red. I sat alone, cursing myself for putting her through such torment.

"Malarek, Victor!"

I got up slowly, wondering why the guard had called my name. The hearing was over but it was still too early to head back to St. Vallier. I went over to the heavy metal desk blocking the doorway.

"Malarek?" the guard asked.

"Yeah."

"Go to the room on the left," he said, pointing down the short corridor.

God, I hope Mom isn't in there. I can't take seeing her right now, I prayed.

The guard removed the handcuffs and I entered the room to find a man sitting on a chair behind a small, bare desk. There was a chair on the other side. I didn't pay any particular attention to him until he spoke.

"I am Dr. Danielli. How do you do?"

"What kind of doctor?" I asked suspiciously.

"I am a psychiatrist."

"I'm not crazy! I don't have to see a headshrink!"

"The judge asked me to see you."

"Why?"

"He wants to know how he can be of some value to you. He wants to understand what is happening with you and try to make things easier for you and your parents."

"I don't need to see any psychiatrist. I'm not nuts!"

"Victor, you don't have to be nuts to talk to a psychiatrist. Now, why don't you sit down and tell me why you are in court today?"

"What do you mean?"

"What has brought you before this court? Why do you seem so upset? Why are you so afraid to speak to a psychiatrist?"

"I'm not afraid. I'm not crazy, that's all." I looked towards the doctor and abruptly turned my gaze to the wall. He was staring intently at me, probably thinking I really was nuts. I sat down.

"So? What do you want me to say?" I asked defensively.

"Anything you feel might be important for me to understand you better. Anything you would like to say."

"I don't know what you mean."

"Tell me about your parents, about your family."

I looked up at him. He was the first real live psychiatrist I had ever encountered and he looked the part. He had penetrating eyes, a pensive expression, and a receding hairline. He kept staring right at me but I avoided his eyes.

"There's not much to say." I felt a lump swelling in the back of my throat. I paused for a moment. "I just don't think I could hack being put away again. It would kill my father. He's sick. He's got cancer and . . ." Tears were streaming down my face. I wiped them away with the sleeve of my shirt. I was angry at myself for being so weak and gutless in front of a total stranger. I cursed myself for breaking down.

"Look, I don't have anything more to say."

"How about if I make arrangements for you to come here tomorrow to speak to me?"

I didn't answer. I was too upset with myself for breaking down. I got up and went back to the waiting room. A short while later, we were herded back onto the detention centre bus and transported back to St. Vallier.

The following day, I was taken to see the shrink at the courthouse clinic. I was surprised. I didn't really expect to ever see him again. I didn't know why, I just had that feeling. Anyway, I didn't trust anyone associated with the court. I felt all they ever really wanted was to pull power trips on kids. I was damned if I was going to let anyone make me squirm or beg.

"Hello, Victor," Dr. Danielli said as the guard led me into his office.

"Hi," I replied, again avoiding his eyes. The psychiatrist waved the guard to leave.

"Why don't you sit down?"

I did as I was told.

"How are things today?" he asked.

"I feel miserable."

"What makes you feel miserable?"

"How would you feel knowing that you were going to be put away?"

"You still have to appear before the judge."

"That doesn't mean anything. I know he's thinking of sending me to adult court. My mother told me last Sunday that they weren't going to let me off. Not this time. I'm in too much trouble. I always get myself into trouble."

"What do you think is the reason you get into trouble?"

"Fighting!"

"Why do you get into so many fights?"

"I don't know. I just get pissed off so fast and bang, I'm in a fight."

Dr. Danielli stared at me a moment. "You seemed pretty worried about your father the last time I spoke with you."

"It's because he's sick."

"Could it be that your getting into trouble has to do with your father's illness?"

"I don't know," I mumbled.

"You seem to be getting into fights so often, stealing."

"You mean the robbery? I didn't do that because of my father. I didn't want to do it. I didn't even need the money. I left the money in the bottom drawer of my dresser at home. I told the police where to find it. I didn't even want to do it. I just got sucked into it. Then, before I knew it, one robbery was pulled and I had to do a second robbery."

"Had to?"

"Well, put it this way. If someone got caught in the second robbery, he would have stooled on the first job if I didn't help."

"Did you tell this to the judge or the probation officer?"

"I'm in so much trouble, they wouldn't believe me. Anyway, Gold never listens to me. He just yells at me. He's a creep. Every time I try to explain myself to him, he starts yelling. It's no use."

Dr. Danielli laughed. Obviously he had met and talked with Gold, so he knew what I was talking about.

"How are things in school?"

"All right, I guess. Except I can't stand some of my teachers."

"What do you mean?"

"Ah, they don't like me and I don't like them."

"What makes you feel they don't like you?"

"I don't know. They get pissed off for stupid reasons like when I don't do my homework or I don't show up for their detentions."

"Why don't you do your homework?"

I shrugged my shoulders. I began wringing my hands.

"Sometimes I get really down. I just don't feel like doing anything. Sometimes things get really bad at home. I just can't. A lot of times my father's in the hospital so I visit him after school. No teacher's going to make me lose a visit over a stupid detention. Anyway, I don't think the reasons those teachers give detentions are fair. If they're pissed off, you suffer. Let them suffer alone."

"Did you ever explain your situation to those teachers?"

"No. They wouldn't give a damn. Most of them are so frustrated in that school. Oh yeah, once I tried to explain why I couldn't take a detention to one teacher last year. I started and he cut me off halfway through saying he didn't have time to listen to excuses. I could have smashed his head in."

"Do you think that being so angry at your probation officer and teachers could have something to do with your relationship with your father?"

"There's nothing wrong between me and my father," I snapped, feeling the acid in my stomach start to boil. He wasn't going to get me to say anything rotten about my father and that was that.

"Maybe it is difficult for you to get angry with him?"

I shrugged my shoulders.

"Knowing that your father is sick must make it difficult for you to express feelings towards him," he continued. "Have you ever tried to talk to your mother and father about the things that upset you?"

I stared at the floor and didn't answer. A barrage of thoughts raced through my mind. How could I talk to my mother and father? How could I tell my mother how unhappy I was? How the situation at home was driving me crazy? How could I point the finger at my father? Then she would use that as an excuse to pack up and leave. I realized a lot of the fights I got into were born out of frustrations at home. Yet I loved my father and was loyal to him, and deep down I knew he loved me despite the fact that he was picking on me incessantly. Somewhere, everything had gone sour and I couldn't understand it. I was confused but I couldn't talk about it. Not to my mother. Especially not to my father and not to this shrink.

Why didn't everything go right when we came back from Weredale? Why did it all fall apart so fast? Why couldn't we make it as a family? Why couldn't my mother love my father again? Why did he have to drink so much? Why did he have to pop so many pain-killers? Why did he pick on me so much? Those questions brought a surge of painful memories. I saw my father stumbling home in a drunk stupor from the tavern just two blocks away. I saw myself slamming down the phone and cursing God after a concerned waiter had called asking me to come and get my father. How embarrassing it was to drag him out of a bar and then hold him up as he careened into walls and garbage cans along the sidewalk. I prayed none of my friends would see us. I wished he were dead as scores of grinning idiots gawked at the two of us. What did they think was so funny? I wondered how they would feel if that was their father. They wouldn't find it so funny then.

I thought of the time when I got off a bus from school one afternoon to see my father hanging onto a street lamppost not knowing where or who he was, blitzed on pills and beer. I watched in disbelief as he tried to wade into a small group of grade school kids who were teasing him. It was the one time I deserted him. I turned and ran away in disgust. How I prayed that day he would die right there on the spot. How terribly guilty I felt for months at the power of my wish.

It was impossible to talk to my father about those things. And how could I talk to my mother about them without cracking up? How could I tell her how I really felt inside when we really hadn't talked in so long about my deep feelings? I really wished I could find the strength to talk to her, but it was too much for me to handle. I didn't know where or how to start. And she had so many problems of her own.

I snapped into consciousness and looked up at Dr. Danielli. He was busy scribbling observations in a notebook. I was extremely tense. I was having trouble swallowing. I wanted to get out of that room. I felt as if it were closing in on me. I was getting angry inside. What the hell was all this about my father anyway, I wondered. What was that shrink trying to get at? He had better watch himself, I thought to myself.

Dr. Danielli looked up and smiled sympathetically. "What would you like to be when you get older?" he asked, breaking through the thick haze around my head.

"It's too late now. I don't know. Maybe a jet pilot."

"Why?"

"So I could fly free in the sky with no worries and no troubles."

Dr. Danielli smiled. "You have brothers?"

"Two. One older, one younger."

"Do you get along with them?"

"Yeah. We have fights occasionally but we stick up for each other."

"Do you have many friends?"

"I know a lot of guys and girls but I have only one very good friend, Lorne. He's in the Marines. He joined last fall. I wanted to join with him but my mother wouldn't sign the papers."

"Why did you want to join?"

"I don't know. Stick around with him. He was my best friend. We had lots of fun together. I really liked him."

There was a long silence.

"Can I ask you a question?"

"Yes," Dr. Danielli said.

"Do you think I'm crazy?"

"No. I think you are very concerned about your father. I think you are very confused and upset. I think you don't know what is making you so angry."

"Do . . . do you think I should see a psychiatrist?"

"It would be very helpful for you to understand what is happening, to understand your feelings."

"Why do you want to see me?"

"I was asked to see you. The judge wants to understand what is happening to you."

"What does he care?"

"You have been brought before him. He has a feeling about you. He doesn't believe you are bad. He wants to understand what is happening to you."

"So what can you do?"

"I could try to help you put things together."

"Ah, what's the use? Judge Gammell is going to put me away anyway."

"The judge is going to do what he believes is best for you."

"Yeah, sure. What . . . what are you going to tell him?"

"That you should see someone at least once a week for a while. That I believe you are very upset about your family. That your behavior seems to be the result of what is happening to your father. That you don't understand what is happening."

"Are you going to tell him to put me away?"

"I will say that I believe the best thing for you is to stay home with your family and try to work things out."

Dr. Danielli stood up. "Victor, I have to go now. I will see you again soon."

"Yeah. Okay." I got up and went to the door.

I hesitated a moment and turned around. "Thanks," I said.

I felt incredibly relieved, even though I was still convinced nothing and no one could get me off. I just felt good after talking to Dr. Danielli. He listened and he didn't yell at me. He seemed interested in what I said and he looked as if he cared. I could actually talk to him, even though some of his questions pissed me off. Maybe he could even help me . . .

19

It seemed as if daylight had come hours ago. I lay on my bunk wishing the guard would come in and yell, "Get up!" Then it would be only an hour before they hustled us off to court.

Friday, February 25, 1966, was my day of reckoning. Soon I would find out what my fate would be. All I wanted was to get it over with. My guts were churning. I kept wringing my hands and biting my nails.

The guard finally grumbled his morning insults and the boys rolled out of their bunks. I didn't touch my breakfast. In the lounge the names of those having to appear in court were called out. We were led downstairs and issued winter coats. Before I was boarded onto the bus, handcuffs were placed on my wrists and I was seated beside a heavy-set guard at the front of the bus.

In the courthouse, time continued to move too slowly for me.

"Come on! Call my name out already! Let's get it over with. Come on!"

Finally! The guard escorted me into the courtroom and stood with me in the centre of the chamber facing the judge's podium. Everything was blurry. I couldn't see anyone clearly. It was like looking at everyone through a fog. My mother sat just behind to my left, looking very sad and yet calm. With her sat my lawyer, looking perplexed. Gold was over to the right, a little in front of me; his expression was serious and pensive. The judge's assistant was filing papers on his desk in front of the podium.

"All rise."

Judge Gammell entered with a thick file folder in his hands.

"Be seated," his assistant said.

"Your honor," my lawyer began. "I would like to —"

"Sir, with all due respect, I've heard all your arguments and have taken them into consideration with the rest of the documents I have here," the judge said.

The lawyer sat down, obviously distraught over the judge's interjection. It was evident he was unfamiliar with the informal workings of juvenile court.

"Victor, do you have anything you would like to say?" the judge asked. I felt as though the death sentence was about to be pronounced.

"No, sir, except that I'm sorry for what I did and the trouble I've caused everyone."

"Victor, I spoke with Dr. Danielli extensively about you and he feels that he could help you and understands your problems. Would you be willing to see him on a regular basis until the court sees fit?"

"Yes, your honor!" I said, looking up into his face. He stared at me a moment and continued.

"I'm going to let you go home."

My heart fluttered. I was sure my ears were playing tricks.

"Thank you, your honor. Thank you," my mother cried out.

"I'm going to let you go home, but you will have to attend the court clinic until we are satisfied with your progress."

"Yes, sir." I was numb. I couldn't believe he was letting me off. I fought an incredible urge to burst out laughing.

"We will be keeping our eye on you. You will also be a ward of this court until you are twenty-one."

"Yes, sir," I answered solemnly.

"One more thing. You are not to chum around with Steven Miller. It's not that he's bad or that you're bad. You two are like two chemicals. Separately they are not dangerous, but put them together and you get a terrific explosion. I mean what I say about staying away from Steven Miller."

"Yes, sir."

"You can go home." The judge got up and disappeared through a side door leading to his private chambers. The guard turned to remove the handcuffs. My mother rushed over and hugged me. Tears were rolling down her cheeks.

"Let's go home," she said. "Dad's waiting for you. He'll be so happy."

My throat swelled as we left the courtroom. All I could think about was I wasn't going to jail. I couldn't understand why but I thanked God.

My mother wanted to take me out for a special dinner, just she and I. "You can have anything you want," she said, putting her arm through mine as we walked out of the courthouse.

We went downtown to a quaint little restaurant. I ordered half a barbecued chicken with fries. I was hungry but my tastebuds were dead. Every time I looked up at my mother, I felt so ashamed for having put her through so much agony. She looked tired and frail. She had cried so many tears. I realized then how much my mother loved me. How much she cared. She didn't have to tell me. Her heart spoke to me through her soft brown eyes. We sat quietly picking at our food for the longest while before she spoke.

"Your father really missed you. He cried so much when he heard what happened to you."

I stared at my plate and didn't answer. I couldn't find any words.

"He said he's going to stop yelling and picking on you. He loves you. You know that."

"I know, Mom."

"How do you feel?"

"Okay, I guess. I don't know. I feel so bad for you. What I put you through. I feel bad for Dad. I wish he was okay. It's hard sometimes. I hate when he picks on me. I hate to see him take all those pills. I hate when he drinks so much. He knows it's bad for him. I hate all that. But I love him. I feel like I'm going crazy sometimes."

"Do you know why you did what you did?"

"No. Not really. But I'm really sorry I did. I think about it sometimes. I know I really didn't want to rob those places. I didn't even spend the money from the first place. I couldn't touch it. I figured only bad would come from it. The fights just happened. I didn't go looking for them. Everything after that just seemed to go out of control."

"Maybe the doctor will help you sort it out."

"Mom, I don't want to see a shrink. I'm not crazy."

"No one said you're crazy, Victor. But maybe he could help you find out what's bothering you inside."

"I know what's bothering me, Mom. I don't need a shrink to tell me. And I don't want to talk to any shrink about it."

"It's been hard for you these past few weeks."

"Yes. That detention centre is a tough place. Its worse than a prison for adults. They treat you like garbage in there. You have no rights."

My thoughts sifted over the time I'd spent in detention. In solitary confinement, I'd had a lot of time to brood, rant and rave, reflect and think about my first seventeen years in this world. After my fits of depression and anger in the cells, I thought I would never find the strength to pick myself up again. Yet I felt cleansed. It was as if I had got in touch with my inner self for the first time. I had finally confronted the source of some of my problems. Before I had always ducked them or pushed them to the back of my mind.

Now what I dreaded most was seeing my father. I didn't know what I would say to him. When we got home, my mother discreetly disappeared into her room. My heart was pounding as I nervously made my way towards the kitchen. My father was sitting at the table engrossed in a Mickey Spillane novel. In front of him on the table was the ever-present quart bottle of Molson's beer.

"Dad, I'm home." My throat was tight.

My father looked up and stared at me for what seemed a long time. His eyes went sad and his hands began to tremble.

I took a deep breath. "Dad, I'm sorry for all the trouble I caused. I'm really sorry."

My father cleared his throat. "It's . . . it's not your fault," he began in a hoarse whisper. "It's my fault. I'm the one who should be sorry. I know I haven't been a good father but I want you to know that I've always loved you. You're my favorite. You've always been my favorite. You always stuck by your old man. You've never deserted me. You were always there when I needed you and I've never forgotten that. Victor, I don't have much time left in this world —"

"Dad, I wish you wouldn't talk like —"

"Let me finish. I know I don't have much time, Victor. I could feel it inside. I just want you to know that I love you and I'm sorry." He stretched out his hand.

I rushed over and threw my arms around him.

EPILOGUE

I was four months away from turning eighteen when Judge Robert Gordon Gammell decided I was worth saving and gave me a break on that fateful day in February 1966. Everyone else in the courtroom had wanted to throw the book at me. When I was released from detention and walked back onto the street, I had made one resolution—to stay out of trouble. I knew it wasn't going to be easy, but I also knew I had to change. Still, I had a huge chip on my shoulder and knocking it off was going to be a major hurdle.

My father was popping painkillers like jelly beans, chasing them down with Molson's and rye, and venting his anger and pent-up frustrations on me. The teachers at the High School of Montreal thought I was dirt. They had all heard about my arrest and incarceration, which added fuel to their firm conviction that I was destined for failure. In their minds, I was a forgone conclusion. It was just a matter of time before I blew it and ended up with somber black numbers under my mug shot. The only group that thought I was cool was my so-called street buddies, and I knew I had to get away from them, their image of me, and their influence. I had had it with the reputation of a tough street kid.

For the longest time, it was awfully lonely and incredibly hard. I pulled away from my street buddies and the comforts of what had been my world—skipping school, hanging around pool halls, living in the moment, and being cool. So often, I could feel the tug of the familiar reeling me back like a seductive drug. But I held out.

For the remainder of the school year, I kept to myself and passed into my final year of high school, with an impressive over-90 per cent average. That floored my teachers! I followed Judge Gammell's order that I get psychiatric help, even though I firmly believed there was no point to it. I attended a few private sessions with Dr. Milton Marcillio (whom I originally referred to in my book as Dr. Danielli) and then a group therapy session once a week for a couple of hours with three other boys and four girls. I didn't say much in those group sessions. I wasn't about to open up and pour my soul out to strangers I didn't know or care about. I was grateful to Marcillio for playing a key role in getting me off by speaking to the judge in my defence. But as soon as I turned eighteen in June and was out of the reach of the juvenile justice system, I bailed.

I was still very angry about my life and the cards I'd been dealt. My main difficulty was my home situation, and no social worker was rushing in to straighten that out. I was like a volcano on the verge of exploding.

That summer, I took a job in shipping and receiving at a women's clothing factory. It was hard, degrading work and the pay was lousy, but at least it kept me occupied, off the hot streets, and helped pay for some private trumpet lessons.

My final year in high school took me in a totally unexpected direction. I was in the auditorium after school, serving a detention for mouthing off at my French teacher. (I was a teenager with opinions!) As I sat in the very back row, I listened with amusement to a group of Grade 8 boys trying out for the role of sailors in the musical *South Pacific*. I couldn't help laughing. The director stopped the audition and asked in a British accent what I thought was so funny. I shot back that it was the image of sailors singing falsetto to "There Is Nothing Like a Dame!" He then challenged me to put out or shut up. So I got on stage, belted out the tune, and nailed a spot in the musical.

Acting and singing in *South Pacific* connected me to a completely different crowd. They were middle-class kids from what seemed to be ordinary families. It was an eye-opener for me. But the key to my acceptance in this foreign setting was Richard Lees, the teacher and director. He saw the rebel in me. He'd heard all about my reputation in the teachers' lounge: that I was a hard-assed kid who mouthed off to teachers, skipped class, and had had a serious brush with the law. He was warned to stay clear—but the red flags didn't matter to him. He never pre-judged me and, unlike so many of my teachers, he refused to write me off. He treated me with respect and kindness. He was a light-hearted man, not a dictator or a bureaucratic stooge. Thanks to this amazing teacher, I started to come out of my protective, iron-riveted armor.

When summer hit Montreal in 1967 and the city was being inundated with tourists for the Expo '67 World's Fair, I boarded a Greyhound bus for a three-day milk run through a half-dozen U.S. states en route to New Orleans. I needed to escape. The situation with my father had become intolerable, and I wanted to play trumpet in a rock blues band. Within a week, I had landed a gig with a band called Satan and His Roses. I was a Rose. Satan was a pale, wiry, greasy-haired, fire-eating, one-beat wonder who appeared on stage just before midnight, shot out flames, and screamed "I'm Satan!" to which his Roses would respond, "He's no, no good!" Then, at the end of the set, he'd disappear into the night.

The wild times ended abruptly with an urgent call from my mother, pleading with me to return home. My father had taken a turn for the worse and was back in hospital. He was asking for me. Grudgingly, I headed home. It turned out all he needed was time to dry out. In the meantime, I went looking for a job. In the *Montreal Star*, I noticed a help wanted ad for an office boy at $45 a week. I applied and landed the position of gofer, toting coffee and copy to editors and writers at the now-defunct *Weekend* magazine. It was there that the seeds of my journalistic ambitions were sown.

On a cold, wet, grey morning in April 1968, a sharp pain shot through my chest. I asked one of the editors if I could go home. I knew in my heart that my father had died. I found him, crumpled on the kitchen floor, a beer glass shattered beside him. He had suffered a massive heart attack. No one was home. It was strange because I'd had a premonition that morning as I kissed his forehead before going to work that something terrible was going to happen. We had a long, drawn-out Ukrainian Orthodox funeral for him. At the end, I kept my long-standing promise to my father, who was a World War II veteran. As his coffin was being lowered into the ground, I played the "Last Post."

After my father's death, the mood at home changed dramatically. The tension had totally evaporated. We were no longer tiptoeing on eggshells, wondering when the next explosion would hit. And yet, I missed my dad.

In between sorting mail, running errands, and doing two coffee runs a day at *Weekend*, I got hit with a bug that was truly foreign to me — writing. I thought it would be cool to be published in *Weekend*. So I started looking for a story idea and found one when I happened to run into a girl who worked as a volunteer at a phone-in suicide crisis center. I approached Paul Rush, the managing editor, and asked if I could write a story on spec. He gave me the nod. Paul and Frank Lowe, the editor-in-chief, liked the article and ran it. For the first time in my life, I was a published writer. I knew right then and there I wanted to be a reporter.

Frank Lowe could see my frustration at going back to toting coffee the day after my article hit the newsstands. Because he liked my work ethic and the passion I had brought to my assignment, he put in a word for me with the *Montreal Star* city editor, Don Foley. After a brief interview, Foley hired me as a police reporter. I began reporting for the *Star* in August 1970, a month after I married my high school sweetheart, Anna. I was one of a team of crime reporters working 24/7, chasing fire trucks, ambulances, and cop cars to fires, accidents, and hold-ups. Then, in October, all hell broke loose when the British trade commissioner, James Richard Cross, was kidnapped and Quebec Labor Minister Pierre Laporte was abducted and murdered by the terrorist Front de Liberation de Quebec (the FLQ).

I was involved in covering this dark moment in Canadian history from start to finish, chasing leads that might take us to where the kidnappers were hiding Cross and Laporte. I stood metres away from the trunk of the vehicle in which Laporte's body was stuffed, then covered his funeral. I watched the nego-tiations outside the duplex in north-end Montreal where Cross was held while a deal was hammered out with his kidnappers.

Then it was back to chasing sirens. Now that I had covered a big story, I was no longer satisfied with reading daily round-up arrest sheets and listening to police radios. I was champing at the bit to investigate more serious stuff. I wanted to write hard-hitting stories. I could feel the pull in my gut. I decided to cull the newspaper's morgue files for articles on a subject I knew well from the inside: Quebec's child welfare system. To my surprise, there was virtually nothing written on the subject. It was as if the issue was taboo.

Donna Logan, a *Star* assistant managing editor, was always looking for features. So I approached her with a proposal for a series on Quebec's juvenile court system. She gave me the green light, but the city editor refused to free me from the police desk. Over the next couple of months, I researched, interviewed experts and victims, and wrote the entire exposé on my own time. On October 30, 1971, the first in a five-part series called "Juvenile Court—Passport to Trouble?" was launched on the front page. It detailed a sorry litany of problems: a juvenile court system bogged down in red tape, overburdened probation officers, overcrowded youth deten-tion centers, untrained guards, and an almost total lack of treatment facilities. At least one positive action that resulted from the series was the closing of St.-Vallier Detention Centre, which was later leveled and turned into a parking lot.

Then, in January 1972, I plunged into the world of investigative journalism. The story involved the suicides of three teenage boys at the Centre Berthelet in Rivière-des-Prairies, fifteen miles northeast of Montreal. Berthelet was billed as a "detention and re-education institution" operated by Quebec's Department of Social Affairs. In plainer language, it was a jail for boys aged fourteen to seventeen.

My investigation began with a rather benign announcement by Quebec's Social Affairs Minister stating that there would be an inquiry into "the conditions of detention at Centre Berthelet." No mention was made of any suicides. Reading the press release, I got a gut feeling that something wasn't right. I started digging and tapped into contacts I had made during my research for the juvenile court series. I called up my old probation officer and beat the drums on the street, hoping a couple of kids recently released from the institution might come forward with information. Then it came, and it was a bombshell: three boys had hanged themselves in their cells by their skate and boot laces.

The first suicide occurred three days before Christmas when a seventeen-year-old from Chicoutimi hanged himself from the bars in his cell with skate laces braided together. On the same day, a sixteen-year-old slashed his wrists with a razor blade. He survived. A week later, a sixteen-year-old orphan was found hanging from a window hook in his cell. And on January 13, a seventeen-year-old ended his life using boot laces. On the same day, another teenager tried to cut his wrists with a jagged piece of glass.

I pounded the keys on my upright Underwood typewriter. I was steaming when I handed the copy over to Foley. He glanced at the first paragraph and tossed the copy into his desk drawer. He muttered that the newspaper "doesn't report on suicides." I argued vehemently that the suicides were at the very core of what was wrong with the juvenile offender system. I pointed out that none of the three boys who had killed themselves had committed a crime. They had been dumped into the detention center because no treatment facility in the province would take them, because they were deemed "too difficult." He didn't get it.

But I was not about to give up. I kept at him like a pit bull until he finally got it and gave in. The story finally ran on the front page across the banner. It was explosive, but little did I know what was to come. Social Affairs Minister Claude Castonguay immediately shot off a press release denying that any deaths had occurred. My feet were put to the fire as the editor prepared to pull the story from the next two editions. Minutes after he gave the kill order, the minister admitted to one death. An hour later he confirmed a second, and by late afternoon, Castonguay had acknowledged all three suicides. An aide to the minister explained that the deaths had been kept secret "because we didn't want to alarm the public and hinder the investigation." A child welfare official added that the government also wanted "to protect the families and ensure that the boys were buried by the church. The Catholic Church will not preside over a funeral of someone who has killed himself or allow the body to be buried in sanctified ground," he offered in a reverent tone.

That investigation set the stage for the rest of my journalistic career. Then and there, I decided that I wanted to be an investigative reporter and nothing else. But my troubles at the newspaper were far from over.

A year later, Foley was gone and a new city editor v s appointed. He was an arrogant individual who informed ᴲ that he didn't like the cut of my "jib," my long hair, or my passion, which he felt clouded my objectivity as a reporter. In a move to push me out, he assigned me to the graveyard shift—midnight to 7 a.m. He was successful. After several months, I quit.

I spent the next three years as a media hack with the federal government—one year with the Secretary of State, two with Health and Welfare Canada. Then, on New Year's Day 1976, I fired off a letter to *The Globe and Mail*'s managing editor, Clark Davey, suggesting the old, grey *Globe* could use a guy like me. To my surprise, he replied with an invitation for an interview. A few weeks later, we met and, fortunately, Davey and I hit it off. I was hired as a senior reporter in Toronto. The moment I walked into the newsroom, I keyed in on children's rights and the juvenile justice system. My first big story targeted the child and adolescent wing of the Lakeshore Psychiatric Hospital. Working key sources, I discovered the unit was a cuckoo's nest run by a wacky psychiatrist who punished uncooperative boys and girls with electroshock, then pumped them with mind-numbing drugs before banishing them to wander the geriatric ward for a month. The front-page story resulted in an inquiry and the shutting down of the unit.

A few months later, I got a tip about a suicide in an Ontario facility: a fourteen-year-old girl by the name of Norma Lee Dean had hanged herself on August 20 at the Kawartha Lakes Training School. Not unexpectedly, officialdom refused to discuss the case, citing privacy issues. My position was unequivocal. Screw them! I knew full well the only privacy issue at stake was the protection of the child welfare system and the probability that their people had messed up big time. With unrelenting zeal, I started digging and slowly peeled back the tragic circumstances leading up to Norma's suicide. The series of stories I wrote on her death revealed a colossal failure in the province's child-care system.

In the newsroom, I soon had the reputation of being "an angry young man." And I was. I was angry at the child welfare system and at what was happening to kids in so-called "care." It was what kept me on fire. And I kept hammering away.

* * *

While my life had taken an amazing turn for the better, I was still shackled by my past. I faced a constant, intense inner struggle over events that had happened to me as a child. Much of it was the result of unresolved issues with my father. Trouble was, he was dead, and I would never be able to confront him about what had made him into such a violent, damaged man. There were a host of other demons tormenting the dark recesses of my mind as well, with the abuse by staff in the boys' home topping the list. No matter how hard I tried, I couldn't seem to find the strength to pull myself out of the pit of self-pity. I would run into guys from the boys' home and we would commiserate endlessly about our time there like it had just happened yesterday.

Here I was, in my late twenties, and I still carried a ton of baggage—huge trunks jam-packed with bad memories of my childhood and teenage years. They would creep into my daily routine and barge into my dreams. I was a prisoner of the tragedy that was my youth. My only salvation would be to find a way to put the past behind me, because if I didn't, I knew I was in for a life of torment and trouble. I was stuck in the muck of the past, living and reliving the garbage, and remaining forever the victim. My past was not allowing me to live or celebrate the present.

I was nearing my thirtieth birthday when I finally realized the truth. It hit me like a lightning bolt. I was not responsible for what had happened to me as a child. I had absolutely no control over those events. I accepted that I was partly the author of my own misfortune as a wayward teenager, but then again, I was already one messed-up kid.

With a lot of self-examination and struggle, I've managed to put the past behind me, but I haven't forgotten or locked it up in some bolted vault in my mind. It's a big mistake to white out any part of your life. You can never go forward by pretending something never happened. Denial disables you. My past is what made and shaped me. Ironically, it's also what gave me a focus.

Often I'd sit on a park bench or at my desk and wonder how I got to where I am when the odds were stacked so high against me. I'd think about the ruined lives of the hundreds of kids I'd met along the beaten child-welfare trail, kids who careened along a track similar to mine. So many Weredale boys hit the skids. So many landed in penitentiary, convicted of assault, break and enter, armed robbery, drug dealing, rape, and murder. Others were killed in violent car crashes. Some were shot in gangland-style hits or by police. Others simply gave up and committed suicide. And far too many followed the paths of their fathers, beating their wives and deserting their families, creating new links in the endless chain of broken homes. Sadly, only a few went on to lead successful lives.

When I look back, I realize that there is no one reason I escaped the tragic fate of so many kids in my situation. I think the most important factor was my recognition that despite everything that had happened to my family, my mother and father loved me. Our family was far from perfect by any stretch, but through thick and thin, my brothers—Fred and Peter—and I stuck together. We always watched each other's backs. The strong bond we felt for each other was rooted deep and gave us all a certain strength.

Curiously, in a way, religion also played a role in my salvation. At a very young age, my psyche was ingrained with the difference between right and wrong. As a child, I was raised to fear God's wrath and certainly didn't want to end up frying in a place called Hell. I'm no longer religious in the church-going, Bible-thumping sense. I have no use for so-called religions whose members cleanse their souls for an hour once a week, then go out and step on anyone who gets in their way. However, I am deeply spiritual and it is my strong sense of justice that drives me.

As far back as my memory takes me, I have always felt there was something more to my self than just this skin wrapped around my body. It was a truth I knew as a child, although I couldn't put it into words. It was something powerful embedded in my soul that I lost touch with when I was tossed onto the treadmill of the child welfare system. In that tumultuous decade, I became numb to this feeling as the casing around my soul hardened. And had it stayed locked up, there is no doubt in my mind that my life would have turned out differently.

Oddly enough, while school played a major role in setting off my short fuse, it was also responsible in part for turning me around. The indifference, smugness, and insensitivity of so many of the teachers I encountered made me lash out. From my own confrontations, I understand bitterly how a teacher can destroy a kid's life by making him or her feel stupid and worthless. Yet, in my final year at the High School of Montreal, things changed for the better. I had a fantastic homeroom teacher in a woman named Mrs. Markell, who took a genuine interest in me. With one warm, understanding smile, she could calm me right down. Henry Wright, the principal, and Jean Brodie, the vice-principal, treated me with understanding as well as a much-needed touch of humor. And then, of course, there was Richard Lees, my drama teacher.

I got a rough ride as a kid, and I wish it hadn't been so painful and miserable. But because of that tough upbringing, I now feel I can deal with just about anything. I took that experience and transformed it. I replaced the anger with passion and put it towards doing good things. It took a lot of time and soul-searching, but in those years, I learned a valuable lesson: if you have the will and put your mind to it, you can turn your life around. For me, it came down to finding the spark and the drive to beat down the demons in my head and calm the rage burning in my body.

In my more than forty years in journalism, I have never stopped fighting for the less fortunate, whether disadvantaged children, battered women, or abused seniors in nursing homes. Whether at *The Globe and Mail*, CBC's *the fifth estate*, or CTV's *W5*, I have always had the strong and unwavering support of my editors and executive producers—even when our personalities clashed and we banged heads. They've allowed me to charge into the fray and swing the sword. For that, I am forever grateful.

* * *

For so many years, I have wondered why the judge let me off when by rights he could have had me locked up in some juvenile prison with orders to throw away the key.

In the spring of 1983, while I was in the throes of writing this book, I decided to look up Judge Robert Gordon Gammell. I found him living in a seniors residence in Montreal. He was a frail, elderly man of seventy-nine years who, surprisingly, remembered me vividly.

"How could I forget you?" he said with a warm smile.

Our visit was short. He was tired and weak, having just come out of hospital after a bout of double pneumonia.

"I remember those boys you fought with. As I recall, it was over some girl who was flirting with you. The boy who started the fight as much as admitted it later. Those boys came into my court with a bunch of lawyers who claimed you were nothing but a young criminal who should be locked up for good. What bothered me about you was the pattern. You were going through a difficult time, a tough adolescence. Adolescence is a very disturbing, disquieting thing. Your body is changing. You're protesting. And I remember that you had been in Weredale and that your family life had not been easy."

Judge Gammell paused and stared at me for a moment.

"It's amazing what you can remember once you start talking. You know, with kids, you've got to play it by ear. I know it sounds like a silly thing to say, but it's true. You've got to use your senses, your instincts. I just knew you weren't a bad kid. I could sense it. I felt that in your case, it was now or never. You were an angry kid walking a tightrope. A wrong push and you'd be lost forever. I felt whatever I did, it was probably your last chance. It's terrible making decisions like that about people's lives, living with this fear of ruining people's lives. It's an awful thing, having to render justice. Yet in your case, I was very fortunate. It was very fortunate that I let you go."

Judge Gammell was getting tired. I looked into his lined face and I could tell he was pleased he had made the right decision.

"I've thought about those days often," I said as I reached the door. "You could have thrown the book at me and I would have deserved it. But you didn't. I'll always be grateful to you for that. Thank you."

One person changed my life and ever since then, it's been my credo: one person can make a difference, and that's what I try to do.